I CANNOT REST O GOD, I CANNOT EAT OR DRINK OR SLEEP,
Till I put forth myself, my prayer, once more to Thee,
Breathe, bathe myself once more in Thee, commune with Thee,
Report myself once more to Thee.

Thou knowest my years entire, my life,
My long and crowded life of active work, not adoration merely;
Thou knowest the prayers and vigils of my youth,
Thou knowest my manhood's solemn and visionary meditations,
Thou knowest how before I commenced I devoted all to come to Thee,
Thou knowest I have in age ratified all those vows and strictly kept them,
Thou knowest I have not once lost nor faith nor ecstasy in Thee,
In shackles, prison'd, in disgrace, repining not,
Accepting all from Thee, as duly come from Thee.

All my emprises have been fill'd with Thee,
My speculations, plans, begun and carried on in thoughts of Thee,
Sailing the deep or journeying the land for Thee;
Intentions, purports, aspirations mine, leaving results to Thee.

O I am sure they really came from Thee,
The urge, the ardor, the unconquerable will,
The potent, felt, interior command, stronger than words,
A message from the Heavens whispering to me even in sleep,
These sped me on.

By me and these the works so far accomplish'd,
By me earth's elder cloy'd and stifled lands uncloy'd, unloos'd,
By me the hemispheres rounded and tied, the unknown to the known.

The end I know not, it is all in Thee,
Or small or great I know not—haply what broad fields, what lands,
Haply the brutish measureless human undergrowth I know,
Transplanted there may rise to stature, knowledge worthy Thee,
Haply the swords I know may there indeed be turn'd to reaping-tools,
Haply the lifeless cross I know, Europe's dead cross, may bud and blossom there.

from PRAYER OF COLUMBUS

SPECIMEN DAYS

BY WALT WHITMAN

BORN IN WEST HILLS, LONG ISLAND, MAY 31, 1819

DIED IN CAMDEN, NEW JERSEY, MARCH 26, 1892

DAVID R. GODINE ❧ PUBLISHER ❧ BOSTON 1971

SPECIMEN DAYS was first published in 1882 by Rees Welch Company of Philadelphia. The 1892 edition published by David McKay, also of Philadelphia, was the source of the present text. The London edition of 1887 was the source of the *Preface to the Reader in the British Islands* on page 1, and the *Note* on page 121. Spelling and punctuation have been changed to conform with modern usage. ❧ The text and photographs are public property, but permission to reproduce the photographs must be obtained from the owners. The design of the present edition has been copyrighted © 1971, by David R. Godine, Brookline, Massachusetts.

THIS EDITION was printed by the Meriden Gravure Company, Meriden, Connecticut. The Stinehour Press, Lunenburg, Vermont, composed the text in Monotype Bembo. The paper for the 1,250 deluxe copies, a laid rag sheet prepared especially for this printing under the supervision of the Hale Paper Company, London, contains watermarks designed by Bram de Does. The remaining 5,000 copies have been printed on Mohawk Superfine, of which 2,500 hardcover and 2,500 softcover were bound by Robert Burlen & Son of Boston. ❧ The book was designed, researched and edited by Lance Hidy. LCC NO. 76–104907.

TABLE OF CONTENTS

LIST OF PHOTOGRAPHS

Henry S. Saunders of Toronto compiled a number of catalogs containing every available photograph of Whitman along with lists of publications in which the portraits appeared. The catalogs are to be found in the major libraries of the eastern states. Although the tiny reproductions are not as fine as the originals, the collection is valuable for its completeness. Saunders arranged the portraits in an approximate chronological sequence and numbered them. *Saunder's number* in the captions under the portraits refers to that numbering. Gay Wilson Allen's *Walt Whitman Handbook* was the source of the biographical information in the captions.

PHOTOGRAPH SOURCES

DUKE UNIVERSITY LIBRARY
Durham, North Carolina

TRENT COLLECTION
Portraits of Walt Whitman, pages 126, 161, 178, 182

LIBRARY OF CONGRESS
Washington, D.C.

CHARLES E. FEINBERG COLLECTION
Whitman's mother and father, page 4.
Birthplace, page 5.
Fulton Ferry, page 9.
George Whitman, page 11.
Christian Commission Contract, page 15.
Eight visiting cards, pages 49, 50, 51, and 52.
Manuscript directions for *Pictures from Life of WW*, page 122.
Manuscript plan for tomb, page 189.
Portraits of Walt Whitman, pages 125, 128, 131, 134, 135, 136, 139, 143, 144, 145, 146, 150, 153, 157, 160, 162, 163, 164, 168, 169, 175, 181, 183, 188.

BRADY COLLECTION
Hospitals, pages 18, 21, 22, 27, 28, 29, 46, 47, 48.
Wounded soldiers, pages 14, 51.
Ambulance train, page 23.
Surgeons, pages 34, 35, 36.
Camps, pages 50, 52, 53, 54, 55, 56, 57, 60.
Contraband camp, page 58.
Prison at Andersonville, page 59.
Soldiers from Richmond Prison, pages 42, 43.

MUSEUM OF FINE ARTS, BOSTON
Boston, Massachusetts

JEAN FRANÇOIS MILLET, THREE OIL PAINTINGS ON CANVAS
The Sower, page 110; 39.75 by 32.5 inches; 17.1485; gift of Quincy Adams Shaw through Q. A. Shaw, Jr. and M. Shaw Haughton.
Peasant Watering Her Cow, Evening, page 111; 32 by 39.25 inches; 17.1531; gift of Quincy Adams Shaw through Q. A. Shaw, Jr., and M. Shaw Haughton.
Harvesters Resting (Ruth and Boaz), page 111; 27.25 by 47.25 inches; 06.2421; signed and dated 1853; bequest of Mrs. Martin Brimmer.

NATIONAL ARCHIVES
Washington, D.C.

BRADY COLLECTION
Portraits of Walt Whitman, pages 129, 137.

NEW YORK PUBLIC LIBRARY
New York City

RARE BOOK DIVISION, OSCAR LION COLLECTION
Portraits of Walt Whitman, pages 130, 141, 147, 148, 154, 155, 156, 158, 165, 167, 171, 174, 184.
Tomb, Harleigh Cemetery, page 190.

PHILADELPHIA MUSEUM OF ART
Philadelphia, Pennsylvania

Portrait of Walt Whitman, page 187.

SMITHSONIAN INSTITUTION
Washington, D.C.

Portraits of Walt Whitman, pages 176, 177.

WALT WHITMAN HOUSE
Camden, New Jersey

Portrait of Walt Whitman, page 124.

YALE UNIVERSITY LIBRARY
New Haven, Connecticut

COLLECTION OF AMERICAN LITERATURE,
BEINECKE RARE BOOK AND MANUSCRIPT LIBRARY
Portraits of Walt Whitman, pages 127, 132, 133, 138, 140, 142, 149, 151, 152, 159, 166, 170, 172, 173, 179, 180, 185, 186.

INTRODUCTION

In 1882, when Walt Whitman finally put into one untidy package, *Specimen Days and Collect*, reminiscences of his youth, his various "memoranda" of the Civil War, his travel diaries and "nature notes" after the war, he was almost at the point of becoming that mythic figure, the universal poet, that he had celebrated in his own poems. In these last years of his life, he had become strangely important to writers in England otherwise so different as Gosse, Tennyson, Hopkins. At home, though his reputation in respectable literary circles was still bad, he was becoming a cause to all sorts of lonely American iconoclasts. Then, after Whitman's death in 1892, he was gradually to be seen as the first truly comprehensive writer America had produced, the first whose imaginative interest concretely included the different peoples in the world. Before Emily Dickinson was recognized as an original poet and Melville as a great mythmaker, Whitman was valued abroad as the American writer who had somehow brought his country into world literature—the poet of a "democracy" not limited to Americans. During the 1914–1918 war, fallen French and German soldiers alike were found in the trenches with Whitman's poems in their uniforms.

This importance to a future concerned (whether through socialism or the early twentieth-century religion of art) with the idea of a world community, this legend of himself as a political-philosophical poet and incarnation of what might yet be everybody's "New World"—this Whitman had foretold in his poetry. Future "greatness" of an almost sublime kind, resting on the idea of redemption through the poet, had been a recurrent motif of Whitman's poetry. He had celebrated himself as a poet by identifying himself with the easy transcendentalist afflatus of the "genius of these states"—and by extension, with every kind of creative leadership conceivable to the stormy literary prophets, entrepreneurs and nation-builders of the nineteenth century.

In 1882, however, Whitman had little tangible reason to expect so much of the future. He was able to make a characteristically uneven, idiosyncratic but finally remarkable self-revelation out of *Specimen Days* largely on the strength of his experiences as a visitor to Washington hospitals during the Civil War, and for this he had to use his old newspaper articles and his already published *Memoranda During The Civil War* (1875). Whitman characteristically introduced these essential war experiences —the heart of the book—with reminiscences of his early life in order to bind future biographers to this self-portrait. Thanks not least to his famous "magnetism"—he was already becoming one of the most photographed men of the nineteenth century—he was betting on the future (for some time he had not had much *but* the future).

But he was, at sixty-three, still unread as well as infamous. He was very poor, partially paralyzed, more or less immobilized by the stroke he had suffered after the Civil War, and which he sometimes attributed to his self-sacrificial hospital visits. He was living in the Camden house of his brother George, and was full of concern for him and for the other members of his immediate family. Whitman was always in close touch with his mother, brothers, their wives, his sister. They depended on him for handouts and steadfastness; the Whitmans had a sickly history of mental illness and of public brawling over money. Whitman eked out his own precarious existence by gifts from distinguished admirers. (Mark Twain among others found it easier to help buy the paralyzed old man a horse and buggy than to praise *Leaves of Grass*.) There were occasional sums from the brave (and always different) publishers who would risk a new edition of *Leaves of Grass*. The Secretary of the Interior himself had discharged Whitman from his clerkship in the Department when he had found *Leaves of Grass* in Whitman's desk; in 1874, Whitman had been discharged from another clerkship, in the Attorney General's Office, which he had held by employing a substitute. In the same year that he put out *Specimen Days*, James Osgood of Boston, who had brought out the eighth edition of *Leaves of Grass*, found himself threatened with prosecution by the Society for the Suppression of Vice, and abandoned publication.

Another publisher, in Philadelphia, was to go ahead with the next edition of the *Leaves*, and in his own foraging, dependent, seductive kind of way, Whitman was able during America's Iron Age to carry on from day to day. But the immediate circumstances of this disabled and isolated old man in Camden, who looked so much older than his years, were in extreme contrast to the poet's ambition to create a last monument to himself in *Specimen Days*.

"Walt Whitman" had been as great a creation in 1855 as *Leaves of Grass*. Nothing so proves Whitman's genius as the fact that he was able to turn into this persona and to make it stick. The poet was to become as important to his readers as his book. From the moment that the "real" Whitman (the hack journalist and unsuccessful editor who had failed at every occupation and probably felt threatened by the mental disturbance marked in his family) was able to create a wholly new existence for himself in and through *Leaves of Grass*, Whitman became one of those "heroes" and "master builders," like Carlyle, Balzac, and Ibsen, who proclaim the scope of the nineteenth century. Whitman the poet had the vision of the whole, the historic "scheme," the national and nationalizing Mythos that one associates with Lincoln, Mazzini, Dostoevsky. This poet of the "modern" (in personal sensation) and of the "future" (as a new sympathy between different races and peoples) actually helped to supply, through all his writings on the Civil War, the rationale for the massive continental power that emerged from the North's victory. The poet of "comradeship," of "manly love," of "adhesiveness," was just now, in 1882, to become as much the bard of blood and soil as Carlyle. Carlyle sneered that Whitman thought he was a big poet because he came from a big country, but Carlyle went on to idolize concentrated Prussian *Macht*. Whitman's America would prove ultimately more powerful and more complex—especially to Walt Whitman.

The Whitman who had created a new self in 1855 was now, with *Specimen Days*, to show what a really determined genius in the nineteenth century could do by way of an "autobiography." If he wanted to create a genial sweet old W.W. for his expected army of biographers, one reason is that he had perceptibly slowed up, had lost his fire, had dropped the fervently suggestive sexuality of his early poems. No doubt he meant to show that he could do something good in the slower, more ruminative style that came with age. But most of all he wanted, by exploiting his experiences in the Washington hospitals, to ennoble and advance his literary reputation by joining it to the drama of war and the "majesty" of the Union cause—by 1882 as sacred a theme as the Passion of Christ, and through Lincoln, often identified with it.

In our century writers have often made their literary fortunes from war. But Whitman is virtually the only important American writer of his day who made so much of the Civil War, who identified himself so directly with it. Emerson was harshly anti-South, from the sidelines. Thoreau and Hawthorne, who died during the war, disbelieved in the holy cause; Henry James could not fight because of the famous "dreadful hurt" he suffered putting out a fire; Howells was American consul in Venice; Mark Twain was to wax comic about his brief inglorious experience as a Confederate volunteer—and after the war became a professional Northerner at banquets of the G.A.R. Of Whitman's literary peers, only Melville left a lasting record—in his privately published poems—of his concern with the war. Melville's "Battle Pieces" are strikingly non-enthusiastic, non-partisan, tragic, sorrowful; they are above the battle. *Specimen Days*, by contrast, shows Whitman always at the scene, in the streets and hospitals of wartime Washington, so intimate and involved an observer that he becomes the important presence he wanted to be—in the war-torn, often "seditious" capital, virtually a participant in the war, at least by his account. *Specimen Days* is thus one book about the Civil War by a first-rate writer of the time that reflects the national fervor of the North, especially as it came to a retrospective glow in the 1880's. But Whitman's spasmodic, curious, fascinating book is most valuable as a record. It is distended, like almost everything else Whitman wrote, but it is not simply a literary creation, like *The Red Badge of Courage*. It is part of the passion of the Civil War itself, of the madness of war, of the victory spirit and the national ego that were to shape the North as much as defeat shaped the South.

Whitman presciently related himself to the popular passion released by war, he gave himself to this passion as the greatest possible political cause, he understood popular opinion in a way that Thoreau, Hawthorne, Melville would never have attempted to understand it. Emerson, who said, like any conventional New England clergyman, that the war was "holy," could not express the war. Whitman was able to get so much out of the war, and to put so much into it, because he knew what the people were feeling. He was not solitary and detached like the Concord writers; not suspicious of the majority like his fellow New Yorker, Melville. Whitman's visits to the hospitals, his actual "war service," in fact, began when he went down to the Virginia front in December 1862 to look for his brother, Captain George Washington Whitman, who had been declared missing. Despite Whitman's mysterious, still elusive personality, he genuinely felt close to the "common man," and he was a notably accessible and sociable creature. He was always to get along better with omnibus drivers, workingmen, printers, "simple" soldiers (especially when they were wounded and open to his ministrations) than with the "genteel" literary class. Whitman, who in his newspaper days had been a radical Democrat, had the instinctive feeling for the Union as the "popular" cause that radicals felt in Europe as well as in America.

But by the time of the Civil War—and as a result of the war—Whitman's politics had become the "nation." One of the essential qualities of *Specimen Days* is Whitman's libidinously powerful urge to associate himself with the great, growing, ever more powerful strength of the Union cause. Whitman's characteristic, lifelong urge to merge, join, combine, to see life in terms of movement, unity, totality, became during the Civil War a kind of actively loving association with the broad masses of the people and "their" war. In his cult of the Civil War, Whitman allies himself with an heroic and creative energy not limited to leaders, as it did to Carlyle and Bismarck, but does see itself spreading out from saintly American leaders (like himself and Lincoln) to be justified, finally, in the mythical connection between these representative men of the people and the people.

In our day, when the United States has so overwhelmingly extended the historic position it achieved after 1865, it seems natural for American writers to be opposed to the Big State and its superpower. Hawthorne and Thoreau were opposed to American bigness in 1861, and the fact that both died during the War is perhaps not unconnected to their horror of the War. But opposition to the Big State was not natural to Whitman. His passion for the Union reflected not only his intense faith in democracy at a time when the United States still represented the revolutionary principles to many European countries, but also his deepest feeling that his own rise from the city streets, his survival as a man, his future as a poet of "democracy," were tied up with the great cause.

Whitman's great gift as a writer was his ability to give an unmistakable vibration, a mysterious significance, to the most commonplace details. He came to this in his poetry by entering boldly into some primary free association with himself, transcribing himself with the greatest possible naturalness, in a fashion that awoke hidden psychic currents in his readers, made them feel the authenticity of their unconscious strivings. In his slovenly, lethargic, passive ruminations, Whitman attained a seemingly directionless but actual mystical bond to the homeliest things at his feet, to street scenes, to accidental impressions and fleeting sensations. He suggested an alliance with powers and forces greater than himself. He could make any of his transactions with the world seem representative, and so made himself to many readers their representative man. He was a kind of lightning conductor to things in the universe that, in the suffocatingly moral universe of so many Americans in the nineteenth century, they were to get only through him. In this sense he really was the "lover" that he proclaimed himself—he started amazingly sympathetic relationships with abstractions, made them as real as popular feelings.

In *Specimen Days* he united himself to the Civil War, he illuminated the war as a striving organism with which even Nature was in sympathy. He made it a living cause by his capacity for turning the homeliest, most common details of his daily life in the Washington hospitals into a vision of the unity of all things. One night, he says in his diary, he stood in the darkness and saw "shadowy columns moving through the night," through deep mud, ladened with their packs and weapons. As they "fil'd by," Whitman suddenly felt that never before had he "realized the majesty and reality of the American people en masse." No American writer now would say that watching soldiers file by, he realized the majesty and reality of the American people en masse. But Whitman was writing from the battlefront in his own country. The very survival of *his* country was at stake. Whitman felt that the Union soldiers, many of them volunteers, were by their sacrifices helping to create an "American people."

Henry James, as a young reviewer in 1865, had condemned *Drum Taps*. By 1898 he finally came around to Whitman by way of his letters about the war. "The beauty of the natural is here, the beauty of the particular nature, the man's own overflow in the deadly dry setting, the personal passion . . . a thousand images of patient, homely American life, else undistinguishable are what its queerness—however startling—happens to express." Whitman's instinct for "the beauty of the natural" is indeed the great key to *Specimen Days*. He had an amazing ability to suggest the "divinity" inherent in ordinary life lived in the midst of the great modern crowd. All things and persons as well as "days" are "specimens" to him—all instances are mysteriously expressive of more than themselves. So it is the passing moment, the rumor of battle, the march at night, a storm over the Capitol, frightened soldiers rushing away from Bull Run to flop down in the Washington streets, Lincoln on a summer morning riding back to the White House after sleeping at the Soldiers' Home to escape the Washington heat—detail after detail that Whitman loves to get down, confident that everything in this national drama will prove the mysterious sympathy of all things in the order of nature.

Again and again in *Specimen Days* Whitman reveals the eery romantic faith—so strange to our generation—that "Nature" is not only part of the drama of war and expressive of martial energies but is sympathetic to man's "purposes." In most realistic writing about war, the more beautiful the weather, the more it symbolizes irrelevance. But Whitman's romantic symbolization of the weather during the Civil War brings home to us the deep, all-absorbing crisis that the war represents to him. He sees as many omens and portents as Caesar before his murder.

There are other features of *Specimen Days* that are far from being realistic. Whitman was a volunteer bringing small gifts and occasionally writing letters, but allowed the picture to stand of a "wound dresser" and Christ-like presence. The wounded soldiers with whom he made special friends, and whom he sometimes kissed, do not talk *to* Whitman; they make patriotic orations at him. Whitman turned his homosexuality, or his motherliness, or whatever it was, into stilted bedside scenes of brave dying soldiers being watched over by a bearded saint. Often enough the wounded seemed exactly alike; one can tell that with just one or two exceptions, Whitman formed no deep personal relationships in the hospitals. But what is "new" and foretelling of certain twentieth-century descriptions of war is exactly this emphasis on the "average." Though Whitman intended it to mean representative of popular greatness, his rapid descriptions of so many faces in the crowded hospitals shows his love of documenting the masses, a modern taste.

Equally so is the utterly spontaneous reporting *sur le vif*, the prose rhythms with which Whitman captures the headlong dash of events. This is the literature not of "realism," as Stephen Crane was to invent it for *The Red Badge of Courage*, but of experience. It is just intensely personal reporting. As Richard Chase said, "Whitman's artistic credo is in the boast from *Song of Myself*, 'I am the man, I suffer'd, I was there.'" But this time Whitman really *was* there. In Winslow Homer's sketches from the field for *Harper's Weekly*, one is always charmed by the immediacy. All his life Whitman had been saying, or trying to say, "I have been everywhere." Now he could glorify his having been in Washington when it counted. And it is this warmth of the moment, his pleasure in being on the spot, that gives the war sections their old-fashioned humanity. One always seems to see Whitman writing the diary; the observer is always in sight, and you know all he is feeling.

Of course, we may suspect today that Whitman made too much of his hospital visits, that he was an interloper even by the relatively primitive hospital standards of the time. The highly organized Sanitary Commission, which Whitman disdains as coldly impersonal, repellent to his favorites, did, in fact, finally establish fundamental principles of modern hospital organization. We know now that the Sanitary Commission inaugurated bureaucratic controls important to government and business after the war. But no professional aide of the Sanitary Commission would have lingered in the hospitals as Whitman did—would have captured so unforgettably what Wilfred Owen would call "the pity of war." It was because Whitman was already an anachronism that he was able to describe in close detail, near to the facts, scenes of individual suffering that would never again matter so much to a writer. But if we compare Whitman in the Washington hospitals with "Walt Whitman" the Godlike seer of the poems, we can see how *Specimen Days* moves us from the archaic America before the Civil War to our own.

In Whitman's account of war, the sense of numbers is fundamental. The overcrowded hospital wards where so many boys are dying in agony, the crowds in the Washington streets, the Grand Army of the Republic in victory finally parading Pennsylvania Avenue for two full days—all this has suddenly filled up the old bare, provincial American scene. We are on the threshold of the modern mass world, where people have become as numerous as leaves of grass and are as indistinguishable and ignorable. But Whitman ignores nothing and nobody; he is no cold "realist." The Civil War, it is true, was the first great modern war of mass armies and mass killing. For Whitman the common soldier, the patiently suffering American, is more a hero than Jeb Stuart was to the South. The wounded are faithfully itemized, with Whitman's strange loving passion for the soldier as archetype. But as we know from his greatest poems, death was of supreme mystical significance to Whitman. When he writes of "the million dead summ'd up," his belief in sacrifice, in death as the fulfillment of "Nature," wins over his horror at so many corpses—

The dead in this war—there they lie, strewing the fields and woods and valleys of the South—Virginia, the Peninsula, Malvern Hill and Fair Oaks—the banks of the Chicahominy—the terraces of Fredericksburgh—Antietam bridge—the grisly ravines of Manassas—the bloody promenade of the Wilderness—the variety of the strayed dead . . . the dead, the dead, the dead, *our* dead—or South or North, ours all (all, all, all, finally dear to me)—or East or West—Atlantic coast of Mississippi Valley—somewhere they crawl'd to die, alone, in bushes, low gullies, or on the sides of hills . . . the infinite dead—(the land entire saturated, perfumed with their impalpable ashes exhalation in Nature's chemistry distill'd, and shall be so forever, in every future grain of wheat or ear of corn, and every flower that grows, and every breath we draw . . .

So the million dead prepared the way, by their "sacrifice," for Lincoln the Christ whom he celebrated in "When Lilacs Last In The Dooryard Bloom'd." The connection of the Civil War with the idea of sacrifice is overwhelming in *Specimen Days*. By extension Whitman includes the sacrifice of his own health. But we cannot mind this, for the theme of sacrifice is fundamental to Whitman's "national" idea of a peoples' war. Whitman's honest sense of his own comparative insignificance, his attempt at the same time to express the willing sacrifice of so many "unknown, forgotten" men, lifts his favorite theme of man's democratic destiny—"One's self I sing, a simple separate person, Yet utter the word Democratic, the word En-Masse"—to a new height of shared emotion.

In the "nature notes" that he wrote up when he became paralyzed after the war, we see Whitman "restoring" himself through Nature. These lovely minor pastorals show Whitman communing with himself and observing Nature as a benevolent presence very friendly to himself. "Nature" is still "Nature" at Timber Creek in the Jersey woods; no pollution. The picture of Whitman in the woods, doggedly trying to brush his failing flesh back to life, does not have the excitement of *Walden* or "Song Of Myself," but it is altogether charming as an old man's last idyll. On the whole, Whitman still finds himself as pleasing as he does nature. There are little set pieces in the book whose titles are already landscapes—"Cedar Apples," "Summer Sights and Indolences," "Sundown Perfume," "Quail Notes," "The Hermit Thrush," "A Sun-Bath," "Nakedness." These sketches are only "notes," but the quick brush stroke is already a picture:

As I journey'd today in a light wagon ten or twelve miles through the country, nothing pleased me more, in their homely beauty and novelty (I had either never seen the little things to such advantage, or had never noticed them before) than that peculiar fruit, with its profuse clear-yellow dangles of inch-long silk or yarn in boundless profusion spotting the dark-green cedar bushes—contrasting well with their bronze tufts—the flossy shreds covering the knobs all over, like a shock of wild hair on elfin pates.

The only modern writer I can think of who wrote with this same quick descriptive response to objects in nature is D. H. Lawrence. As with Lawrence, writing about nature seems as good to Whitman as breathing; you can even say of many sketches in *Specimen Days* that he breathes by writing *them*. But unlike Lawrence, who was always imperiously direct, Whitman often wanders back into unformed thoughts. He suffers from that strange inarticulateness at times which Howells, as a young critic, thought was inherent in the nature of Whitman's affinity with music. Yet since Whitman, even when he nodded, was a wholly original writer, he could often, despite his strange lethargies and divagations, find the idiosyncratically right word and phrase that was his essential strength—the symbol of his wholly personal way of seeing. His span of attention in these notes is short but delightful. What Whitman always did best was to make the reader partake of his homely, mysteriously effective creative process. *Specimen Days* gives us contact with his mind at its source.

ALFRED KAZIN
May 15, 1970

Walt Whitman
June. 1 '87

PREFACE TO THE READER IN THE BRITISH ISLANDS

If you will only take the following pages, as you do some long and gossippy letter written for you by a relative or friend traveling through distant scenes and incidents, and jotting them down lazily and informally, but ever veraciously (with occasional diversions of critical thought about somebody or something), it might remove all formal or literary impediments at once, and bring you and me close together in the spirit in which the jottings were collated to be read. You have had, and have, plenty of public events and facts and general statistics of America;—in the following book is a common individual New World *private life,* its birth and growth, its struggles for a living, its goings and comings and observations (or representative portions of them) amid the United States of America the last thirty or forty years, with their varied war and peace, their local coloring, the unavoidable egotism, and the lights and shades and sights and joys and pains and sympathies common to humanity. Further introductory light may be found in the paragraph, "A Happy Hour's Command," and the bottom note belonging to it, at the beginning of the book. I have said in the text that if I were required to give good reason-for-being of *Specimen Days,* I should be unable to do so. Let me fondly hope that it has at least the reason and excuse of such off-hand gossippy letter as just alluded to, portraying American life-sights and incidents as they actually occurred—their presentation, making additions as far as it goes, to the simple experience and association of your soul, from a comrade soul;—and that also, in the volume, as below any page of mine, anywhere, ever remains, for seen or unseen basis-phrase,

good-will between the common people of all nations.

WALT WHITMAN
LONDON EDITION, JUNE, 1887

SPECIMEN DAYS

A HAPPY HOUR'S COMMAND ✤ DOWN IN THE WOODS, JULY 2D, 1882 ✤ If I do it at all I must delay no longer. Incongruous and full of skips and jumps as is that huddle of diary-jottings, war memoranda of 1862–'65, Nature notes of 1877–'81, with Western and Canadian observations afterward, all bundled up and tied by a big string, the resolution and indeed mandate comes to me this day, this hour (and what a day! what an hour just passing! the luxury of riant grass and blowing breeze, with all the shows of sun and sky and perfect temperature, never before so filling me body and soul) —to go home, untie the bundle, reel out diary scraps and memoranda, just as they are, large or small, one after another, into print pages,* and let the mélange's lackings and wants of connection take care of themselves. It will illustrate one phase of humanity anyhow: how few of life's days and hours (and they not by relative value or proportion, but by chance) are ever noted. Probably another point, too, how we give long preparations for some object, planning and delving and fashioning, and then, when the actual hour for doing arrives, find ourselves still quite unprepared, and tumble the things together, letting hurry and crudeness tell the story better than fine work. At any rate I obey my happy hour's command, which seems curiously imperative. Maybe, if I don't do anything else, I shall send out the most wayward, spontaneous, fragmentary book ever printed.

ANSWER TO AN INSISTING FRIEND ✤ You ask for items, details of my early life—of genealogy and parentage, particularly of the women of my ancestry, and of its far-back Netherlands stock on the maternal side—of the region where I was born and raised, and my father and mother before me, and theirs before them —with a word about Brooklyn and New York cities, the times I lived there as lad and young man. You say you want to get at these details mainly as the go-befores and embryos of *Leaves of Grass*. Very good; you shall have at least some specimens of them all. I have often thought of the meaning of such things—that one can only encompass and complete matters of that kind by exploring behind, perhaps far behind, themselves directly, and so into their genesis, antecedents, and cumulative stages. Then as luck would have it, I lately whiled away the tedium of a week's half-sickness and confinement by collating these very items for another (yet unfulfilled, probably abandoned) purpose; and if you will be satisfied with them, authentic in date-occurrence and fact simply, and told my own way, garrulous-like, here they are. I shall not hesitate to make extracts, for I catch at anything to save labor; but those will be the best versions of what I want to convey.

GENEALOGY—VAN VELSOR AND WHITMAN ✤ The later years of the last century found the Van Velsor family, my mother's side, living on their

---

* The pages from 3 to 11 are nearly verbatim an offhand letter of mine in January, 1882, to an insisting friend. Following, I give some gloomy experiences. The war of attempted secession has, of course, been the distinguishing event of my time. I commenced at the close of 1862, and continued steadily through '63, '64, and '65, to visit the sick and wounded of the army, both on the field and in the hospitals in and around Washington city. From the first I kept little notebooks for impromptu jottings in pencil to refresh my memory of names and circumstances, and what was specially wanted, etc. In these I briefed cases, persons, sights, occurrences in camp, by the bedside, and not seldom by the corpses of the dead. Some were scratched down from narratives I heard and itemized while watching, or waiting, or tending somebody amid those scenes. I have dozens of such little notebooks left, never to be possibly said or sung. I wish I could convey to the reader the associations that attach to these soiled and creased livraisons, each composed of a sheet or two of paper, folded small to carry in the pocket, and fastened with a pin. I leave them just as I threw them by after the war, blotched here and there with more than one bloodstain, hurriedly written, sometimes at the clinic, not seldom amid the excitement of uncertainty, or defeat, or of action, or getting ready for it, or a march. Most of the pages from 14 to 60 are

verbatim copies of those lurid & blood-smutched little notebooks.

Very different are most of the memoranda that follow. Some time after the war ended I had a paralytic stroke, which prostrated me for several years. In 1876 I began to get over the worst of it. From this date, portions of several seasons, especially summers, I spent at a secluded haunt down in Camden County, New Jersey— Timber Creek, quite a little river (it enters from the great Delaware, twelve miles away)—with primitive solitudes, winding stream, recluse and woody banks, sweet-feeding springs, and all the charms that birds, grass, wildflowers, rabbits and squirrels, old oaks, walnut trees, etc., can bring. Through these times, and on these spots, the diary from page 61 onward was mostly written.

(The COLLECT afterward gathers up the odds and ends of whatever pieces I can now lay hands on, written at various times past, and swoops all together like fish in a net.)

I suppose I publish and leave the whole gathering, first, from that eternal tendency to perpetuate and preserve which is behind all Nature, authors included; second, to symbolize two or three specimen interiors, personal and other, out of the myriads of my time, the middle range of the nineteenth century in the New World: a strange, unloosened, wondrous time. But the book is probably without any definite purpose that can be told in a statement.

own farm at Cold Spring, Long Island, New York State, near the eastern edge of Queens County, about a mile from the harbor.* My father's side—probably the fifth generation from the first English arrivals in New England—were at the same time farmers on their own land—(and a fine domain it was, 500 acres, all good soil, gently sloping east and south, about one-tenth woods, plenty of grand old trees), two or three miles off, at West Hills, Suffolk County. The Whitman name in the eastern states, and so branching west and south, starts undoubtedly from one John Whitman, born 1602, in Old England, where he grew up, married, and his eldest son was born in 1629. He came over in the *True Love* in 1640 to America, and lived in Weymouth, Mass., which place became the mother hive of the New Englanders of the name; he died in 1692. His brother, Rev. Zechariah Whitman, also came over in the *True Love*, either at that time or soon after, and lived at Milford, Conn. A son of this Zechariah, named Joseph, migrated to Hun-

tington, Long Island, and permanently settled there. Savage's *Genealogical Dictionary* (Vol. iv, p. 524) gets the Whitman family established at Huntington, per this Joseph, before 1664. It is quite certain that from that beginning, and from Joseph, the West Hill Whitmans, and all others in Suffolk County, have since radiated, myself among the number. John and Zechariah both went to England and back again divers times; they had large families, and several of their children were born in the old country. We hear of the father of John and Zechariah, Abijah Whitman, who goes over into the 1500's, but we know little about him, except that he also was for some time in America. ❧ These old pedigree reminiscences come up to me vividly from a visit I made not long since (in my 63d year) to West Hills, and to the burial grounds of my ancestry, both sides. I extract from notes of that visit, written there and then:

THE OLD WHITMAN AND VAN VELSOR CEMETERIES ❧ JULY 29, 1881 ❧ After more than forty years' absence (except a brief visit, to take my father there once more, two years before he died), went down Long Island on a week's jaunt to the place where I was born, thirty miles from New York City. Rode

LOUISA VAN VELSOR WHITMAN, 1795 TO 1863

WALTER WHITMAN, SR., 1789 TO 1855

[4]

around the old familiar spots, viewing and pondering and dwelling long upon them, everything coming back to me. Went to the old Whitman homestead on the upland and took a view eastward, inclining south, over the broad and beautiful farm lands of my grandfather (1780) and my father. There was the new house (1810), the big oak a hundred and fifty or two hundred years old; there the well, the sloping kitchen garden, and a little way off even the well-kept remains of the dwelling of my great-grandfather (1750–'60) still standing, with its mighty timbers and low ceilings. Near by, a stately grove of tall, vigorous black walnuts, beautiful, Apollo-like, the sons or grandsons, no doubt, of black walnuts during or before 1776. On the other side of the road spread the famous apple orchard, over twenty acres, the trees planted by hands long moldering in the grave (my uncle Jesse's), but quite many of them evidently capable of throwing out their annual blossoms and fruit yet. ๏ I now write these lines seated on an old grave (doubtless of a century since at least) on the burial hill of the Whitmans of many generations. Fifty and more graves are quite plainly traceable, and as many more decayed out of all form—depressed mounds, crumbled and broken stones, covered with moss—the gray and sterile hill, the clumps of chestnuts outside, the silence, just varied by the soughing wind. There is always the deepest eloquence of sermon or poem in any of these ancient graveyards of which Long Island has so many; so what must this one have been to me? My whole family history, with its succession of links, from the first settlement down to date, told here—three centuries concentrate on this sterile acre. ๏ The next day, July 30, I devoted to the maternal locality, and if possible was still more penetrated and impressed. I write this paragraph on the burial hill of the Van Velsors, near Cold Spring, the most significant depository of the dead that could be imagined, without the slightest help from art, but far ahead of it, soil sterile, a mostly bare plateau-flat of half an acre, the top of a hill, brush and well-grown trees and dense woods bordering all around, very primitive, secluded, no visitors, no road (you cannot drive here; you have to bring the dead on foot, and follow on foot). Two- or threescore graves quite plain; as many more almost rubbed out. My grandfather Cornelius and my grandmother Amy (Naomi) and numerous relatives nearer or remoter, on my mother's side, lie buried here. The scene as I stood or sat, the delicate and wild odor of the woods, a slightly drizzling rain, the emotional atmosphere of the place, and the inferred reminiscences, were fitting accompaniments.

WALT WHITMAN'S BIRTHPLACE, WEST HILLS, LONG ISLAND, 1890

THE MATERNAL HOMESTEAD ‽ I went down from this ancient grave place eighty or ninety rods to the site of the Van Velsor homestead, where my mother was born (1795) and where every spot had been familiar to me as a child and youth (1825-'40). Then stood there a long, rambling, dark gray, shingle-sided house, with sheds, pens, a great barn, and much open road-space. Now of all those not a vestige left; all had been pulled down, erased, and the plough and harrow passed over foundations, road-spaces, and everything, for many summers; fenced in at present, and grain and clover growing like any other fine fields. Only a big hole from the cellar, with some little heaps of broken stone, green with grass and weeds, identified the place. Even the copious old brook and spring seemed to have mostly dwindled away. The whole scene, with what it aroused, memories of my young days there half a century ago, the vast kitchen and ample fireplace and the sitting room adjoining, the plain furniture, the meals, the house full of merry people, my grandmother Amy's sweet old face in its Quaker cap, my grandfather "the Major," jovial, red, stout, with sonorous voice and characteristic physiognomy, with the actual sights themselves, made the most pronounced half-day's experience of my whole jaunt. ‽ For there with all those wooded, hilly, healthy surroundings, my dearest mother, Louisa Van Velsor, grew up (her mother, Amy Williams, of the Friends' or Quakers' denomination—the Williams family, seven sisters and one brother—the father and brother sailors, both of whom met their deaths at sea). The Van Velsor people were noted for fine horses, which the men bred and trained from blooded stock. My mother, as a young woman, was a daily and daring rider. As to the head of the family himself, the old race of the Netherlands, so deeply grafted on Manhattan Island and in Kings and Queens Counties, never yielded a more marked and full Americanized specimen than Major Cornelius Van Velsor.

TWO OLD FAMILY INTERIORS ‽ Of the domestic and inside life of the middle of Long Island, at and just before that time, here are two samples: *The Whitmans, at the beginning of the present century, lived in a long story-and-a-half farm-house, hugely timber'd, which is still standing. A great smoke-canopied kitchen, with vast hearth and chimney, form'd one end of the house. The existence of slavery in New York at that time, and the possession by the family of some twelve or fifteen slaves, house and field servants, gave things quite a patriarchal look. The very young darkies could be seen, a swarm of them, toward sundown, in this kitchen, squatted in a circle on the floor, eating their supper of Indian pudding and milk. In the house, and in food and furniture, all was rude, but substantial. No carpets or stoves were known, and no coffee, and tea or sugar only for the women. Rousing wood fires gave both warmth and light on winter nights. Pork, poultry, beef, and all the ordinary vegetables and grains were plentiful. Cider was the men's common drink, and used at meals. The clothes were mainly homespun. Journeys were made by both men and women on horseback. Both sexes labored with their own hands—the men on the farm, the women in the house and around it. Books were scarce. The annual copy of the almanac was a treat, and was pored over through the long winter evenings. I must not forget to mention that both these families were near enough to sea to behold it from the high places, and to hear in still hours the roar of the surf; the latter, after a storm, giving a peculiar sound at night. Then all hands, male and female, went down frequently on beach and bathing parties, and the men on practical expeditions for cutting salt hay, and for clamming and fishing.—John Burroughs's* NOTES. ‽ *The ancestors of Walt Whitman, on both the paternal and maternal sides, kept a good table, sustained the hospitalities, decorums, and an excellent social reputation in the county, and they were often of marked individuality. If space permitted, I should consider some of the men worthy special description, and still more some of the women. His great-grandmother on the paternal side, for instance, was a large swarthy woman, who lived to a very old age. She smoked tobacco, rode on horseback like a man, managed the most vicious horse, and, becoming a widow in later life, went forth every day over her farmlands, frequently in the saddle, directing the labor of her slaves, with language in which, on exciting occasions, oaths were not spared. The two immediate grandmothers were, in the best sense, superior women. The maternal one (Amy Williams before marriage) was a Friend, or Quakeress, of sweet, sensible character, housewifely proclivities, and deeply intuitive and spiritual. The other (Hannah Brush) was an equally noble, perhaps stronger character, lived to be very old, had quite a family of sons, was a natural lady, was in early life a schoolmistress, and had great solidity of mind. W. W. himself makes much of the women of his ancestry.—The same.* ‽ Out from these arrières of persons and scenes, I was born May 31, 1819. And now to dwell a while on the locality itself—as the successive growth-stages of my infancy, childhood, youth, and manhood were all passed on Long Island, which I sometimes feel as if I had incorporated. I roamed as boy and man, and have lived in nearly all parts, from Brooklyn to Montauk Point.

PAUMANOK, AND MY LIFE ON IT AS CHILD AND YOUNG MAN ‽ Worth fully and particularly investigating indeed, this Paumanok (to give the spot its aboriginal name*), stretching east

---

* "Paumanok (or Paumanake, or Paumanack, the Indian name of Long Island), over a hundred miles long; shaped like a fish—plenty

through Kings, Queens and Suffolk Counties, 120 miles altogether. On the north, Long Island Sound, a beautiful, varied and picturesque series of inlets, "necks," and sealike expansions, for a hundred miles to Orient Point. On the ocean side the great south bay dotted with countless hummocks, mostly small, some quite large, occasionally long bars of sand out two hundred rods to a mile and a half from the shore, while now and then, as at Rockaway and far east along the Hamptons, the beach makes right on the island, the sea dashing up without intervention. Several lighthouses on the shores east; a long history of wrecks tragedies, some even of late years. As a youngster, I was in the atmosphere and traditions of many of these wrecks—of one or two almost an observer. Off Hempstead beach for example, was the loss of the ship *Mexico* in 1840 (alluded to in "The Sleepers" in *L. of G.*). And at Hampton, some years later, the destruction of the brig *Elizabeth*, a fearful affair, in one of the worst winter gales, where Margaret Fuller went down with her husband and child. ৩৩ Inside the outer bars or beach this south bay is everywhere comparatively shallow; of cold winters all thick ice on the surface. As a boy I often went forth with a chum or two, on those frozen fields, with hand sled, axe, and eel-spear, after messes of eels. We would cut holes in the ice, sometimes striking quite an eel bonanza, and filling our baskets with great, fat, sweet, white-meated fellows. The scenes, the ice, drawing the hand sled, cutting holes, spearing the eels, etc., were of course just such fun as is dearest to boyhood. The shores of this bay, winter and summer, and my doings there in early life, are woven all through *L. of G.* One sport I was very fond of was to go on a bay party in summer to gather sea gulls' eggs. (The gulls lay two or three eggs, more than half the size of hens' eggs, right on the sand, and leave the sun's heat to hatch them.) ৩৩ The eastern end of Long Island, the Peconic Bay region, I knew quite well, too—sailed more than once around Shelter Island, and down to Montauk—spent many an hour on Turtle Hill by the old lighthouse, on the extreme point, looking out over the ceaseless roll of the Atlantic. I used to like to go down there and fraternize with the bluefishers, or the annual squads of sea-bass takers. Sometimes, along Montauk peninsula (it is some 15 miles long, and good

grazing), met the strange, unkempt, half-barbarous herdsmen, at that time living there entirely aloof from society or civilization, in charge, on those rich pasturages, of vast droves of horses, kine, or sheep owned by farmers of the eastern towns. Sometimes, too, the few remaining Indians, or half-breeds, at that period left on Montauk peninsula, but now I believe altogether extinct. ৩৩ More in the middle of the Island were the spreading Hempstead plains, then (1830-'40) quite prairielike, open, uninhabited, rather sterile, covered with kill-calf and huckleberry bushes, yet plenty of fair pasture for the cattle, mostly milch cows, who fed there by hundreds, even thousands, and at evening (the plains too were owned by the towns, and this was the use of them in common) might be seen taking their way home, branching off regularly in the right places. I have often been out on the edges of these plains toward sundown, and can yet recall in fancy the interminable cow processions, and hear the music of the tin or copper bells clanking far or near, and breathe the cool of the sweet and slightly aromatic evening air, and note the sunset. ৩৩ Through the same region of the island, but further east, extended wide central tracts of pine and scrub oak (charcoal was largely made here), monotonous and sterile. But many a good day or half-day did I have, wandering through those solitary crossroads, inhaling the peculiar and wild aroma. Here, and all along the island and its shores, I spent intervals many years, all seasons, sometimes riding, sometimes boating, but generally afoot (I was always then a good walker), absorbing fields, shores, marine incidents, characters, the bay men, farmers, pilots—always had a plentiful acquaintance with the latter, and with fishermen—went every summer on sailing trips—always liked the bare sea beach, south side, and have some of my happiest hours on it to this day. ৩৩ As I write, the whole experience comes back to me after the lapse of forty and more years—the soothing rustle of the waves, and the saline smell—boyhood's times, the clam-digging, barefoot, and with trousers rolled up—hauling down the creek—the perfume of the sedge meadows—the hay-boat, and the chowder and fishing excursions; or, of later years, little voyages down and out New York Bay, in the pilot boats. Those same later years, also, while living in Brooklyn (1836-'50), I went regularly every week in the mild seasons down to Coney Island, at that time a long, bare, unfrequented shore, which I had all to myself, and where I loved, after bathing, to race up and down the hard sand, and declaim Homer or Shakespeare to the surf and sea gulls by the hour. But I am getting ahead too rapidly, and must keep more in my traces.

---

of seashore, sandy, stormy, uninviting, the horizon boundless, the air too strong for invalids, the bays a wonderful resort for aquatic birds, the south-side meadows covered with salt hay, the soil of the island generally tough, but good for the locust tree, the apple orchard, and the blackberry, and with numberless springs of the sweetest water in the world. Years ago, among the bay men—a strong, wild race, now extinct, or rather entirely changed—a native of Long Island was called a *Paumanacker*, or *Creole Paumanacker*."—John Burroughs.

MY FIRST READING—LAFAYETTE ⁊ From 1824 to '28 our family lived in Brooklyn in Front, Cranberry, and Johnson Streets. In the latter my father built a nice house for a home, and afterward another in Tillary Street. We occupied them, one after the other, but they were mortgaged, and we lost them. I yet remember Lafayette's visit.* Most of these years I went to the public schools. It must have been about 1829 to '30 that I went with my father and mother to hear Elias Hicks preach in a ballroom on Brooklyn Heights. At about the same time employed as a boy in an office, lawyers', father and two sons, Clarke's, Fulton Street, near Orange. I had a nice desk and window nook to myself; Edward C. kindly helped me at my handwriting and composition, and (the signal event of my life up to that time) subscribed for me to a big circulating library. For a time I now reveled in romance reading of all kinds, first *The Arabian Nights*, all the volumes, an amazing treat. Then, with sorties in very many other directions, took in Walter Scott's novels, one after another, and his poetry (and continue to enjoy novels and poetry to this day).

PRINTING OFFICE—OLD BROOKLYN ⁊ After about two years went to work in a weekly newspaper and printing office, to learn the trade. The paper was the *Long Island Patriot*, owned by S. E. Clements, who was also postmaster. An old printer in the office, William Hartshorne, a Revolutionary character, who had seen Washington, was a special friend of mine, and I had many a talk with him about long-past times. The apprentices, including myself, boarded with his granddaughter. I used occasionally to go out riding with the boss, who was very kind to us boys; Sundays he took us all to a great old rough, fortress-looking stone church, on Joralemon Street, near where the Brooklyn City Hall now is (at that time broad fields and country roads everywhere around†). Afterward I worked on the *Long Island Star*, Alden Spooner's paper. My father all these years pursuing his trade as carpenter and builder, with varying fortune. There was a growing family of children—eight of us—my brother Jesse the oldest, myself the second, my dear sisters Mary and Hannah Louisa, my brothers Andrew, George, Thomas Jefferson, and then my youngest brother, Edward, born 1835, and always badly crippled, as I am myself of late years.

GROWTH—HEALTH—WORK ⁊ I developed (1833-4-5) into a healthy, strong youth (grew too fast, though, was nearly as big as a man at 15 or 16). Our family at this period moved back to the country, my dear mother very ill for a long time, but recovered. All these years I was down Long Island more or less every summer, now east, now west, sometimes months at a stretch. At 16, 17, and so on, was fond of debating societies, and had an active membership with them, off and on, in Brooklyn and one or two country towns on the island. A most omnivorous novel-reader, these and later years, devoured everything I could get. Fond of the theater, also, in New York, went whenever I could—sometimes witnessing fine performances. ⁊ 1836-7, worked as compositor in printing offices in New York City. Then, when little more than eighteen, and for a while afterward, went to teaching country schools down in Queens and Suffolk Counties, Long Island, and "boarded round." (This latter I consider one of my best experiences and deepest lessons in human nature behind the scenes, and in the masses.) In '39-'40, I started and published a weekly paper in my native town, Huntington. Then returning to New York City and Brooklyn, worked on as printer and writer, mostly prose, but an occasional shy at "poetry."

MY PASSION FOR FERRIES ⁊ Living in Brooklyn or New York City from this time forward,

---

* "On the visit of General Lafayette to this country, in 1824, he came over to Brooklyn in state, and rode through the city. The children of the schools turned out to join in the welcome. An edifice for a free public library for youths was just then commencing, and Lafayette consented to stop on his way and lay the cornerstone. Numerous children arriving on the ground, where a huge irregular excavation for the building was already dug, surrounded with heaps of rough stone, several gentlemen assisted in lifting the children to safe or convenient spots to see the ceremony. Among the rest, Lafayette, also helping the children, took up the five-year-old Walt Whitman, and pressing the child a moment to his breast, and giving him a kiss, handed him down to a safe spot in the excavation."—John Burroughs.

† Of the Brooklyn of that time (1830-40) hardly anything remains, except the lines of the old streets. The population was then between ten and twelve thousand. For a mile Fulton Street was lined with magnificent elm trees. The character of the place was thoroughly rural. As a sample of comparative values, it may be mentioned that twenty-five acres in what is now the most costly part of the city, bounded by Flatbush and Fulton Avenues, were then bought by Mr. Parmentier, a French *émigré*, for $4000. Who remembers the old places as they were? Who remembers the old citizens of that time? Among the former were Smith & Wood's, Coe Downing's, and other public houses at the ferry, the old ferry itself, Love Lane, the Heights and then, the Wallabout with the wooden bridge, and the road out beyond Fulton Street to the old toll gate. Among the latter were the majestic and genial General Jeremiah Johnson, with others, Gabriel Furman, Rev. E. M. Johnson, Alden Spooner, Mr. Pierrepont, Mr. Joralemon, Samuel Willoughby, Jonathan Trotter, George Hall, Cyrus P. Smith, N. B. Morse, John Dikeman, Adrian Hegeman, William Udall, and old Mr. Duflon, with his military garden.

my life, then, and still more the following years, was curiously identified with Fulton Ferry, already becoming the greatest of its sort in the world for general importance, volume, variety, rapidity, and picturesqueness. Almost daily, later ('50 to '60), I crossed on the boats, often up in the pilot houses where I could get a full sweep, absorbing shows, accompaniments, surroundings. What oceanic currents, eddies, underneath—the great tides of humanity also, with ever-shifting movements. Indeed, I have always had a passion for ferries; to me they afford inimitable, streaming, never-failing, living poems. The river and bay scenery, all about New York island, any time of a fine day—the hurrying, splashing sea tides—the changing panorama of steamers, all sizes, often a string of big ones outward bound to distant ports—the myriads of white-sailed schooners, sloops, skiffs, and the marvelously beautiful yachts—the majestic Sound boats as they rounded the Battery and came along toward 5, afternoon, eastward bound—the prospect off toward Staten Island, or down the Narrows, or the other way up the Hudson—what refreshment of spirit such sights and experiences gave me years ago (and many a time since). My old pilot friends, the Balsirs, Johnny Cole, Ira Smith, William White, and my young ferry friend, Tom Gere—how well I remember them all.

BROADWAY SIGHTS ❧ Besides Fulton Ferry, off and on for years, I knew and frequented Broadway—that noted avenue of New York's crowded and mixed humanity, and of so many notables. Here I saw, during those times, Andrew Jackson, Webster, Clay, Seward, Martin Van Buren, filibuster Walker, Kossuth, Fitz-Greene Halleck, Bryant, the Prince of Wales, Charles Dickens, the first Japanese ambassadors, and lots of other celebrities of the time. Always something novel or inspiriting, yet mostly to me the hurrying and vast amplitude of those never-ending human currents. I remember seeing James Fenimore Cooper in a courtroom in Chambers Street, back of the City Hall, where he was carrying on a law case (I think it was a charge of libel he had brought against some one). I also remember seeing Edgar A. Poe, and having a short interview with him (it must have been in 1845 or '6) in his office, second story of a corner building (Duane or Pearl Street.) He was editor and owner or part owner of *The Broadway Journal*. The visit was about a piece of mine he had published. Poe was very cordial, in a quiet way, appeared well in person, dress, etc. I have a distinct and pleasing remembrance of his looks, voice, manner, and matter; very

THE FULTON FERRY, 1890

kindly and human, but subdued, perhaps a little jaded. For another of my reminiscences, here on the west side, just below Houston Street, I once saw (it must have been about 1832, of a sharp, bright January day) a bent, feeble but stout-built very old man, bearded, swathed in rich furs, with a great ermine cap on his head, led and assisted, almost carried, down the steps of his high front stoop (a dozen friends and servants, emulous, carefully holding, guiding him) and then lifted and tucked in a gorgeous sleigh, enveloped in other furs, for a ride. The sleigh was drawn by as fine a team of horses as I ever saw. (You needn't think all the best animals are brought up nowadays; never was such horseflesh as fifty years ago on Long Island, or south, or in New York City; folks looked for spirit and mettle in a nag, not tame speed merely.) Well, I, a boy of perhaps thirteen or fourteen, stopped and gazed long at the spectacle of that fur-swathed old man, surrounded by friends and servants, and the careful seating of him in the sleigh. I remember the spirited, champing horses, the driver with his whip, and a fellow driver by his side, for extra prudence. The old man, the subject of so much attention, I can almost see now. It was John Jacob Astor. ᕯ The years 1846, '47, and there along, see me still in New York City, working as writer and printer, having my usual good health, and a good time generally.

OMNIBUS JAUNTS AND DRIVERS ᕯ One phase of those days must by no means go unrecorded—namely, the Broadway omnibuses, with their drivers. The vehicles still (I write this paragraph in 1881) give a portion of the character of Broadway—the Fifth Avenue, Madison Avenue, and Twenty-third Street lines yet running. But the flush days of the old Broadway stages, characteristic and copious, are over. The Yellow-birds, the Red-birds, the original Broadway, the Fourth Avenue, the Knickerbocker, and a dozen others of twenty or thirty years ago, are all gone. And the men specially identified with them, and giving vitality and meaning to them—the drivers—a strange, natural, quick-eyed and wondrous race (not only Rabelais and Cervantes would have gloated upon them, but Homer and Shakespeare would)—how well I remember them, and must here give a word about them. How many hours, forenoons, and afternoons—how many exhilarating night-times I have had—perhaps June or July, in cooler air—riding the whole length of Broadway, listening to some yarn (and the most vivid yarns ever spun, and the rarest mimicry)—or perhaps I declaiming some stormy passage from Julius Caesar or Richard (you could roar as loudly as you chose in that heavy, dense, uninterrupted street bass). Yes, I knew all the drivers then, Broadway Jack, Dressmaker, Balky Bill, George

Storms, Old Elephant, his brother Young Elephant (who came afterward), Tippy, Pop Rice, Big Frank, Yellow Joe, Pete Callahan, Patsy Dee, and dozens more; for there were hundreds. They had immense qualities, largely animal—eating, drinking, women—great personal pride, in their way—perhaps a few slouches here and there, but I should have trusted the general run of them, in their simple good will and honor, under all circumstances. Not only for comradeship, and sometimes affection—great studies I found them also. (I suppose the critics will laugh heartily, but the influence of those Broadway omnibus jaunts and drivers and declamations and escapades undoubtedly entered into the gestation of *Leaves of Grass*.)

PLAYS AND OPERAS TOO ᕯ And certain actors and singers had a good deal to do with the business. All through these years, off and on, I frequented the old Park, the Bowery, Broadway, and Chatham Square Theaters, and the Italian operas at Chambers Street, Astor Place, or the Battery—many seasons was on the free list, writing for papers even as quite a youth. The old Park Theater—what names, reminiscences, the words bring back! Placide, Clarke, Mrs. Vernon Fisher, Clara F., Mrs. Wood, Mrs. Sequin, Ellen Tree, Hackett, the younger Kean, Macready, Mrs. Richardson, Rice—singers, tragedians, comedians. What perfect acting! Henry Placide in *Napoleon's Old Guard* or *Grandfather Whitehead*—or *The Provoked Husband* of Cibber, with Fanny Kemble as Lady Townley—or Sheridan Knowles in his own *Virginius*—or inimitable Power in *Born to Good Luck*. These, and many more, the years of youth and onward. Fanny Kemble—name to conjure up great mimic scenes withal—perhaps the greatest. I remember well her rendering of Bianca in *Fazio*, and Marianna in *The Wife*. Nothing finer did ever stage exhibit—the veterans of all nations said so, and my boyish heart and head felt it in every minute cell. The lady was just matured, strong, better than merely beautiful, born from the footlights, had had three years' practice in London and through the British towns, and then she came to give America that young maturity and roseate power in all their noon, or rather forenoon, flush. It was my good luck to see her nearly every night she played at the old Park—certainly in all her principal characters. ᕯ I heard, these years, well rendered, all the Italian and other operas in vogue, *Sonnambula, The Puritans, Der Freischutz, Huguenots, Fille du Régiment, Faust, Etoile du Nord, Poliuto*, and others. Verdi's *Ernani, Rigoletto*, and *Trovatore*, with Donnizetti's *Lucia* or *Favorita* or *Lucrezia*, and Auber's *Massaniello*, or Rossini's *William Tell* and *Gazza Ladra*, were among my special enjoyments. I heard Alboni every time she sang in New York and vicinity—

also Grisi, the tenor Mario, and the baritone Badiali, the finest in the world. ෩ This musical passion followed my theatrical one. As boy or young man I had seen (reading them carefully the day beforehand) quite all Shakespeare's acting dramas, played wonderfully well. Even yet I cannot conceive anything finer than old Booth in *Richard Third*, or *Lear* (I don't know which was best), or Iago (or Pescara, or Sir Giles Overreach, to go outside of Shakespeare)—or Tom Hamblin in *Macbeth*—or old Clarke, either as the ghost in *Hamlet*, or as Prospero in *The Tempest*, with Mrs. Austin as Ariel, and Peter Richings as Caliban. Then other dramas, and fine players in them, Forrest as Metamora or Damon or Brutus—John R. Scott as Tom Cringle or Rolla—or Charlotte Cushman's Lady Gay Spanker in *London Assurance*. Then of some years later, at Castle Garden, Battery, I yet recall the splendid seasons of the Havana musical troupe under Maretzek—the fine band, the cool sea breezes, the unsurpassed vocalism—Steffanone, Bosio, Truffi, Marini in *Marino Faliero, Don Pasquale*, or *Favorita*. No better playing or singing ever in New York. It was here too I afterward heard Jenny Lind. (The Battery—its past associations—what tales those old trees and walks and sea walls could tell!)

THROUGH EIGHT YEARS ෩ In 1848–'49, I was occupied as editor of the *Daily Eagle* newspaper, in Brooklyn. The latter year went off on a leisurely journey and working expedition (my brother Jeff with me) through all the middle states, and down the Ohio and Mississippi Rivers. Lived awhile in New Orleans, and worked there on the editorial staff of *Daily Crescent* newspaper. After a time plodded back northward, up the Mississippi, and around to and by way of the Great Lakes, Michigan, Huron, and Erie, to Niagara Falls and lower Canada, finally returning through central New York and down the Hudson; traveling altogether probably 8,000 miles this trip, to and fro. '51, '53, occupied in housebuilding in Brooklyn. (For a little of the first part of that time in printing a daily and weekly paper, *The Freeman*.) '55, lost my dear father this year by death. Commenced putting *Leaves of Grass* to press for good, at the job-printing office of my friends, the brothers Rome, in Brooklyn, after many ms. doings and undoings (I had great trouble in leaving out the stock "poetical" touches, but succeeded at last). I am now (1856–'7) passing through my 37th year.

SOURCES OF CHARACTER—RESULTS— 1860 ෩ To sum up the foregoing from the outset (and, of course, far, far more unrecorded), I estimate three leading sources and formative stamps of my own character, now solidified for good or bad, and its subsequent literary and other outgrowth—the maternal nativity stock brought hither from faraway Netherlands, for one (doubtless the best)—the subterranean tenacity and central bony structure (obstinacy, willfulness) which I get from my paternal English elements, for another—and the combination of my Long Island birth-spot, seashores, childhood's scenes, absorptions, with teeming Brooklyn and New York—with, I suppose, my experiences afterward in the secession outbreak, for the third. ෩ For, in 1862, startled by news that my brother George, an officer in the 51st New York Volunteers, had been seriously wounded (first Fredericksburg battle, December 13th), I hurriedly went down to the field of war in Virginia. But I must go back a little.

GEORGE WASHINGTON WHITMAN

OPENING OF THE SECESSION WAR ෩ News of the attack on Fort Sumter and *the flag* at Charleston Harbor, S.C., was received in New York City late at night (13th April, 1861) and was immediately sent out in extras of the newspapers. I had been to the opera in Fourteenth Street that night, and after the performance was walking down Broadway toward twelve o'clock, on my way to Brooklyn, when I heard in the distance the loud cries of the newsboys, who came presently tearing and yelling up the street, rushing from side to side even more furiously than usual. I bought an extra and crossed to the Metropolitan Hotel (Niblo's), where the great lamps were still brightly blazing, and, with a crowd of others, who gathered impromptu, read the news, which was evidently authentic. For the benefit of some who had no papers, one of us read the telegram aloud, while all listened silently and attentively. No remark was made by any of the crowd, which had increased to thirty or forty, but all stood a minute or two, I remember, before they dispersed. I can almost see them there now, under the lamps at midnight again.

NATIONAL UPRISING AND VOLUN-
TEERING ᕦ I have said somewhere that the three
Presidentiads preceding 1861 showed how the weakness
and wickedness of rulers are just as eligible here in America under republican, as in Europe under dynastic influences. But what can I say of that prompt and splendid
wrestling with secession slavery, the archenemy person-
ified, the instant he unmistakably showed his face? The
volcanic upheaval of the nation, after that firing on the
flag at Charleston, proved for certain something which
had been previously in great doubt, and at once substantially settled the question of disunion. In my judgment it will remain as the grandest and most encourag-
ing spectacle yet vouchsafed in any age, old or new, to
political progress and democracy. It was not for what
came to the surface merely—though that was important
—but what it indicated below, which was of eternal
importance. Down in the abysms of New World humanity there had formed and hardened a primal hardpan of national Union will, determined and in the
majority, refusing to be tampered with or argued
against, confronting all emergencies, and capable at any
time of bursting all surface bonds and breaking out like
an earthquake. It is, indeed, the best lesson of the century, or of America, and it is a mighty privilege to have
been part of it. (Two great spectacles, immortal proofs
of democracy, unequaled in all the history of the past,
are furnished by the secession war—one at the beginning, the other at its close. Those are, the general, voluntary, armed upheaval, and the peaceful and harmoni-
ous disbanding of the armies in the summer of 1865.)

CONTEMPTUOUS FEELING ᕦ Even after the
bombardment of Sumter, however, the gravity of the
revolt, and the power and will of the slave states for a
strong and continued military resistance to national authority, were not at all realized at the North, except by
a few. Nine-tenths of the people of the free states looked
upon the rebellion, as started in South Carolina, from a
feeling one-half of contempt and the other half composed of anger and incredulity. It was not thought it
would be joined in by Virginia, North Carolina, or
Georgia. A great and cautious national official predicted
that it would blow over "in sixty days," and folks generally believed the prediction. I remember talking about
it on a Fulton Ferryboat with the Brooklyn mayor, who
said he only "hoped the Southern fire-eaters would
commit some overt act of resistance, as they would then
be at once so effectually squelched, we would never
hear of secession again—but he was afraid they never
would have the pluck to really do anything." I remember, too, that a couple of companies of the Thirteenth
Brooklyn, who rendezvou'd at the city armory, and
started thence as thirty-day men, were all provided with
pieces of rope, conspicuously tied to their musket bar-
rels, with which to bring back each man a prisoner from
the audacious South, to be led in a noose, on our men's
early and triumphant return!

BATTLE OF BULL RUN, JULY, 1861 ᕦ All
this sort of feeling was destined to be arrested and re-
versed by a terrible shock—the battle of first Bull Run—
certainly, as we now know it, one of the most singular
fights on record. (All battles, and their results, are far
more matters of accident than is generally thought; but
this was throughout a casualty, a chance. Each side supposed it had won, till the last moment. One had, in
point of fact, just the same right to be routed as the
other. By a fiction, or series of fictions, the national
forces at the last moment exploded in a panic and fled
from the field.) The defeated troops commenced pouring into Washington over the Long Bridge at daylight
on Monday, 22d—day drizzling all through with rain.
The Saturday and Sunday of the battle (20th, 21st) had
been parched and hot to an extreme—the dust, the
grime and smoke, in layers, sweated in, followed by
other layers again sweated in, absorbed by those excited
souls—their clothes all saturated with the clay powder
filling the air—stirred up everywhere on the dry roads
and trodden fields by the regiments, swarming wagons,
artillery, etc.—all the men with this coating of murk
and sweat and rain, now recoiling back, pouring over
the Long Bridge—a horrible march of twenty miles,
returning to Washington baffled, humiliated, panic-
struck. Where are the vaunts, and the proud boasts with
which you went forth? Where are your banners, and
your bands of music, and your ropes to bring back your
prisoners? Well, there isn't a band playing—and there
isn't a flag but clings ashamed and lank to its staff. ᕦ The
sun rises, but shines not. The men appear, at first sparsely
and shamefaced enough, then thicker, in the streets of
Washington—appear in Pennsylvania Avenue, and on
the steps and basement entrances. They come along in
disorderly mobs, some in squads, stragglers, companies.
Occasionally, a rare regiment, in perfect order, with its
officers (some gaps, dead, the true braves) marching in
silence, with lowering faces, stern, weary to sinking, all
black and dirty, but every man with his musket, and
stepping alive; but these are the exceptions. Sidewalks
of Pennsylvania Avenue, Fourteenth Street, etc.,
crowded, jammed with citizens, darkies, clerks, everybody, lookers-on; women in the windows, curious expressions from faces, as those swarms of dirt-covered
returned soldiers there (will they never end?) move by;
but nothing said, no comments (half our lookers-on
secesh of the most venomous kind—they say nothing;

but the devil snickers in their faces). During the forenoon Washington gets all-over motley with these defeated soldiers—queer looking objects, strange eyes and faces, drenched (the steady rain drizzles on all day) and fearfully worn, hungry, haggard, blistered in the feet. Good people (but not over-many of them either) hurry up something for their grub. They put wash-kettles on the fire, for soup, for coffee. They set tables on the sidewalks—wagonloads of bread are purchased, swiftly cut in stout chunks. Here are two aged ladies, beautiful, the first in the city for culture and charm; they stand with store of eating and drink at an improvised table of rough plank, and give food, and have the store replenished from their house every half-hour all that day; and there in the rain they stand, active, silent, white-haired, and give food, though the tears stream down their cheeks, almost without intermission, the whole time. Amid the deep excitement, crowds and motion, and desperate eagerness, it seems strange to see many, very many, of the soldiers sleeping—in the midst of all, sleeping sound. They drop down anywhere, on the steps of houses, up close by the basements or fences, on the sidewalk, aside on some vacant lot, and deeply sleep. A poor seventeen or eighteen-year-old boy lies there, on the stoop of a grand house; he sleeps so calmly, so profoundly. Some clutch their muskets firmly even in sleep. Some in squads; comrades, brothers, close together—and on them, as they lie, sulkily drips the rain. ‿ As afternoon passed, and evening came, the streets, the barrooms, knots everywhere, listeners, questioners, terrible yarns, bugaboo, masked batteries, our regiment all cut up, etc. —stories and storytellers, windy, bragging, vain centers of street crowds. Resolution, manliness, seem to have abandoned Washington. The principal hotel, Willard's, is full of shoulder straps—thick, crushed, creeping with shoulder straps. (I see them, and must have a word with them. There you are, shoulder straps! But where are your companies? Where are your men? Incompetents! Never tell me of chances of battle, of getting strayed, and the like. I think this is your work, this retreat, after all. Sneak, blow, put on airs there in Willard's sumptuous parlors and barrooms, or anywhere—no explanation shall save you. Bull Run is your work; had you been half or one-tenth worthy your men, this would never have happened.) ‿ Meantime, in Washington, among the great persons and their entourage, a mixture of awful consternation, uncertainty, rage, shame, helplessness, and stupefying disappointment. The worst is not only imminent, but already here. In a few hours—perhaps before the next meal—the secesh generals, with their victorious hordes, will be upon us. The dream of humanity, the vaunted Union we thought so strong, so impregnable—lo! it seems already smashed like a china plate. One bitter, bitter hour—perhaps proud America will never again know such an hour. She must pack and fly—no time to spare. Those white palaces—the dome-crowned Capitol there on the hill, so stately over the trees—shall they be left—or destroyed first? For it is certain that the talk among certain of the magnates and officers and clerks and officials everywhere, for twenty-four hours in and around Washington after Bull Run, was loud and undisguised for yielding out and out, and substituting the southern rule, and Lincoln promptly abdicating and departing. If the secesh officers and forces had immediately followed, and by a bold Napoleonic movement had entered Washington the first day (or even the second), they could have had things their own way, and a powerful faction north to back them. One of our returning colonels expressed in public that night, amid a swarm of officers and gentlemen in a crowded room, the opinion that it was useless to fight, that the southerners had made their title clear, and that the best course for the national government to pursue was to desist from any further attempt at stopping them, and admit them again to the lead, on the best terms they were willing to grant. Not a voice was raised against this judgment, amid that large crowd of officers and gentlemen. (The fact is, the hour was one of the three or four of those crises we had then and afterward, during the fluctuations of four years, when human eyes appeared at least just as likely to see the last breath of the Union as to see it continue.)

THE STUPOR PASSES—SOMETHING ELSE BEGINS ‿ But the hour, the day, the night passed, and whatever returns, an hour, a day, a night like that can never again return. The President, recovering himself, begins that very night—sternly, rapidly sets about the task of reorganizing his forces and placing himself in positions for future and surer work. If there were nothing else of Abraham Lincoln for history to stamp him with, it is enough to send him with his wreath to the memory of all future time, that he endured that hour, that day, bitterer than gall—indeed a crucifixion day—that it did not conquer him—that he unflinchingly stemmed it, and resolved to lift himself and the Union out of it. ‿ Then the great New York papers at once appeared (commencing that evening, and following it up the next morning, and incessantly through many days afterward), with leaders that rang out over the land with the loudest, most reverberating ring of clearest bugles, full of encouragement, hope, inspiration, unfaltering defiance. Those magnificent editorials! They never flagged for a fortnight. The *Herald* commenced them—I remember the articles well. The *Tribune* was equally cogent and inspiriting—and the *Times, Evening*

Post, and other principal papers were not a whit behind. They came in good time, for they were needed. For in the humiliation of Bull Run, the popular feeling north, from its extreme of superciliousness, recoiled to the depth of gloom and apprehension. ᠅ (Of all the days of the war, there are two especially I can never forget. Those were the days following the news, in New York and Brooklyn, of that first Bull Run defeat, and the day of Abraham Lincoln's death. I was home in Brooklyn on both occasions. The day of the murder we heard the news very early in the morning. Mother prepared breakfast—and other meals afterward—as usual; but not a mouthful was eaten all day by either of us. We each drank half a cup of coffee; that was all. Little was said. We got every newspaper, morning and evening, and the frequent extras of that period, and passed them silently to each other.)

DOWN AT THE FRONT ᠅ FALMOUTH, VA., OPPOSITE FREDERICKSBURG, DECEMBER 21, 1862 ᠅ Begin my visits among the camp hospitals in the Army of the Potomac. Spend a good part of the day in a large brick mansion on the banks of the Rappahannock, used as a hospital since the battle—seems to have received only the worst cases. Outdoors, at the foot of a tree, within ten yards of the front of the house, I notice a heap of amputated feet, legs, arms, hands, etc., a full load for a one-horse cart. Several dead bodies lie near, each covered with its brown woolen blanket. In the dooryard, toward the river, are fresh graves, mostly of officers, their names on pieces of barrel staves or broken boards, stuck in the dirt. (Most of these bodies were subsequently taken up and transported north to their friends.) The large mansion is quite crowded upstairs and down, everything impromptu, no system, all bad enough, but I have no doubt the best that can be done; all the wounds pretty bad, some frightful, the men in their old clothes, unclean and bloody. Some of the wounded are rebel soldiers and officers, prisoners. One, a Mississippian, a captain, hit badly in leg, I talked with some time; he asked me for papers, which I gave him. (I saw him three months afterward in Washington, with his leg amputated, doing well.) I went through the rooms, downstairs and up. Some of the men were dying. I had nothing to give at that visit, but wrote a few letters

WOUNDED SOLDIERS OUTSIDE HOSPITAL IN FREDERICKSBURG, VIRGINIA

No. *155*

Office Christian Commission,

No. 13 Bank Street.

Philadelphia, *Jany 20th 1863*

To Officers of the Army and Navy of the United States, and others:

The **CHRISTIAN COMMISSION,** organized by a Convention of the Young Men's Christian Associations of the loyal States, to promote the spiritual and temporal welfare and improvement of the men of the Army and Navy, acting under the approbation and commendation of the President, the Secretaries of the Army and the Navy, and of the Generals in command, have appointed

Walt Whitman of Brooklyn N.Y.

A Delegate, to act in accordance with instructions furnished herewith, under direction of the proper officers, in furtherance of the objects of the Christian Commission.

His services will be rendered in behalf of the Christian Commission, without remuneration from, or expense to, the Government.

His work will be that of distributing stores where needed, in hospitals and camps; circulating good reading matter amongst soldiers and sailors; visiting the sick and wounded, to instruct, comfort and cheer them, and aid them in correspondence with their friends at home; aiding Surgeons on the battle-field and elsewhere in the care and conveyance of the wounded to hospitals; helping Chaplains in their ministrations and influence for the good of the men under their care; and addressing soldiers and sailors, individually and collectively, in explanation of the work of the Christian Commission and its Delegates, and for their personal instruction and benefit, temporal and eternal.

All possible facilities, and all due courtesies, are asked for him, in the proper pursuance of any or all of these duties.

Geo. H. Stuart

Chairman Christian Commission.

to folks home, mothers, etc. Also talked to three or four, who seemed most susceptible to it, and needing it.

AFTER FIRST FREDERICKSBURG ᵱᵃ DECEMBER 23 TO 31 ᵱᵃ The results of the late battle are exhibited everywhere about here in thousands of cases (hundreds die every day) in the camp, brigade, and division hospitals. These are merely tents, and sometimes very poor ones, the wounded lying on the ground, lucky if their blankets are spread on layers of pine or hemlock twigs, or small leaves. No cots, seldom even a mattress. It is pretty cold. The ground is frozen hard, and there is occasional snow. I go around from one case to another. I do not see that I do much good to these wounded and dying, but I cannot leave them. Once in a while some youngster holds on to me convulsively, and I do what I can for him; at any rate, stop with him and sit near him for hours, if he wishes it. ᵱᵃ Besides the hospitals, I also go occasionally on long tours through the camps, talking with the men, etc. Sometimes at night among the groups around the fires, in their shebang enclosure of bushes. These are curious shows, full of characters and groups. I soon get acquainted anywhere in camp, with officers or men, and am always well used. Sometimes I go down on picket with the regiments I know best. As to rations, the army here at present seems to be tolerably well supplied, and the men have enough, such as it is, mainly salt pork and hardtack. Most of the regiments lodge in the flimsy little shelter tents. A few have built themselves huts of logs and mud, with fireplaces.

BACK TO WASHINGTON ᵱᵃ JANUARY, '63 ᵱᵃ Left camp at Falmouth, with some wounded, a few days since, and came here by Aquia Creek railroad, and so on government steamer up the Potomac. Many wounded were with us on the cars and boat. The cars were just common platform ones. The railroad journey of ten or twelve miles was made mostly before sunrise. The soldiers guarding the road came out from their tents or shebangs of bushes with rumpled hair and half-awake look. Those on duty were walking their posts, some on banks over us, others down far below the level of the track. I saw large cavalry camps off the road. At Aquia Creek landing were numbers of wounded going north. While I waited some three hours, I went around among them. Several wanted word sent home to parents, brothers, wives, etc., which I did for them (by mail the next day from Washington). On the boat I had my hands full. One poor fellow died going up. ᵱᵃ I am now remaining in and around Washington, daily visiting the hospitals. Am much in Patent Office, Eighth Street, H Street, Armory Square, and others. Am now able to do

a little good, having money (as almoner of others home) and getting experience. Today, Sunday afternoon and till nine in the evening, visited Campbell Hospital; attended specially to one case in Ward I, very sick with pleurisy and typhoid fever, young man, farmer's son, D. F. Russell, Company E, 60th New York, downhearted and feeble; a long time before he would take any interest; wrote a letter home to his mother, in Malone, Franklin County, N.Y., at his request; gave him some fruit and one or two other gifts; enveloped and directed his letter, etc. Then went thoroughly through Ward 6, observed every case in the ward, without, I think, missing one; gave perhaps from twenty to thirty persons, each one some little gift, such as oranges, apples, sweet crackers, figs, etc. ᵱᵃ THURSDAY, JAN. 21 ᵱᵃ Devoted the main part of the day to Armory Square hospital; went pretty thoroughly through Wards F, G, H, and I; some fifty cases in each ward. In Ward F supplied the men throughout with writing paper and stamped envelope each; distributed in small portions to proper subjects, a large jar of first-rate preserved berries, which had been donated to me by a lady—her own cooking. Found several cases I thought good subjects for small sums of money, which I furnished. (The wounded men often come up broke, and it helps their spirits to have even the small sum I give them.) My paper and envelopes all gone, but distributed a good lot of amusing reading matter; also, as I thought judicious, tobacco, oranges, apples, etc. Interesting cases in Ward I: Charles Miller, Bed 19, Company D, 53d Pennsylvania, is only sixteen years of age, very bright, courageous boy, left leg amputated below the knee; next bed to him, another young lad, very sick; gave each appropriate gifts. In the bed above, also, amputation of the left leg; gave him a little jar of raspberries; Bed 1, this ward, gave a small sum; also to a soldier on crutches, sitting on his bed near . . . (I am more and more surprised at the very great proportion of youngsters from fifteen to twenty-one in the army. I afterward found a still greater proportion among the southerners.) ᵱᵃ Evening, same day, went to see D. F. R., before alluded to; found him remarkably changed for the better; up and dressed—quite a triumph; he afterward got well, and went back to his regiment. Distributed in the wards a quantity of note paper, and forty or fifty stamped envelopes, of which I had recruited my stock and the men were much in need.

FIFTY HOURS LEFT WOUNDED ON THE FIELD ᵱᵃ Here is a case of a soldier I found among the crowded cots in the Patent Office. He likes to have some one to talk to, and we will listen to him. He got badly hit in his leg and side at Fredericksburg that eventful Saturday, 13th of December. He lay the succeeding two days and nights helpless on the field, between the city and those grim terraces of batteries; his company and regiment had been compelled to leave him to his fate. To make matters worse, it happened he lay with his head slightly downhill, and could not help himself. At the end of some fifty hours he was brought off, with other wounded, under a flag of truce. I ask him how the rebels treated him as he lay during those two days and nights within reach of them—whether they came to him—whether they abused him. He answers that several of the rebels, soldiers and others, came to him at one time and another. A couple of them, who were together, spoke roughly and sarcastically, but nothing worse. One middle-aged man, however, who seemed to be moving around the field, among the dead and wounded, for benevolent purposes, came to him in a way he will never forget; treated our soldier kindly, bound up his wounds, cheered him, gave him a couple of biscuits and a drink of whiskey and water; asked him if he could eat some beef. This good secesh, however, did not change our soldier's position, for it might have caused the blood to burst from the wounds, clotted and stagnated. Our soldier is from Pennsylvania; has had a pretty severe time; the wounds proved to be bad ones. But he retains a good heart, and is at present on the gain. (It is not uncommon for the men to remain on the field this way, one, two, or even four or five days.)

HOSPITAL SCENES AND PERSONS ∂ LETTER WRITING ∂ When eligible, I encourage the men to write, and myself, when called upon, write all sorts of letters for them (including love letters, very tender ones). Almost as I reel off these memoranda, I write for a new patient to his wife. M. de F., of the 17th Connecticut, Company H, has just come up (February 17th) from Windmill Point, and is received in Ward H, Armory Square. He is an intelligent-looking man, has a foreign accent, black-eyed and -haired, a Hebraic appearance. Wants a telegraphic message sent to his wife, New Canaan, Conn. I agree to send the message—but to make things sure I also sit down and write the wife a letter, and dispatch it to the Post Office immediately, as he fears she will come on, and he does not wish her to, as he will surely get well. ∂ SATURDAY, JANUARY 30TH ∂ Afternoon, visited Campbell Hospital. Scene of cleaning up the ward, and giving the men all clean clothes—through the ward (6), the patients dressing or being dressed—the naked upper half of the bodies—the good humor and fun—the shirts, drawers, sheets of beds, etc., and the general fixing up for Sunday. Gave J. L. 50 cents. ∂ WEDNESDAY, FEBRUARY 4TH ∂ Visited Armory Square hospital, went pretty thoroughly through Wards E and D. Supplied paper and enve-

lopes to all who wished—as usual, found plenty of men who needed these articles. Wrote letters. Saw and talked with two or three members of the Brooklyn 14th Regt. A poor fellow in Ward D, with a fearful wound in a fearful condition, was having some loose splinters of bone taken from the neighborhood of the wound. The operation was long, and one of great pain—yet, after it was well commenced, the soldier bore it in silence. He sat up, propped—was much wasted—had lain a long time quiet in one position (not for days only but weeks), a bloodless, brown-skinned face, with eyes full of determination—belonged to a New York regiment. There was an unusual cluster of surgeons, medical cadets, nurses, etc., around his bed—I thought the whole thing was done with tenderness, and done well. In one case, the wife sat by the side of her husband, his sickness typhoid fever, pretty bad. In another, by the side of her son, a mother—she told me she had seven children, and this was the youngest. (A fine, kind, healthy, gentle mother, good-looking, not very old, with a cap on her head, and dressed like home—what a charm it gave to the whole ward.) I liked the woman nurse in Ward E— I noticed how she sat a long time by a poor fellow who just had, that morning, in addition to his other sickness, bad hemorrhage—she gently assisted him, relieved him of the blood, holding a cloth to his mouth, as he coughed it up—he was so weak he could only just turn his head over on the pillow. ∂ One young New York man, with a bright, handsome face, had been lying several months from a most disagreeable wound received at Bull Run. A bullet had shot him right through the bladder, hitting him front, low in the belly, and coming out back. He had suffered much—the water came out of the wound, by slow but steady quantities, for many weeks—so that he lay almost constantly in a sort of puddle—and there were other disagreeable circumstances. He was of good heart, however. At present comparatively comfortable, had a bad throat, was delighted with a stick of horehound candy I gave him, with one or two other trifles.

PATENT OFFICE HOSPITAL ∂ FEBRUARY 23 ∂ I must not let the great hospital at the Patent Office pass away without some mention. A few weeks ago the vast area of the second story of that noblest of Washington buildings was crowded close with rows of sick, badly wounded and dying soldiers. They were placed in three very large apartments. I went there many times. It was a strange, solemn, and, with all its features of suffering and death, a sort of fascinating sight. I go sometimes at night to soothe and relieve particular cases. Two of the immense apartments are filled with high and ponderous glass cases, crowded with models in miniature of every kind of utensil, machine, or invention it ever entered into the mind of man to conceive; and with curiosities and foreign presents. Between these cases are lateral openings, perhaps eight feet wide and quite deep, and in these were placed the sick, besides a great long double row of them up and down through the middle of the hall. Many of them were very bad cases, wounds and amputations. Then there was a gallery running above the hall in which there were beds also. It was, indeed, a curious scene, especially at night when lit up. The glass cases, the beds, the forms lying there, the gallery above, and the marble pavement underfoot—the suffering, and the fortitude to bear it in various degrees—occasionally, from some, the groan that could not be repressed—sometimes a poor fellow dying, with emaciated face and glassy eye, the nurse by his side, the doctor also there, but no friend, no relative—such were the sights but lately in the Patent Office. (The wounded have since been removed from there, and it is now vacant again.)

THE WHITE HOUSE BY MOONLIGHT ⅌ FEBRUARY 24TH ⅌ A spell of fine soft weather. I wander about a good deal, sometimes at night under the moon. Tonight took a long look at the President's house. The white portico—the palacelike, tall, round columns,

spotless as snow—the walls also—the tender and soft moonlight, flooding the pale marble, and making peculiar faint languishing shades, not shadows—everywhere a soft, transparent, hazy, thin, blue moon lace, hanging in the air—the brilliant and extra-plentiful clusters of gas, on and around the façade, columns, portico, etc.—everything so white, so marbly pure and dazzling, yet soft—the White House of future poems, and of dreams and dramas, there in the soft and copious moon—the gorgeous front, in the trees, under the lustrous flooding moon, full of reality, full of illusion—the forms of the trees, leafless, silent, in trunk and myriad angles of branches, under the stars and sky—the White House of the land, and of beauty and night—sentries at the gates, and by the portico, silent, pacing there in blue overcoats —stopping you not at all, but eyeing you with sharp eyes, whichever way you move.

AN ARMY HOSPITAL WARD ⅌ Let me specialize a visit I made to the collection of barracklike one-story edifices, Campbell Hospital, out on the flats, at the end of the then horse railway route, on Seventh Street. There is a long building appropriated to each ward. Let us go into Ward 6. It contains today, I should judge, eighty or a hundred patients, half sick, half wounded.

CAMPBELL HOSPITAL

The edifice is nothing but boards, well whitewashed inside, and the usual slender-framed iron bedsteads, narrow and plain. You walk down the central passage, with a row on either side, their feet toward you, and their heads to the wall. There are fires in large stoves, and the prevailing white of the walls is relieved by some ornaments, stars, circles, etc., made of evergreens. The view of the whole edifice and occupants can be taken at once, for there is no partition. You may hear groans or other sounds of unendurable suffering from two or three of the cots, but in the main there is quiet—almost a painful absence of demonstration; but the pallid face, the dulled eye, and the moisture on the lip, are demonstration enough. Most of these sick or hurt are evidently young fellows from the country, farmers' sons, and such like. Look at the fine large frames, the bright and broad countenances, and the many yet lingering proofs of strong constitution and physique. Look at the patient and mute manner of our American wounded as they lie in such a sad collection; representatives from all New England, and from New York, and New Jersey, and Pennsylvania—indeed from all the states and all the cities—largely from the West. Most of them are entirely without friends or acquaintants here—no familiar face, and hardly a word of judicious sympathy or cheer, through their sometimes long and tedious sickness, or the pangs of aggravated wounds.

A CONNECTICUT CASE ℘ This young man in Bed 25 is H. D. B., of the 27th Connecticut, Company B. His folks live at Northford, near New Haven. Though not more than twenty-one, or thereabouts, he has knocked much around the world, on sea and land, and has seen some fighting on both. When I first saw him he was very sick, with no appetite. He declined offers of money—said he did not need anything. As I was quite anxious to do something, he confessed that he had a hankering for a good homemade rice pudding—thought he could relish it better than anything. At this time his stomach was very weak. (The doctor, whom I consulted, said nourishment would do him more good than anything; but things in the hospital, though better than usual, revolted him.) I soon procured B. his rice pudding. A Washington lady (Mrs. O'C.), hearing his wish, made the pudding herself, and I took it up to him the next day. He subsequently told me he lived upon it for three or four days. This B. is a good sample of the American eastern young man—the typical Yankee. I took a fancy to him, and gave him a nice pipe for a keepsake. He received afterward a box of things from home, and nothing would do but I must take dinner with him, which I did, and a very good one it was.

TWO BROOKLYN BOYS ℘ Here in this same ward are two young men from Brooklyn, members of the 51st New York. I had known both the two as young lads at home, so they seem near to me. One of them, J. L., lies there with an amputated arm, the stump healing pretty well. (I saw him lying on the ground at Fredericksburg last December, all bloody, just after the arm was taken off. He was very phlegmatic about it, munching away at a cracker in the remaining hand—made no fuss.) He will recover, and thinks and talks yet of meeting the Johnny Rebs.

A SECESH BRAVE ℘ The grand soldiers are not comprised in those of one side, any more than the other. Here is a sample of an unknown southerner, a lad of seventeen. At the War Department, a few days ago, I witnessed a presentation of captured flags to the Secretary. Among others a soldier named Gant, of the 104th Ohio Volunteers, presented a rebel battle flag, which one of the officers stated to me was borne to the mouth of our cannon and planted there by a boy but seventeen years of age, who actually endeavored to stop the muzzle of the gun with fence rails. He was killed in the effort, and the flagstaff was severed by a shot from one of our men.

THE WOUNDED FROM CHANCELLORSVILLE ℘ MAY, '63 ℘ As I write this, the wounded have begun to arrive from Hooker's command from bloody Chancellorsville. I was down among the first arrivals. The men in charge told me the bad cases were yet to come. If that is so I pity them, for these are bad enough. You ought to see the scene of the wounded arriving at the landing here at the foot of Sixth Street, at night. Two boatloads came about half past seven last night. A little after eight it rained a long and violent shower. The pale, helpless soldiers had been debarked, and lay around on the wharf and neighborhood anywhere. The rain was, probably, grateful to them; at any rate they were exposed to it. The few torches light up the spectacle. All around—on the wharf, on the ground, out on side places—the men are lying on blankets, old quilts, etc., with bloody rags bound round heads, arms, and legs. The attendants are few, and at night few outsiders also—only a few hard-worked transportation men and drivers. (The wounded are getting to be common, and people grew callous.) The men, whatever their condition, lie there, and patiently wait till their turn comes to be taken up. Near by, the ambulances are now arriving in clusters, and one after another is called to back up and take its load. Extreme cases are sent off on stretchers. The men generally make little or no ado, whatever their sufferings. A few groans that cannot be suppressed, and occasionally a scream of pain as they lift a man into the ambulance. Today, as I write, hundreds more are expected, and tomorrow and the next day more, and so on for many days. Quite often they arrive at the rate of 1,000 a day.

A NIGHT BATTLE, OVER A WEEK SINCE

ॐ MAY 12 ॐ There was part of the late battle at Chancellorsville (second Fredericksburg), a little over a week ago, Saturday, Saturday night, and Sunday, under Gen. Joe Hooker, I would like to give just a glimpse of (a moment's look in a terrible storm at sea—of which a few suggestions are enough, and full details impossible). The fighting had been very hot during the day and, after an intermission the latter part, was resumed at night, and kept up with furious energy till 3 o'clock in the morning. That afternoon (Saturday) an attack sudden and strong by Stonewall Jackson had gained a great advantage to the Southern army, and broken our lines, entering us like a wedge, and leaving things in that position at dark. But Hooker at 11 at night made a desperate push, drove the secesh forces back, restored his original lines, and resumed his plans. This night scrimmage was very exciting, and afforded countless strange and fearful pictures. The fighting had been general both at Chancellorsville and northeast at Fredericksburg. (We hear of some poor fighting, episodes, skedaddling on our part. I think not of it. I think of the fierce bravery, the general rule.) One corps, the 6th, Sedgewick's, fights four dashing and bloody battles in thirty-six hours, retreating in great jeopardy, losing largely but maintaining itself, fighting with the sternest desperation under all circumstances, getting over the Rappahannock only by the skin of its teeth, yet getting over. It lost many, many brave men, yet it took vengeance, ample vengeance. ॐ But it was the tug of Saturday evening, and through the night and Sunday morning, I wanted to make a special note of. It was largely in the woods, and quite a general engagement. The night was very pleasant, at times the moon shining out full and clear, all Nature so calm in itself, the early summer grass so rich, and foliage of the trees—yet there the battle raging, and many good fellows lying helpless, with new accessions to them, and every minute amid the rattle of muskets and crash of cannon (for there was an artillery contest too) the red life-blood oozing out from heads or trunks or limbs upon that green and dew-cool grass. Patches of the woods take fire, and several of the wounded, unable to move, are consumed—quite large spaces are swept over, burning the dead also—some of the men have their hair and beards singed—some, burns on their faces and hands —others holes burnt in their clothing. The flashes of fire from the cannon, the quick flaring flames and smoke,

and the immense roar—the musketry so general, the light nearly bright enough for each side to see the other —the crashing, tramping of men—the yelling—close quarters—we hear the secesh yells—our men cheer loudly back, especially if Hooker is in sight—hand-to-hand conflicts, each side stands up to it, brave, determined as demons, they often charge upon us—a thousand deeds are done, worth to write newer greater poems on—and still the woods on fire—still many are not only scorched —too many, unable to move, are burned to death. ॐ Then the camps of the wounded—O heavens, what scene is this?—is this indeed *humanity*—these butchers' shambles? There are several of them. There they lie, in the largest, in an open space in the woods, from 200 to 300 poor fellows—the groans and screams—the odor of blood, mixed with the fresh scent of the night, the grass, the trees—that slaughterhouse! O well is it their mothers, their sisters cannot see them—cannot conceive, and never conceived, these things. One man is shot by a shell, both in the arm and leg—both are amputated— there lie the rejected members. Some have their legs blown off—some bullets through the breast—some indescribably horrid wounds in the face or head, all mutilated, sickening, torn, gouged out—some in the abdomen—some mere boys—many rebels, badly hurt—they take their regular turns with the rest, just the same as any —the surgeons use them just the same. Such is the camp of the wounded—such a fragment, a reflection afar off of the bloody scene—while over all the clear, large moon comes out at times softly, quietly shining. Amid the woods, that scene of flitting souls—amid the crack and crash and yelling sounds—the impalpable perfume of the woods—and yet the pungent, stifling smoke—the radiance of the moon, looking from heaven at intervals so placid—the sky so heavenly—the clear-obscure up there, those buoyant upper oceans—a few large placid stars beyond, coming silently and languidly out, and then disappearing—the melancholy, draperied night above, around. And there, upon the roads, the fields, and in those woods, that contest, never one more desperate in any age or land—both parties now in force— masses—no fancy battle, no semiplay, but fierce and savage demons fighting there—courage and scorn of death the rule, exceptions almost none. ॐ What history, I say, can ever give—for who can know—the mad, determined tussle of the armies, in all their separate large and little squads—as this—each steeped from crown to toe in desperate, mortal purports? Who know the conflict, hand-to-hand—the many conflicts in the dark, those shadowy-tangled, flashing-moonbeamed woods —the writhing groups and squads—the cries, the din, the cracking guns and pistols—the distant cannon—the cheers and calls and threats and awful music of the oaths

—the indescribable mix—the officers' orders, persuasions, encouragements—the devils fully roused in human hearts—the strong shout, *Charge, men, charge*—the flash of the naked sword, and rolling flame and smoke? And still the broken, clear and clouded heaven—and still again the moonlight pouring silvery soft its radiant patches over all. Who paint the scene, the sudden partial panic of the afternoon, at dusk? Who paint the irrepressible advance of the second division of the Third Corps, under Hooker himself, suddenly ordered up—those rapid-filing phantoms through the woods? Who show what moves there in the shadows, fluid and firm—to save, (and it did save) the army's name, perhaps the nation? as there the veterans hold the field. (Brave Berry falls not yet—but death has marked him—soon he falls.)

UNNAMED REMAINS THE BRAVEST SOLDIER ᵱ Of scenes like these, I say, who writes—whoe'er can write the story? Of many a score—aye, thousands, north and south, of unwrit heroes, unknown heroisms, incredible, impromptu, first-class desperations—who tells? No history ever—no poem sings, no music sounds, those bravest men of all—those deeds. No formal general's report, nor book in the library, nor

column in the paper, embalms the bravest, north or south, east or west. Unnamed, unknown, remain, and still remain, the bravest soldiers. Our manliest—our boys—our hardy darlings; no picture gives them. Likely, the typic one of them (standing, no doubt, for hundreds, thousands) crawls aside to some bush-clump, or ferny tuft, on receiving his death shot—there sheltering a little while, soaking roots, grass and soil, with red blood—the battle advances, retreats, flits from the scene, sweeps by—and there, haply with pain and suffering (yet less, far less, than is supposed), the last lethargy winds like a serpent round him—the eyes glaze in death—none recks—perhaps the burial squads, in truce, a week afterwards, search not the secluded spot—and there, at last, the Bravest Soldier crumbles in mother earth, unburied and unknown.

SOME SPECIMEN CASES ᵱ JUNE 18TH ᵱ In one of the hospitals I find Thomas Haley, Company M, 4th New York Cavalry—a regular Irish boy, a fine specimen of youthful physical manliness—shot through the lungs—inevitably dying—came over to this country from Ireland to enlist—has not a single friend or acquaintance here—is sleeping soundly at this moment (but it is the sleep of death)—has a bullet hole straight

ARMORY SQUARE HOSPITAL, WARD K

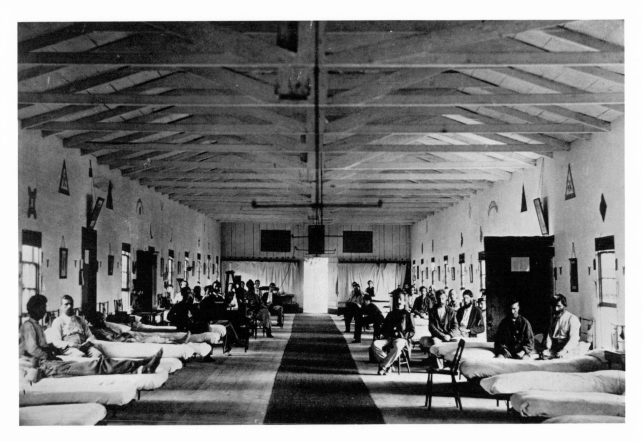

through the lung. I saw Tom when first brought here, three days since, and didn't suppose he could live twelve hours (yet he looks well enough in the face to a casual observer). He lies there with his frame exposed above the waist, all naked, for coolness, a fine-built man, the tan not yet bleached from his cheeks and neck. It is useless to talk to him, as with his sad hurt, and the stimulants they give him, and the utter strangeness of every object, face, furniture, etc., the poor fellow, even when awake, is like some frightened, shy animal. Much of the time he sleeps, or half-sleeps. (Sometimes I thought he knew more than he showed.) I often come and sit by him in perfect silence; he will breathe for ten minutes as softly and evenly as a young babe asleep. Poor youth, so handsome, athletic, with profuse beautiful shining hair. One time as I sat looking at him while he lay asleep, he suddenly, without the least start, awakened, opened his eyes, gave me a long steady look, turning his face very slightly to gaze easier—one long, clear, silent look—a slight sigh—then turned back and went into his doze again. Little he knew, poor death-stricken boy, the heart of the stranger that hovered near. ?? W. H. E., CO. F., 2D N.J. ?? His disease is pneumonia. He lay sick at the wretched hospital below Aquia Creek, for seven or eight days before brought here. He was detailed from his regiment to go there and help as nurse, but was soon taken down himself. Is an elderly, sallow-faced, rather gaunt, gray-haired man, a widower, with children. He expressed a great desire for good, strong green tea. An excellent lady, Mrs. W., of Washington, soon sent him a package; also a small sum of money. The doctor said give him the tea at pleasure; it lay on the table by his side, and he used it every day. He slept a great deal; could not talk much, as he grew deaf. Occupied Bed 15, Ward I, Armory. (The same lady above, Mrs. W., sent the men a large package of tobacco.) ?? J. G. lies in Bed 52, Ward I; is of Company B, 7th Pennsylvania. I gave him a small sum of money, some tobacco, and envelopes. To a man adjoining also gave twenty-five cents; he flushed in the face when I offered it—refused at first, but as I found he had not a cent, and was very fond of having the daily papers to read, I pressed it on him. He was evidently very grateful, but said little. ?? J. T. L., of Company F., 9th New Hampshire, lies in Bed 37, Ward I. Is very fond of tobacco. I furnish him some: also with a little money. Has gangrene of the feet, a pretty bad case; will surely have to lose three toes. Is a regular specimen of an old-fashioned, rude, hearty, New England countryman, impressing me with his likeness to that celebrated singed cat who was better than she looked. ?? Bed 3, Ward E,

ARMORY SQUARE HOSPITAL, WARD K

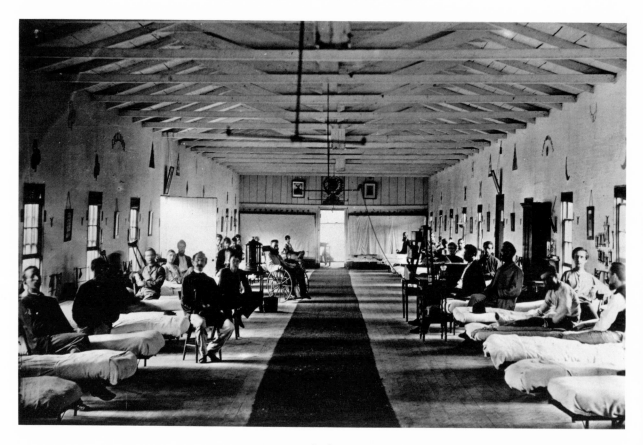

Armory, has a great hankering for pickles, something pungent. After consulting the doctor, I gave him a small bottle of horseradish, also some apples, also a book. Some of the nurses are excellent. The woman nurse in this ward I like very much. (Mrs. Wright—a year afterward I found her in Mansion House Hospital, Alexandria—she is a perfect nurse.) ॐ In one bed a young man, Marcus Small, Company K, 7th Maine—sick with dysentery and typhoid fever—pretty critical case—I talk with him often—he thinks he will die—looks like it, indeed. I write a letter for him home to East Livermore, Maine—I let him talk to me a little, but not much, advise him to keep very quiet—do most of the talking myself—stay quite a while with him, as he holds on to my hand—talk to him in a cheering, but slow, low, and measured manner—talk about his furlough, and going home as soon as he is able to travel. ॐ Thomas Lindly, 1st Pennsylvania Cavalry, shot very badly through the foot—poor young man, he suffers horribly, has to be constantly dosed with morphine, his face ashy and glazed, bright young eyes—I give him a large handsome apple, lay it in sight, tell him to have it roasted in the morning, as he generally feels easier then, and can eat a little breakfast. I write two letters for him. ॐ Opposite, an old Quaker lady is sitting by the side of her son, Amer

Moore, 2d U.S. Artillery—shot in the head two weeks since, very low, quite rational—from hips down paralyzed—he will surely die. I speak a very few words to him every day and evening—he answers pleasantly—wants nothing (he told me soon after he came about his home affairs, his mother had been an invalid, and he feared to let her know his condition). He died soon after she came.

MY PREPARATIONS FOR VISITS ॐ In my visits to the hospitals I found it was in the simple matter of personal presence, and emanating ordinary cheer and magnetism, that I succeeded and helped more than by medical nursing, or delicacies, or gifts of money, or anything else. During the war I possessed the perfection of physical health. My habit, when practicable, was to prepare for starting out on one of those daily or nightly tours of from a couple to four or five hours by fortifying myself with previous rest, the bath, clean clothes, a good meal, and as cheerful an appearance as possible.

AMBULANCE PROCESSIONS ॐ JUNE 25, SUNDOWN ॐ As I sit writing this paragraph I see a train of about thirty huge four-horse wagons, used as ambulances, filled with wounded, passing up Fourteenth

AMBULANCE TRAIN AT CITY POINT HOSPITAL

[23]

Street, on their way, probably, to Columbian, Carver, and Mount Pleasant Hospitals. This is the way the men come in now, seldom in small numbers, but almost always in these long, sad processions. Through the past winter, while our army lay opposite Fredericksburg, the like strings of ambulances were of frequent occurrence along Seventh Street, passing slowly up from the steamboat wharf, with loads from Aquia Creek.

BAD WOUNDS—THE YOUNG ⁊ The soldiers are nearly all young men, and far more American than is generally supposed—I should say nine-tenths are native-born. Among the arrivals from Chancellorsville I find a large proportion of Ohio, Indiana, and Illinois men. As usual, there are all sorts of wounds. Some of the men fearfully burned from the explosions of artillery caissons. One ward has a long row of officers, some with ugly hurts. Yesterday was perhaps worse than usual. Amputations are going on—the attendants are dressing wounds. As you pass by, you must be on your guard where you look. I saw the other day a gentleman, a visitor apparently from curiosity, in one of the wards, stop and turn a moment to look at an awful wound they were probing. He turned pale, and in a moment more he had fainted away and fallen on the floor.

THE MOST INSPIRITING OF ALL WAR'S SHOWS ⁊ JUNE 29 ⁊ Just before sundown this evening a very large cavalry force went by—a fine sight. The men evidently had seen service. First came a mounted band of sixteen bugles, drums, and cymbals, playing wild martial tunes—made my heart jump. Then the principal officers, then company after company, with their officers at their heads, making of course the main part of the cavalcade; then a long train of men with led horses, lots of mounted Negroes with special horses—and a long string of baggage wagons, each drawn by four horses—and then a motley rear guard. It was a pronouncedly warlike and gay show; the sabers clanked, the men looked young and healthy and strong; the electric tramping of so many horses on the hard road, and the gallant bearing, fine seat, and bright-faced appearance of a thousand and more handsome young American men, were so good to see. An hour later another troop went by, smaller in numbers, perhaps three hundred men. They too looked like serviceable men, campaigners used to field and fight. ⁊ JULY 3 ⁊ This forenoon, for more than an hour, again long strings of cavalry, several regiments, very fine men and horses, four or five abreast. I saw them in Fourteenth Street, coming in town from north. Several hundred extra horses, some of the mares with colts, trotting along. (Appeared to be a number of prisoners too.) How in-

spiriting always the cavalry regiments. Our men are generally well mounted, feel good, are young, gay on the saddle, their blankets in a roll behind them, their sabers clanking at their sides. This noise and movement and the tramp of many horses' hoofs has a curious effect upon one. The bugles play—presently you hear them afar off, deadened, mixed with other noises. Then just as they had all passed, a string of ambulances commenced from the other way, moving up Fourteenth Street north, slowly wending along, bearing a large lot of wounded to the hospitals.

BATTLE OF GETTYSBURG ⁊ JULY 4TH ⁊ The weather today, upon the whole, is very fine, warm, but from a smart rain last night, fresh enough, and no dust, which is a great relief for this city. I saw the parade about noon, Pennsylvania Avenue, from Fifteenth Street down toward the Capitol. There were three regiments of infantry (I suppose the ones doing patrol duty here), two or three societies of Odd Fellows, a lot of children in barouches, and a squad of policemen. (A useless imposition upon the soldiers—they have work enough on their backs without piling the like of this.) As I went down the Avenue, saw a big flaring placard on the bulletin board of a newspaper office, announcing "Glorious Victory for the Union Army!" Meade had fought Lee at Gettysburg, Pennsylvania, yesterday and day before, and repulsed him most signally, taken 3,000 prisoners, etc. (I afterwards saw Meade's dispatch, very modest, and a sort of order of the day from the President himself, quite religious, giving thanks to the Supreme, and calling on the people to do the same.) I walked on to Armory Hospital—took along with me several bottles of blackberry and cherry syrup, good and strong, but innocent. Went through several of the wards, announced to the soldiers the news from Meade, and gave them all a good drink of the syrups with ice water, quite refreshing —prepared it all myself, and served it around. Meanwhile the Washington bells are ringing their sundown peals for Fourth of July, and the usual fusillades of boys' pistols, crackers, and guns.

A CAVALRY CAMP ⁊ I am writing this, nearly sundown, watching a cavalry company (acting Signal Service), just come in through a shower, making their night's camp ready on some broad, vacant ground, a sort of hill, in full view opposite my window. There are the men in their yellow-striped jackets. All are dismounted; the freed horses stand with drooping heads and wet sides; they are to be led off presently in groups, to water. The little wall tents and shelter tents spring up quickly. I see the fires already blazing, and pots and kettles over them. Some among the men are driving in tent poles, wielding their axes with strong, slow blows. I see great huddles of horses, bundles of hay, groups of men (some with unbuckled sabers yet on their sides), a few officers, piles of wood, the flames of the fires, saddles, harness, etc. The smoke streams upward, additional men arrive and dismount—some drive in stakes, and tie their horses to them; some go with buckets for water, some are chopping wood, and so on. ᎧᎧ JULY 6TH ᎧᎧ A steady rain, dark and thick and warm. A train of six-mule wagons has just passed bearing pontoons, great square-end flat boats, and the heavy planking for overlaying them. We hear that the Potomac above here is flooded, and are wondering whether Lee will be able to get back across again, or whether Meade will indeed break him to pieces. The cavalry camp on the hill is a ceaseless field of observation for me. This forenoon there stand the horses, tethered together, dripping, steaming, chewing their hay. The men emerge from their tents, dripping also. The fires are half quenched. ᎧᎧ JULY 10TH ᎧᎧ Still the camp opposite—perhaps fifty or sixty tents. Some of the men are cleaning their sabers (pleasant today), some brushing boots, some laying off, reading, writing—some cooking, some sleeping. On long temporary cross-sticks back of the tents are cavalry accoutrements—blankets and overcoats are hung out to air—there are the squads of horses tethered, feeding, continually stamping and whisking their tails to keep off flies. I sit long in my third-story window and look at the scene—a hundred little things going on—peculiar objects connected with the camp that could not be described, any of them, justly, without much minute drawing and coloring in words.

A NEW YORK SOLDIER ᎧᎧ This afternoon, July 22d, I have spent a long time with Oscar F. Wilber, Company G, 154th New York, low with chronic diarrhea, and a bad wound also. He asked me to read him a chapter in the New Testament. I complied, and asked him what I should read. He said, "Make your own choice." I opened at the close of one of the first books of the evangelists, and read the chapters describing the latters hours of Christ, and the scenes at the crucifixion. The poor, wasted young man asked me to read the following chapter also, how Christ rose again. I read very slowly, for Oscar was feeble. It pleased him very much, yet the tears were in his eyes. He asked me if I enjoyed religion. I said, "Perhaps not, my dear, in the way you mean, and yet, maybe, it is the same thing." He said, "It is my chief reliance." He talked of death, and said he did not fear it. I said, "Why, Oscar, don't you think you will get well?" He said, "I may, but it is not probable." He spoke calmly of his condition. The wound was very bad, it discharged much. Then the diarrhea had pros-

trated him, and I felt that he was even then the same as dying. He behaved very manly and affectionate. The kiss I gave him as I was about leaving he returned fourfold. He gave me his mother's address, Mrs. Sally D. Wilber, Alleghany Post Office, Cattaraugus County, N.Y. I had several such interviews with him. He died a few days after the one just described.

HOME-MADE MUSIC ᎧᎧ AUGUST 8TH ᎧᎧ Tonight, as I was trying to keep cool, sitting by a wounded soldier in Armory Square, I was attracted by some pleasant singing in an adjoining ward. As my soldier was asleep, I left him, and entering the ward where the music was, I walked halfway down and took a seat by the cot of a young Brooklyn friend, S. R., badly wounded in the hand at Chancellorsville, and who has suffered much, but at that moment in the evening was wide awake and comparatively easy. He had turned over on his left side to get a better view of the singers, but the mosquito curtains of the adjoining cots obstructed the sight. I stepped round and looped them all up, so that he had a clear show, and then sat down again by him, and looked and listened. The principal singer was a young lady nurse of one of the wards, accompanying on a melodeon, and joined by the lady nurses of other wards. They sat there, making a charming group, with their handsome, healthy faces, and standing up a little behind them were some ten or fifteen of the convalescent soldiers, young men, nurses, etc., with books in their hands, singing. Of course it was not such a performance as the great soloists at the New York Opera House take a hand in, yet I am not sure but I received as much pleasure under the circumstances, sitting there, as I have had from the best Italian compositions, expressed by world-famous performers. The men lying up and down the hospital, in their cots (some badly wounded—some never to rise thence), the cots themselves, with their drapery of white curtains, and the shadows down the lower and upper parts of the ward; then the silence of the men, and the attitudes they took—the whole was a sight to look around upon again and again. And there sweetly rose those voices up to the high, whitewashed wooden roof, and pleasantly the roof sent it all back again. They sang very well, mostly quaint old songs and declamatory hymns, to fitting tunes. Here, for instance:

My days are swiftly gliding by, and I a pilgrim stranger,
Would not detain them as they fly, those hours of toil and
* danger;*
For O we stand on Jordan's strand, our friends are passing
* over,*
And just before, the shining shore we may almost discover.

We'll gird our loins, my brethren dear, our distant home
  discerning,
Our absent Lord has left us word, let every lamp be burning.
For O we stand on Jordan's strand, our friends are passing
  over,
And just before, the shining shore we may almost discover.

ABRAHAM LINCOLN ᕀ AUGUST 12TH ᕀ I see the President almost every day, as I happen to live where he passes to or from his lodgings out of town. He never sleeps at the White House during the hot season, but has quarters at a healthy location some three miles north of the city, the Soldier's Home, a United States military establishment. I saw him this morning about 8:30, coming in to business, riding on Vermont Avenue, near L Street. He always has a company of twenty-five or thirty cavalry, with sabers drawn and held upright over their shoulders. They say this guard was against his personal wish, but he lets his counselors have their way. The party makes no great show in uniform or horses. Mr. Lincoln on the saddle generally rides a good-sized, easy-going gray horse, is dressed in plain black, somewhat rusty and dusty, wears a black stiff hat, and looks about as ordinary in attire, etc., as the commonest man. A lieutenant, with yellow straps, rides at his left, and following behind, two by two, come the cavalry men, in their yellow-striped jackets. They are generally going at a slow trot, as that is the pace set them by the one they wait upon. The sabers and accoutrements clank, and the entirely unornamental cortège as it trots toward Lafayette Square arouses no sensation, only some curious stranger stops and gazes. I see very plainly ABRAHAM LINCOLN's dark brown face, with the deep-cut lines, the eyes, always to me with a deep latent sadness in the expression. We have got so that we exchange bows, and very cordial ones. Sometimes the President goes and comes in an open barouche. The cavalry always accompany him, with drawn sabers. Often I notice as he goes out evenings—and sometimes in the morning, when he returns early—he turns off and halts at the large and handsome residence of the Secretary of War, on K Street, and holds conference there. If in his barouche, I can see from my window he does not alight, but sits in his vehicle, and Mr. Stanton comes out to attend him. Sometimes one of his sons, a boy of ten or twelve, accompanies him, riding at his right on a pony. Earlier in the summer I occasionally saw the President and his wife, toward the latter part of the afternoon, out in a barouche, on a pleasure ride through the city. Mrs. Lincoln was dressed in complete black, with a long crape veil. The equipage is of the plainest kind, only two horses, and they nothing extra. They passed me once very close, and I saw the President in the face fully, as they were moving slowly, and his look, though abstracted, happened to be directed steadily in my eye. He bowed and smiled, but far beneath his smile I noticed well the expression I have alluded to. None of the artists or pictures has caught the deep, though subtle and indirect, expression of this man's face. There is something else there. One of the great portrait painters of two or three centuries ago is needed.

HEATED TERM ᕀ There has lately been much suffering here from heat; we have had it upon us now eleven days. I go around with an umbrella and a fan. I saw two cases of sunstroke yesterday, one in Pennsylvania Avenue and another in Seventh Street. The city railroad company loses some horses every day. Yet Washington is having a livelier August and is probably putting in a more energetic and satisfactory summer, than ever before during its existence. There is probably more human electricity, more population to make it, more business, more light heartedness, than ever before. The armies that swiftly circumambiated from Fredericksburg—marched, struggled, fought, had out their mighty clinch and hurl at Gettysburg—wheeled, circumambiated again, returned to their ways, touching us not, either at their going or coming. And Washington feels that she has passed the worst, perhaps feels that she is henceforth mistress. So here she sits with her surrounding hills spotted with guns, and is conscious of a character and identity different from what it was five or six short weeks ago, and very considerably pleasanter and prouder.

SOLDIERS AND TALKS ᕀ Soldiers, soldiers, soldiers, you meet everywhere about the city, often superb-looking men, though invalids dressed in worn uniforms, and carrying canes or crutches. I often have talks with them, occasionally quite long and interesting. One, for instance, will have been all through the peninsula under McClellan—narrates to me the fights, the marches, the strange, quick changes of that eventful campaign, and gives glimpses of many things untold in any official reports or books or journals. These, indeed, are the things that are genuine and precious. The man was there, has been out two years, has been through a dozen fights, the superfluous flesh of talking is long worked off him, and he gives me little but the hard meat and sinew. I find it refreshing, these hardy, bright, intuitive, American young men (experienced soldiers with all their youth). The vocal play and significance moves one more than books. Then there hangs something majestic about a man who has borne his part in battles, especially if he is very quiet regarding it when you desire him to unbosom. I am continually lost at the

[26]

absence of blowing and blowers among these old-young American militaires. I have found some man or other who has been in every battle since the war began, and have talked with them about each one in every part of the United States, and many of the engagements on the rivers and harbors too. I find men here from every state in the Union, without exception. (There are more Southerners, especially border-state men, in the Union Army than is generally supposed.*) I now doubt whether one can get a fair idea of what this war practically is, or what genuine America is, and her character, without some such experience as this I am having.

DEATH OF A WISCONSIN OFFICER ᴓ Another characteristic scene of that dark and bloody 1863, from notes of my visit to Armory Square Hospital, one hot but pleasant summer day. In Ward H we approach the cot of a young lieutenant of one of the Wisconsin regiments. Tread the bare board floor lightly here, for the pain and panting of death are in this cot. I saw the lieutenant when he was first brought here from Chancellorsville, and have been with him occasionally from day to day and night to night. He had been getting along pretty well till night before last, when a sudden hemorrhage that could not be stopped came upon him, and today it still continues at intervals. Notice that water pail by the side of the bed, with a quantity of blood and

---

* Mr. Garfield (*in the House of Representatives, April 15, '79*): "Do gentlemen know that (leaving out all the border states) there were fifty regiments and seven companies of white men in our army fighting for the Union from the states that went into rebellion? Do they know that from the single state of Kentucky more Union soldiers fought under our flag than Napoleon took into the battle of Waterloo? more than Wellington took with all the allied armies against Napoleon? Do they remember that 186,000 colored men fought under our flag against the rebellion and for the Union, and that of that number 90,000 were from the states which went into rebellion?"

bloody pieces of muslin, nearly full; that tells the story. The poor young man is struggling painfully for breath, his great dark eyes with a glaze already upon them, and the choking faint but audible in his throat. An attendant sits by him, and will not leave him till the last; yet little or nothing can be done. He will die here in an hour or two, without the presence of kith or kin. Meantime the ordinary chat and business of the ward a little way off goes on indifferently. Some of the inmates are laughing and joking, others are playing checkers or cards, others are reading, etc. ᴓ I have noticed through most of the hospitals that as long as there is any chance for a man, no matter how bad he may be, the surgeon and nurses work hard, sometimes with curious tenacity, for his life, doing everything, and keeping somebody by him to execute the doctor's orders, and minister to him every minute night and day. See that screen there. As you advance through the dusk of early candlelight, a nurse will step forth on tiptoe and silently but imperiously forbid you to make any noise, or perhaps to come near at all. Some soldier's life is flickering there, suspended between recovery and death. Perhaps at this moment the exhausted frame has just fallen into a light sleep that a step might shake. You must retire. The neighboring patients must move in their stocking feet. I have been several times struck with such marked efforts—everything bent to save a life from the very grip of the destroyer. But when that grip is once firmly fixed, leaving no hope or chance at all, the surgeon abandons the patient. If it is a case where stimulus is any relief, the nurse gives milk punch or brandy, or whatever is wanted, *ad libitum*. There is no fuss made. Not a bit of sentimentalism or whining have I seen about a single deathbed in hospital or on the field, but generally impassive indifference. All is over, as far as any efforts can avail; it is useless to expend emotions or labors. While there is a prospect they strive hard—at least most surgeons do; but, death certain and evident, they yield the field.

ARMORY SQUARE HOSPITAL

[27]

HOSPITALS ENSEMBLE ᵱ AUG., SEPT., AND OCT., '63 ᵱ I am in the habit of going to all, and to Fairfax Seminary, Alexandria, and over Long Bridge to the great Convalescent Camp. The journals publish a regular directory of them—a long list. As a specimen of almost any one of the larger of these hospitals, fancy to yourself a space of three to twenty acres of ground, on which are grouped ten or twelve very large wooden barracks, with, perhaps, a dozen or twenty, and sometimes more than that number, small buildings, capable altogether of accommodating from five hundred to a thousand or fifteen hundred persons. Sometimes these wooden barracks or wards, each of them perhaps from a hundred to a hundred and fifty feet long, are ranged in a straight row, evenly fronting the street; others are planned so as to form an immense V; and others again are ranged around a hollow square. They make altogether a huge cluster, with the additional tents, extra wards for contagious diseases, guardhouses, sutler's stores, chaplain's house; in the middle will probably be an edifice devoted to the offices of the surgeon in charge and the ward surgeons, principal attachés, clerks, etc. The wards are either lettered alphabetically, Ward G, Ward K, or else numerically, 1, 2, 3, etc. Each has its ward surgeon and corps of nurses. Of course, there is, in the aggregate, quite a muster of employees, and over all the surgeon in charge. Here in Washington, when these army hospitals are all filled (as they have been already several times), they contain a population more numerous in itself than the whole of Washington of ten or fifteen years ago. Within sight of the Capitol, as I write, are some thirty or forty such collections, at times holding from fifty to seventy thousand men. Looking from any eminence and studying the topography in my rambles, I use them as landmarks. Through the rich August verdure of the trees, see that white group of buildings off yonder in the outskirts; then another cluster half a mile to the left of the first; then another a mile to the right, and another a mile beyond, and still another between us and the first. Indeed, we can hardly look in any direction but these clusters are dotting the landscape and environs. That little town, as you might suppose it, off there on the brow of a hill, is indeed a town, but of wounds, sickness, and death. It is Finley Hospital, northeast of the city, on Kendall Green, as it used to be called. That other is Campbell Hospital. Both are large establishments. I have known these two alone to have from two thousand to twenty-five hundred inmates. Then there is Carver Hospital, larger still, a walled and military city regularly laid out, and guarded by squads of sentries. Again, off east, Lincoln Hospital, a still larger one; and half a mile farther Emory Hospital. Still sweeping the eye around down the river toward Alexandria, we see, to the right, the locality where the Convalescent Camp stands, with its five, eight, or sometimes ten thousand inmates. Even all these are but a portion. The Harewood, Mount Pleasant, Armory Square, Judiciary Hospitals are some of the rest, and all large collections.

CONVALESCENT CAMP, ALEXANDRIA, VIRGINIA

A SILENT NIGHT RAMBLE ❧ OCTOBER 20TH
❧ Tonight, after leaving the hospital at 10 o'clock (I
had been on self-imposed duty some five hours, pretty
closely confined), I wandered a long time around Washington. The night was sweet, very clear, sufficiently
cool, a voluptuous half-moon, slightly golden, the space
near it of a transparent blue-gray tinge. I walked up
Pennsylvania Avenue, and then to Seventh Street, and a
long while around the Patent Office. Somehow it looked
rebukefully strong, majestic, there in the delicate moonlight. The sky, the planets, the constellations all so
bright, so calm, so expressively silent, so soothing, after
those hospital scenes. I wandered to and fro till the moist
moon set, long after midnight.

SPIRITUAL CHARACTERS AMONG THE
SOLDIERS ❧ Every now and then, in hospital or
camp, there are beings I meet—specimens of unworldli-
ness, disinterestedness, and animal purity and heroism—
perhaps some unconscious Indianian, or from Ohio or
Tennessee—on whose birth the calmness of heaven
seems to have descended, and whose gradual growing
up, whatever the circumstances of work-life or change,
or hardship, or small or no education that attended it,
the power of a strange spiritual sweetness, fiber, and inward health have also attended. Something veiled and
abstracted is often a part of the manners of these beings.
I have met them, I say, not seldom in the army, in camp,
and in the hospitals. The Western regiments contain

many of them. They are often young men, obeying the
events and occasions about them, marching, soldiering,
fighting, foraging, cooking, working on farms or at
some trade before the war—unaware of their own nature (as to that, who is aware of his own nature?), their
companions only understanding that they are different
from the rest, more silent, "something odd about them,"
and apt to go off and meditate and muse in solitude.

CATTLE DROVES ABOUT WASHINGTON
❧ Among other sights are immense droves of cattle
with their drivers, passing through the streets of the
city. Some of the men have a way of leading the cattle
by a peculiar call, a wild, pensive hoot, quite musical,
prolonged, indescribable, sounding something between
the cooing of a pigeon and the hoot of an owl. I like to
stand and look at the sight of one of these immense
droves—a little way off (as the dust is great). There are
always men on horseback, cracking their whips and
shouting—the cattle low—some obstinate ox or steer
attempts to escape—then a lively scene—the mounted
men, always excellent riders and on good horses, dash
after the recusant, and wheel and turn—a dozen mounted drovers, their great slouched, broad-brimmed hats,
very picturesque—another dozen on foot—everybody
covered with dust—long goads in their hands—an immense drove of perhaps 1,000 cattle—the shouting,
hooting, movement, etc.

HOSPITAL TENTS BEHIND DOUGLAS HOSPITAL

[29]

HOSPITAL PERPLEXITY ❧ To add to other troubles, amid the confusion of this great army of sick, it is almost impossible for a stranger to find any friend or relative, unless he has the patient's specific address to start upon. Besides the directory printed in the newspapers here, there are one or two general directories of the hospitals kept at provost's headquarters, but they are nothing like complete; they are never up-to-date, and, as things are, with the daily streams of coming and going and changing, cannot be. I have known cases, for instance, such as a farmer coming here from northern New York to find a wounded brother, faithfully hunting round for a week, and then compelled to leave and go home without getting any trace of him. When he got home he found a letter from the brother giving the right address.

DOWN AT THE FRONT ❧ CULPEPER, VA., FEB. '64 ❧ Here I am pretty well down toward the extreme front. Three or four days ago General S., who is now in chief command (I believe Meade is absent, sick), moved a strong force southward from Camp as if intending business. They went to the Rapidan; there has since been some maneuvering and a little fighting, but nothing of consequence. The telegraphic accounts given Monday morning last make entirely too much of it, I should say. What General S. intended here we know not, but we trust in that competent commander. We were somewhat excited (but not so very much either) on Sunday, during the day and night, as orders were sent out to pack up and harness, and be ready to evacuate, to fall back toward Washington. But I was very sleepy and went to bed. Some tremendous shouts arousing me during the night, I went forth and found it was from the men above mentioned, who were returning. I talked with some of the men; as usual I found them full of gaiety, endurance, and many fine little out-shows, the signs of the most excellent good manliness of the world. It was a curious sight to see those shadowy columns moving through the night. I stood unobserved in the darkness and watched them long. The mud was very deep. The men had their usual burdens, overcoats, knapsacks, guns, and blankets. Along and along they filed by me, with often a laugh, a song, a cheerful word, but never once a murmur. It may have been odd, but I never before so realized the majesty and reality of the American people *en masse*. It fell upon me like a great awe. The strong ranks moved neither fast nor slow. They had marched seven or eight miles already through the slipping unctuous mud. The brave First Corps stopped here. The equally brave Third Corps moved on to Brandy station. The famous Brooklyn 14th are here, guarding the town. You see their red

legs actively moving everywhere. Then they have a theater of their own here. They give musical performances, nearly everything done capitally. Of course the audience is a jam. It is good sport to attend one of these entertainments of the 14th. I like to look around at the soldiers, and the general collection in front of the curtain, more than the scene on the stage.

PAYING THE BOUNTIES ❧ One of the things to note here now is the arrival of the paymaster with his strong box, and the payment of bounties to veterans re-enlisting. Major H. is here today, with a small mountain of greenbacks, rejoicing the hearts of the 2d Division of the First Corps. In the midst of a rickety shanty, behind a little table, sit the major and Clerk Eldridge, with the rolls before them and much moneys. A re-enlisted man gets in cash about $200 down (and heavy installments following, as the paydays arrive, one after another). The show of the men crowding around is quite exhilarating; I like to stand and look. They feel elated, their pockets full, and the ensuing furlough, the visit home. It is a scene of sparkling eyes and flushed cheeks. The soldier has many gloomy and harsh experiences, and this makes up for some of them. Major H. is ordered to pay first all the re-enlisted men of the First Corps their bounties and back pay, and then the rest. You hear the peculiar sound of the rustling of the new and crisp greenbacks by the hour, through the nimble fingers of the major and my friend Clerk E.

RUMORS, CHANGES, ETC. ❧ About the excitement of Sunday, and the orders to be ready to start, I have heard since that the said orders came from some cautious minor commander, and that the high principalities knew not and thought not of any such move; which is likely. The rumor and fear here intimated a long circuit by Lee, and flank attack on our right. But I cast my eyes at the mud, which was then at its deepest and palmiest condition, and retired composedly to rest. Still it is about time for Culpeper to have a change. Authorities have chased each other here like clouds in a stormy sky. Before the first Bull Run this was the rendezvous and camp of instruction of the secession troops. I am stopping at the house of a lady who has witnessed all the eventful changes of the war, along this route of contending armies. She is a widow, with a family of young children, and lives here with her sister in a large handsome house. A number of army officers board with them.

VIRGINIA ❧ Dilapidated, fenceless, and trodden with war as Virginia is, wherever I move across her surface I find myself roused to surprise and admiration. What capacity for products, improvements, human life, nourishment, and expansion. Everywhere that I have been in the Old Dominion (the subtle mockery of that title now!) such thoughts have filled me. The soil is yet far above the average of any of the Northern states. And how full of breadth the scenery, everywhere distant mountains, everywhere convenient rivers. Even yet prodigal in forest woods, and surely eligible for all the fruits, orchards, and flowers. The skies and atmosphere most luscious, as I feel certain, from more than a year's residence in the state, and movements hither and yon. I should say very healthy, as a general thing. Then a rich and elastic quality, by night and by day. The sun rejoices in his strength, dazzling and burning, and yet, to me, never unpleasantly weakening. It is not the panting tropical heat, but invigorates. The north tempers it. The nights are often unsurpassable. Last evening (Feb. 8) I saw the first of the new moon, the outlined old moon clear along with it; the sky and air so clear, such transparent hues of color, it seemed to me I had never really seen the new moon before. It was the thinnest cut crescent possible. It hung delicate just above the sulky shadow of the Blue Mountains. Ah, if it might prove an omen and good prophecy for this unhappy state.

SUMMER OF 1864 ?? I am back again in Washington, on my regular daily and nightly rounds. Of course there are many specialties. Dotting a ward here and there are always cases of poor fellows, long-suffering under obstinate wounds, or weak and disheartened from typhoid fever, or the like; marked cases, needing special and sympathetic nourishment. These I sit down and either talk to, or silently cheer them up. They always like it hugely (and so do I). Each case has its peculiarities, and needs some new adaptation. I have learned to thus conform—learned a good deal of hospital wisdom. Some of the poor young chaps, away from home for the first time in their lives, hunger and thirst for affection; this is sometimes the only thing that will reach their condition. The men like to have a pencil, and something to write in. I have given them cheap pocket diaries, and almanacs for 1864, interleaved with blank paper. For reading I generally have some old pictorial magazines or story papers—they are always acceptable. Also the morning or evening papers of the day. The best books I do not give, but lend to read through the wards, and then take them to others, and so on; they are very punctual about returning the books. In these wards, or in the field, as I thus continue to go round, I have come to adapt myself to each emergency, after its kind or call, however trivial, however solemn, every one justified and made real under its circumstances—not only visits

and cheering talk and little gifts—not only washing and dressing wounds (I have some cases where the patient is unwilling any one should do this but me)—but passages from the Bible, expounding them, prayer at the bedside, explanations of doctrine, etc. (I think I see my friends smiling at this confession, but I was never more in earnest in my life.) In camp and everywhere, I was in the habit of reading or giving recitations to the men. They were very fond of it, and liked declamatory poetical pieces. We would gather in a large group by ourselves, after supper, and spend the time in such readings, or in talking, and occasionally by an amusing game called the Game of Twenty Questions.

A NEW ARMY ORGANIZATION FIT FOR AMERICA ?? It is plain to me out of the events of the war, north and south, and out of all considerations, that the current military theory, practice, rules, and organization (adopted from Europe from the feudal institutes, with, of course, the "modern improvements," largely from the French), though tacitly followed, and believed in by the officers generally, are not at all consonant with the United States, nor our people, nor our days. What it will be I know not—but I know that as entire an abnegation of the present military system, and the naval too, and a building up from radically different root bases and centers appropriate to us, must eventually result, as that our political system has resulted and become established, different from feudal Europe, and built up on itself from original, perennial, democratic premises. We have undoubtedly in the United States the greatest military power—an exhaustless, intelligent, brave, and reliable rank and file—in the world, any land, perhaps all lands. The problem is to organize this in the manner fully appropriate to it, to the principles of the republic, and to get the best service out of it. In the present struggle, as already seen and reviewed, probably three-fourths of the losses, men, lives, etc., have been sheer superfluity, extravagance, waste.

DEATH OF A HERO ?? I wonder if I could ever convey to another—to you, for instance, reader dear—the tender and terrible realities of such cases (many, many happened) as the one I am now going to mention. Stewart C. Glover, Company E, 5th Wisconsin—was wounded May 5, in one of those fierce tussles of the Wilderness—died May 21—aged about 20. He was a small and beardless young man—a splendid soldier—in fact almost an ideal American, of his age. He had served nearly three years, and would have been entitled to his discharge in a few days. He was in Hancock's corps. The fighting had about ceased for the day, and the general commanding the brigade rode by and called for volunteers to bring in the wounded. Glover responded among the first—went out gaily—but while in the act of bearing in a wounded sergeant to our lines, was shot in the knee by a rebel sharpshooter; consequence, amputation and death. He had resided with his father, John Glover, an aged and feeble man, in Batavia, Genesee County, N.Y., but was at school in Wisconsin, after the war broke out, and there enlisted—soon took to soldier life, liked it, was very manly, was beloved by officers and comrades. He kept a little diary, like so many of the soldiers. On the day of his death he wrote the following in it: *Today the doctor says I must die—all is over with me—ah, so young to die.* On another blank leaf he penciled to his brother: *Dear brother Thomas, I have been brave but wicked—pray for me.*

HOSPITAL SCENES—INCIDENTS ஐ It is Sunday afternoon, middle of summer, hot and oppressive, and very silent through the ward. I am taking care of a critical case, now lying in a half-lethargy. Near where I sit is a suffering rebel, from the 8th Louisiana; his name is Irving. He has been here a long time, badly wounded, and lately had his leg amputated; it is not doing very well. Right opposite me is a sick soldier boy, laid down with his clothes on, sleeping, looking much wasted, his pallid face on his arm. I see by the yellow trimming on his jacket that he is a cavalry boy. I step softly over and find by his card that he is named William Cone, of the 1st Maine Cavalry, and his folks live in Skowhegan. ஐ ICE CREAM TREAT ஐ One hot day toward the middle of June, I gave the inmates of Carver Hospital a general ice cream treat, purchasing a large quantity, and, under convoy of the doctor or head nurse, going around personally through the wards to see to its distribution. ஐ AN INCIDENT ஐ In one of the fights before Atlanta, a rebel soldier, of large size, evidently a young man, was mortally wounded top of the head, so that the brains partially exuded. He lived three days, lying on his back on the spot where he first dropped. He dug with his heel in the ground during that time a hole big enough to put in a couple of ordinary knapsacks. He just lay there in the open air, and with little intermission kept his heel going night and day. Some of our soldiers then moved him to a house, but he died in a few minutes. ஐ ANOTHER ஐ After the battles at Columbia, Tennessee, where we repulsed about a score of vehement rebel charges, they left a great many wounded on the ground, mostly within our range. Whenever any of these wounded attempted to move away by any means, generally by crawling off, our men without exception brought them down by a bullet. They let none crawl away, no matter what his condition.

A YANKEE SOLDIER ஐ As I turned off the Avenue one cool October evening into Thirteenth Street, a soldier with knapsack and overcoat stood at the corner inquiring his way. I found he wanted to go part of the road in my direction, so we walked on together. We soon fell into conversation. He was small and not very young, and a tough little fellow, as I judged in the evening light, catching glimpses by the lamps we passed. His answers were short, but clear. His name was Charles Carroll; he belonged to one of the Massachusetts regiments, and was born in or near Lynn. His parents were living, but were very old. There were four sons, and all had enlisted. Two had died of starvation and misery in the prison at Andersonville, and one had been killed in the West. He only was left. He was now going home and by the way he talked I inferred that his time was nearly out. He made great calculations on being with his parents to comfort them the rest of their days.

UNION PRISONERS SOUTH ஐ Michael Stansbury, 48 years of age, a seafaring man, a Southerner by birth and raising, formerly captain of the U.S. Light Ship *Long Shoal*, stationed at Long Shoal Point, Pamlico Sound—though a Southerner, a firm Union man—was captured Feb. 17, 1863, and has been nearly two years in the Confederate prisons; was at one time ordered released by Governor Vance, but a rebel officer rearrested him; then sent on to Richmond for exchange—but instead of being exchanged was sent down (as a Southern citizen, not a soldier) to Salisbury, N.C., where he remained until lately, when he escaped among the exchanged by assuming the name of a dead soldier, and coming up via Wilmington with the rest. Was about sixteen months in Salisbury. Subsequent to October, '64, there were about 11,000 Union prisoners in the stockade; about 100 of them Southern unionists, 200 U.S. deserters. During the past winter 1,500 of the prisoners, to save their lives, joined the Confederacy, on condition of being assigned merely to guard duty. Out of the 11,000 not more than 2,500 came out; 500 of these were pitiable, helpless wretches—the rest were in a condition to travel. There were often 60 dead bodies to be buried in the morning; the daily average would be about 40. The regular food was a meal of corn, the cob and husk ground together, and sometimes once a week a ration of sorghum molasses. A diminutive ration of meat might possibly come once a month, not oftener. In the stockade, containing the 11,000 men, there was a partial show of tents, not enough for 2,000. A large proportion of the men lived in holes in the ground, in the utmost wretchedness. Some froze to death, others had their hands and feet frozen. The rebel guards would occasionally, and on the least pretense, fire into the prison from mere demonism and wantonness. All the horrors that can be named, starvation, lassitude, filth, vermin, despair, swift loss of self-respect, idiocy, insanity, and frequent murder, were there. Stansbury has a wife and child living in Newbern—has written to them from here—is in the U.S. lighthouse employ still (had been home to Newbern to see his family, and on his return to the ship was captured in his boat). Has seen men brought there to Salisbury as hearty as you ever see in your life—in a few weeks completely dead gone, much of it from thinking on their condition—hope all gone. Has himself a hard, sad, strangely deadened kind of look, as of one chilled for years in the cold and dark, where his good manly nature had no room to exercise itself.

DESERTERS ◐ OCT. 24 ◐ Saw a large squad of our own deserters (over 300) surrounded with a cordon of armed guards, marching along Pennsylvania Avenue. The most motley collection I ever saw, all sorts of rig, all sorts of hats and caps, many fine-looking young fellows, some of them shamefaced, some sickly, most of them dirty, shirts very dirty and long worn, etc. They tramped along without order, a huge huddling mass, not in ranks. I saw some of the spectators laughing, but I felt like anything else but laughing. These deserters are far more numerous than would be thought. Almost every day I see squads of them, sometimes two or three at a time, with a small guard; sometimes ten or twelve, under a larger one. (I hear that desertions from the army now in the field have often averaged 10,000 a month. One of the commonest sights in Washington is a squad of deserters.)

A GLIMPSE OF WAR'S HELL-SCENES ◐
In one of the late movements of our troops in the valley (near Upperville, I think), a strong force of Moseby's mounted guerrillas attacked a train of wounded and the guard of cavalry convoying them. The ambulances contained about 60 wounded, quite a number of them officers of rank. The rebels were in strength, and the capture of the train and its partial guard after a short snap was effectually accomplished. No sooner had our men surrendered, the rebels instantly commenced robbing the train and murdering their prisoners, even the wounded. Here is the scene or a sample of it, ten minutes after. Among the wounded officers in the ambulances were one, a lieutenant of regulars, and another of higher rank. These two were dragged out on the ground on their backs, and were now surrounded by the guerrillas, a demoniac crowd, each member of which was stabbing them in different parts of their bodies. One of the officers had his feet pinned firmly to the ground by bayonets

stuck through them and thrust into the ground. These two officers, as afterward found on examination, had received about twenty such thrusts, some of them through the mouth, face, etc. The wounded had all been dragged (to give a better chance also for plunder) out of their wagons; some had been effectually dispatched, and their bodies were lying there lifeless and bloody. Others, not yet dead, but horribly mutilated, were moaning or groaning. Of our men who surrendered, most had been thus maimed or slaughtered. ◐ At this instant a force of our cavalry, who had been following the train at some interval, charged suddenly upon the secesh captors, who proceeded at once to make the best escape they could. Most of them got away, but we gobbled two officers and seventeen men, in the very act just described. The sight was one which admitted of little discussion, as may be imagined. The seventeen captured men and two officers were put under guard for the night, but it was decided there and then that they should die. The next morning the two officers were taken in the town, separate places, put in the center of the street, and shot. The seventeen men were taken to an open ground, a little one side. They were placed in a hollow square, half-encompassed by two of our cavalry regiments, one of which regiments had three days before found the bloody corpses of three of their men hamstrung and hung up by the heels to limbs of trees by Moseby's guerrillas, and the other had not long before had twelve men, after surrendering, shot and then hung by the neck to limbs of trees, and jeering inscriptions pinned to the breast of one of the corpses, who had been a sergeant. Those three, and those twelve, had been found, I say, by these environing regiments. Now, with revolvers, they formed the grim cordon of the seventeen prisoners. The latter were placed in the midst of the hollow square, unfastened, and the ironical remark made to them that they were now to be given "a chance for themselves." A few ran for it. But what use? From every side the deadly pills came. In a few minutes the seventeen corpses strewed the hollow square. I was curious to know whether some of the Union soldiers, some few (some one or two at least of the youngsters), did not abstain from shooting on the helpless men. Not one. There was no exultation, very little said, almost nothing, yet every man there contributed his shot. ◐ Multiply the above by scores, aye hundreds—verify it in all the forms that different circumstances, individuals, places, could afford—light it with every lurid passion, the wolf's, the lion's lapping thirst for blood—the passionate, boiling volcanoes of human revenge for comrades, brothers slain—with the light of burning farms, and heaps of smutting, smoldering black embers—and in the human heart everywhere black, worse embers—& you have an inkling of this war.

GIFTS—MONEY—DISCRIMINATION 𝕝 As a very large proportion of the wounded came up from the front without a cent of money in their pockets, I soon discovered that it was about the best thing I could do to raise their spirits, and show them that somebody cared for them, and practically felt a fatherly or brotherly interest in them, to give them small sums in such cases, using tact and discretion about it. I am regularly supplied with funds for this purpose by good women and men in Boston, Salem, Providence, Brooklyn, and New York. I provide myself with a quantity of bright new ten-cent and five-cent bills, and, when I think it incumbent, I give 25 or 30 cents, or perhaps 50 cents, and occasionally a still larger sum to some particular case. As I have started this subject, I take opportunity to ventilate the financial question. My supplies, altogether voluntary, mostly confidential, often seeming quite Providential, were numerous and varied. For instance, there were two distant and wealthy ladies, sisters, who sent regularly, for two years, quite heavy sums, enjoining that their names should be kept secret. The same delicacy was indeed a frequent condition. From several I had *carte blanche*. Many were entire strangers. From these sources, during from two to three years, in the manner described, in the hospitals, I bestowed, as almoner for others, many, many thousands of dollars. I learned one thing conclusively—that beneath all the ostensible greed and heartlessness of our times there is no end to the generous benevolence of men and women in the United States, when once sure of their object. Another thing became clear to me—while *cash* is not amiss to bring up the rear, tact and magnetic sympathy and unction are, and ever will be, sovereign still.

ITEMS FROM MY NOTEBOOKS 𝕝 Some of the half-erased, and not overlegible when made, memoranda of things wanted by one patient or another, will convey quite a fair idea. D. S. G., Bed 52, wants a good book; has a sore, weak throat; would like some horehound candy; is from New Jersey, 28th Regiment. C. H. L., 145th Pennsylvania, lies in Bed 6, with jaundice and erysipelas; also wounded; stomach easily nauseated; bring him some oranges, also a little tart jelly; hearty, full-blooded young fellow (he got better in a few days, and is now home on a furlough). J. H. G., Bed 24, wants an undershirt, drawers, and socks; has not had a change for quite a while; is evidently a neat, clean boy from New England (I supplied him; also with a comb, toothbrush, and some soap and towels; I noticed afterward he was the cleanest of the whole ward). Mrs. G., lady nurse, Ward F, wants a bottle of brandy—has two patients imperatively requiring stimulus—low with wounds and exhaustion. (I supplied her with a bottle of first-rate brandy from the Christian commission rooms.)

A CASE FROM SECOND BULL RUN 𝕝 Well, poor John Mahay is dead. He died yesterday. His was a painful and long-lingering case (see p. 17 *ante*). I have been with him at times for the past fifteen months. He belonged to Company A, 101st New York, and was shot through the lower region of the abdomen at second Bull Run, August, '62. One scene at his bedside will suffice for the agonies of nearly two years. The bladder had been perforated by a bullet going entirely through him. Not long since I sat a good part of the morning by his bedside, Ward E, Armory Square. The water ran out of his eyes from the intense pain, and the muscles of his face were distorted, but he uttered nothing except a low groan now and then. Hot, moist cloths were applied, and relieved him somewhat. Poor Mahay, a mere boy in age, but old in misfortune. He never knew the love of parents, was placed in infancy in one of the New York charitable institutions, and subsequently bound out to a tyrannical master in Sullivan County

MAJOR A. N. DOUGHERTY, SURGEON, U.S.V.

(the scars of whose cowhide and club remained yet on his back). His wound here was a most disagreeable one, for he was a gentle, cleanly, and affectionate boy. He found friends in his hospital life, and, indeed, was a universal favorite. He had quite a funeral ceremony.

ARMY SURGEONS—AID DEFICIENCIES
꿍 I must bear my most emphatic testimony to the zeal, manliness, and professional spirit and capacity generally prevailing among the surgeons, many of them young men, in the hospitals and the army. I will not say much about the exceptions, for they are few (but I have met some of those few, and very incompetent and airish they were). I never ceased to find the best men, and the hardest and most disinterested workers, among the surgeons in the hospitals. They are full of genius, too. I have seen many hundreds of them, and this is my testimony. There are, however, serious deficiencies, wastes, sad want of system in the commissions, contributions, and in all the voluntary and a great part of the governmental

nursing, edibles, medicines, stores, etc. (I do not say surgical attendance, because the surgeons cannot do more than human endurance permits.) Whatever puffing accounts there may be in the papers of the North, this is the actual fact. No thorough previous preparation, no system, no foresight, no genius. Always plenty of stores, no doubt, but never where they are needed, and never the proper application. Of all harrowing experiences, none is greater than that of the days following a heavy battle. Scores, hundreds of the noblest men on earth, uncomplaining, lie helpless, mangled, faint, alone, and so bleed to death, or die from exhaustion, either actually untouched at all, or merely the laying of them down and leaving them, when there ought to be means provided to save them.

THE BLUE EVERYWHERE 꿍 This city, its suburbs, the Capitol, the front of the White House, the places of amusement, the Avenue, and all the main streets swarm with soldiers this winter, more than ever before. Some are out from the hospitals, some from the

LIEUTENANT COLONEL PETER PINEO
MEDICAL INSPECTOR, U.S.A.

MAJOR L. QUICK, SURGEON, U.S.V.

neighboring camps, etc. One source or another, they pour plenteously, and make, I should say, the marked feature in the human movement and costume appearance of our national city. Their blue pants and overcoats are everywhere. The clump of crutches is heard up the stairs of the paymasters' offices, and there are characteristic groups around the doors of the same, often waiting long and wearily in the cold. Toward the latter part of the afternoon, you see the furloughed men, sometimes singly, sometimes in small squads, making their way to the Baltimore depot. At all times, except early in the morning, the patrol detachments are moving around, especially during the earlier hours of evening, examining passes, and arresting all soldiers without them. They do not question the one-legged, or men badly disabled or maimed, but all others are stopped. They also go around evenings through the auditoriums of the theaters, and make officers and all show their passes, or other authority, for being there.

A MODEL HOSPITAL ꝏ SUNDAY, JANUARY 29TH, 1865 ꝏ

Have been in Armory Square this afternoon. The wards are very comfortable, new floors and plaster walls, and models of neatness. I am not sure but this is a model hospital after all, in important respects. I found several sad cases of old lingering wounds. One Delaware soldier, William H. Millis, from Bridgeville, whom I had been with after the battles of the Wilderness, last May, where he received a very bad wound in the chest, with another in the left arm, and whose case was serious (pneumonia had set in) all last June and July, I now find well enough to do light duty. For three weeks at the time mentioned he just hovered between life and death.

BOYS IN THE ARMY ꝏ

As I walked home about sunset, I saw in Fourteenth Street a very young soldier, thinly clad, standing near the house I was about to enter. I stopped a moment in front of the door and called him to me. I knew that an old Tennessee regiment, and also an Indiana regiment, were temporarily stopping in new barracks, near Fourteenth Street. This boy I found belonged to the Tennessee regiment. But I could hardly believe he carried a musket. He was but 15 years old, yet had been twelve months a soldier, and had borne his part in several battles, even historic ones. I asked him if he did not suffer from the cold, and if he had no overcoat. No, he did not suffer from cold, and had no over-

coat, but could draw one whenever he wished. His father was dead, and his mother living in some part of East Tennessee; all the men were from that part of the country. The next forenoon I saw the Tennessee and Indiana regiments marching down the Avenue. My boy was with the former, stepping along with the rest. There were many other boys no older. I stood and watched them as they tramped along with slow, strong, heavy, regular steps. There did not appear to be a man over 30 years of age, and a large proportion were from 15 to perhaps 22 or 23. They had all the look of veterans, worn, stained, impassive, and a certain unbent, lounging gait, carrying in addition to their regular arms and knapsacks, frequently a frying pan, broom, etc. They were all of pleasant physiognomy; no refinement, nor blanched with intellect, but as my eye picked them, moving along, rank by rank, there did not seem to be a single repulsive, brutal, or markedly stupid face among them.

BURIAL OF A LADY NURSE ꝏ

Here is an incident just occurred in one of the hospitals. A lady named Miss or Mrs. Billings, who has long been a practical friend of soldiers, and nurse in the army, and had become attached to it in a way that no one can realize but him or her who has had experience, was taken sick, early this winter, lingered some time, and finally died in the hospital. It was her request that she should be buried among the soldiers, and after the military method. This request was fully carried out. Her coffin was carried to the grave by soldiers, with the usual escort, buried, and a salute fired over the grave. This was at Annapolis a few days since.

FEMALE NURSES FOR SOLDIERS ꝏ

There are many women in one position or another, among the hospitals, mostly as nurses here in Washington and among the military stations; quite a number of them young ladies acting as volunteers. They are a help in certain ways, and deserve to be mentioned with respect. Then it remains to be distinctly said that few or no young ladies, under the irresistible conventions of society, answer the practical requirements of nurses for soldiers. Middle-aged or healthy and good-conditioned elderly women, mothers of children, are always best. Many of the wounded must be handled. A hundred things which cannot be gainsaid, must occur and must be done. The presence of a good middle-aged or elderly woman, the magnetic touch of hands, the expressive features of the mother, the silent soothing of her presence, her words, her knowledge and privileges arrived at only through having had children, are precious and final qualifications. It is a natural faculty that is required; it is not merely having a genteel young woman at a table in a ward. One of the finest nurses I met was a red-faced illiterate old Irishwoman; I have seen her take the poor wasted naked boys so tenderly up in her arms. There are plenty of excellent clean old black woman that would make tiptop nurses.

SOUTHERN ESCAPEES ᴥ FEB. 23, '65 ᴥ I saw a large procession of young men from the rebel army (deserters they are called, but the usual meaning of the word does not apply to them) passing the Avenue today. There were nearly 200, come up yesterday by boat from James River. I stood and watched them as they shuffled along, in a slow, tired, worn sort of way; a large proportion of light-haired, blond, light gray-eyed young men among them. Their costumes had a dirt-stained uniformity; most had been originally gray; some had articles of our uniform, pants on one, vest or coat on another; I think they were mostly Georgia and North Carolina boys. They excited little or no attention. As I stood quite close to them, several good-looking enough youths (but O what a tale of misery their appearance told) nodded or just spoke to me, without doubt divining pity and fatherliness out of my face, for my heart was full enough of it. Several of the couples trudged along with their arms about each other, some probably brothers, as if they were afraid they might somehow get separated. They nearly all looked what one might call simple, yet intelligent, too. Some had pieces of old carpet, some blankets, and others old bags around their shoulders. Some of them here and there had fine faces; still, it was a procession of misery. The two hundred had with them about half a dozen armed guards. Along this week I saw some such procession, more or less in numbers, every day, as they were brought up by the boat. The government does what it can for them, and sends them north and west. ᴥ FEB. 27 ᴥ Some three or four hundred more escapees from the Confederate Army came up on the boat. As the day has been very pleasant indeed (after a long spell of bad weather), I have been wandering around a good deal, without any other object than to be outdoors and enjoy it; have met these escaped men in all directions. Their apparel is the same ragged, long-worn motley as before described. I talked with a number of the men. Some are quite bright and stylish, for all their poor clothes—walking with an air, wearing their old head coverings on one side, quite saucily, I find the old, unquestionable proofs, as all along the past four years, of the unscrupulous tyranny exercised by the secession government in conscripting the common people by absolute force everywhere, and paying no attention whatever to the men's time being up—keeping them in military service just the same. One

gigantic young fellow, a Georgian, at least six feet three inches high, broad-sized in proportion, attired in the dirtiest, drab, well-smeared rags, tied with strings, his trousers at the knees all strips and streamers, was complacently standing eating some bread and meat. He appeared contented enough. Then a few minutes after I saw him slowly walking along. It was plain he did not take anything to heart. ᴥ FEB. 28 ᴥ As I passed the military headquarters of the city, not far from the President's house, I stopped to interview some of the crowd of escapees who were lounging there. In appearance they were the same as previously mentioned. Two of them, one about 17, and the other perhaps 25 or '6, I talked with some time. They were from North Carolina, born and raised there, and had folks there. The elder had been in the rebel service four years. He was first conscripted for two years. He was then kept arbitrarily in the ranks. This is the case with a large proportion of the secession army. There was nothing downcast in these young men's manners; the younger had been soldiering about a year; he was conscripted; there were six brothers (all the boys of the family) in the army, part of them as conscripts, part as volunteers; three had been killed; one had escaped about four months ago, and now this one had got away; he was a pleasant and well-talking lad, with the peculiar North Carolina idiom (not at all disagreeable to my ears). He and the elder one were of the same company, and escaped together—and wished to remain together. They thought of getting transportation away to Missouri, and working there; but were not sure it was judicious. I advised them rather to go to some of the directly Northern states, and get farm work for the present. The younger had made six dollars on the boat, with some tobacco he brought; he had three and a half left. The elder had nothing; I gave him a trifle. Soon after, met John Wormley, 9th Alabama, a West Tennessee raised boy, parents both dead—had the look of one for a long time on short allowance—said very little—chewed tobacco at a fearful rate, spitting in proportion—large, clear dark-brown eyes, very fine—didn't know what to make of me—told me at last he wanted much to get some clean underclothes and a pair of decent pants. Didn't care about coat or hat fixings. Wanted a chance to wash himself well, and put on the underclothes. I had the very great pleasure of helping him to accomplish all those wholesome designs. ᴥ MARCH 1ST ᴥ Plenty more butternut or clay-colored escapees every day. About 160 came in today, a large portion South Carolinians. They generally take the oath of allegiance, and are sent north, west, or extreme southwest if they wish. Several of them told me that the desertions in their army, or men going home, leave or no leave, are far more numerous than their desertions to our side. I saw a very forlorn-looking squad of about a hundred, late this afternoon, on their way to the Baltimore depot.

THE CAPITOL BY GASLIGHT ᴀ Tonight I have been wandering awhile in the Capitol, which is all lit up. The illuminated rotunda looks fine. I like to stand aside and look a long, long while up at the dome; it comforts me somehow. The House and Senate were both in session till very late. I looked in upon them, but only a few moments; they were hard at work on tax and appropriation bills. I wandered through the long and rich corridors and apartments under the Senate; an old habit of mine, former winters, and now more satisfaction than ever. Not many persons down there, occasionally a flitting figure in the distance.

THE INAUGURATION ᴀ MARCH 4 ᴀ The President very quietly rode down to the Capitol in his own carriage, by himself, on a sharp trot, about noon, either because he wished to be on hand to sign bills, or to get rid of marching in line with the absurd procession, the muslin temple of liberty, and pasteboard monitor. I saw him on his return, at three o'clock, after the performance was over. He was in his plain two-horse barouche, and looked very much worn and tired; the lines, indeed, of vast responsibilities, intricate questions, and demands of life and death cut deeper than ever upon his dark brown face; yet all the old goodness, tenderness, sadness, and canny shrewdness underneath the furrows. (I never see that man without feeling that he is one to become personally attached to, for his combination of purest, heartiest tenderness, and native western form of manliness.) By his side, sat his little boy, of ten years. There were no soldiers, only a lot of civilians on horseback, with huge yellow scarfs over their shoulders, riding around the carriage. (At the inauguration four years ago, he rode down and back again surrounded by a dense mass of armed cavalrymen, eight deep with drawn sabers; and there were sharpshooters stationed at every corner on the route.) I ought to make mention of the closing levee of Saturday night last. Never before was such a compact jam in front of the White House— all the grounds filled, and away out to the spacious sidewalks. I was there, as I took a notion to go—was in the rush inside with the crowds—urged along the passageways, the Blue and other rooms, and through the great East Room. Crowds of country people, some very funny. Fine music from the Marine Band off in a side place. I saw Mr. Lincoln, dressed all in black, with white kid gloves and a claw-hammer coat, receiving, as in duty bound, shaking hands, looking very disconsolate, and as if he would give anything to be somewhere else.

ATTITUDE OF FOREIGN GOVERNMENTS DURING THE WAR ᴀ Looking over my scraps, I find I wrote the following during 1864. The happening to our America, abroad as well as at home, these years, is indeed most strange. The democratic republic has paid her today the terrible and resplendent compliment of the united wish of all the nations of the world that her union should be broken, her future cut off, and that she should be compelled to descend to the level of kingdoms and empires ordinarily great. There is certainly not one government in Europe but is now watching the war in this country, with the ardent prayer that the United States may be effectually split, crippled, and dismembered by it. There is not one but would help toward that dismemberment, if it dared. I say such is the ardent wish today of England and of France, as governments, and of all the nations of Europe, as governments. I think indeed it is today the real, heartfelt wish of all the nations of the world, with the single exception of Mexico—Mexico, the only one to whom we have ever really done wrong, and now the only one who prays for us and for our triumph with genuine prayer. Is it not indeed strange? America, made up of all, cheerfully from the beginning opening her arms to all, the result and justifier of all, of Britain, Germany, France, and Spain—all here—the accepter, the friend, hope, last resource, and general house of all—she who has harmed none, but been bounteous to so many, to millions, the mother of strangers and exiles, all nations—should now, I say, be paid this dread compliment of general governmental fear and hatred. Are we indignant? alarmed? Do we feel jeopardized? No; helped, braced, concentrated, rather. We are all too prone to wander from ourselves, to affect Europe, and watch her frowns and smiles. We need this hot lesson of general hatred, and henceforth must never forget it. Never again will we trust the moral sense nor abstract friendliness of a single *government* of the old world.

THE WEATHER—DOES IT SYMPATHIZE WITH THESE TIMES? ᴀ Whether the rains, the heat and cold, and what underlies them all, are affected with what affects man in masses, and follow his play of passionate action, strained stronger than usual, and on a larger scale than usual—whether this or no—it is certain that there is now, and has been for twenty months or more, on this American continent north, many a remarkable, many an unprecedented expression of the subtle world of air above us and around us. There, since this war, and the wide and deep national agitation, strange analogies, different combinations, a different sunlight, or absence of it; different products even out of the ground. After every great battle, a great storm. Even civic events the same. On Saturday last, a forenoon like whirling demons, dark, with slanting rain, full of rage; and then the afternoon, so calm, so bathed with flooding splendor from heaven's most excellent sun, with atmosphere of sweetness; so clear, it showed the stars, long, long before they were due. As the President came out on the Capitol portico, a curious little white cloud, the only one in that part of the sky, appeared like a hovering bird, right over him. ℘ Indeed, the heavens, the elements, all the meteorological influences, have run riot for weeks past. Such caprices, abruptest alternation of frowns and beauty, I never knew. It is a common remark that (as last summer was different in its spells of intense heat from any preceding it) the winter just completed has been without parallel. It has remained so down to the hour I am writing. Much of the daytime of the past month was sulky, with leaden heaviness, fog, interstices of bitter cold, and some insane storms. But there have been samples of another description. Nor earth nor sky ever knew spectacles of superber beauty than some of the nights lately here. The western star, Venus, in the earlier hours of evening, has never been so large, so clear; it seems as if it told something, as if it held rapport indulgent with humanity, with us Americans. Five or six nights since, it hung close by the moon, then a little past its first quarter. The star was wonderful, the moon like a young mother. The sky, dark blue, the transparent night, the planets, the moderate west wind, the elastic temperature, the miracle of that great star, and the young and swelling moon swimming in the west, suffused the soul. Then I heard slow and clear, the deliberate notes of a bugle come up out of the silence, sounding so good through the night's mystery, no hurry, but firm and faithful, floating along, rising, falling leisurely, with here and there a long-drawn note; the bugle, well played, sounding tattoo, in one of the army hospitals near here, where the wounded (some of them personally so dear to me) are lying in their cots, and many a sick boy come down to the war from Illinois, Michigan, Wisconsin, Iowa, and the rest.

INAUGURATION BALL ℘ MARCH 6 ℘ I have been up to look at the dance and supper rooms, for the inauguration ball at the Patent Office; and I could not help thinking what a different scene they presented to my view a while since, filled with a crowded mass of the worst wounded of the war, brought in from second Bull Run, Antietam, and Fredericksburg. Tonight, beautiful women, perfumes, the violins' sweetness, the polka and the waltz; then the amputation, the blue face, the groan, the glassy eye of the dying, the clotted rag, the odor of wounds and blood, and many a mother's son amid strangers, passing away untended there (for the crowd

of the badly hurt was great, and much for nurse to do, and much for surgeon).

SCENE AT THE CAPITOL ℘ I must mention a strange scene at the Capitol, the hall of Representatives, the morning of Saturday last (March 4th). The day just dawned, but in half-darkness, everything dim, leaden, and soaking. In that dim light, the members nervous from long-drawn duty, exhausted, some asleep, and many half asleep. The gaslight, mixed with the dingy daybreak, produced an unearthly effect. The poor little sleepy, stumbling pages, the smell of the hall, the members with heads leaning on their desks, the sounds of the voices speaking, with unusual intonations—the general moral atmosphere also of the close of this important session—the strong hope that the war is approaching its close—the tantalizing dread lest the hope may be a false one—the grandeur of the hall itself, with its effect of vast shadows up toward the panels and spaces over the galleries—all made a marked combination. ℘ In the midst of this, with the suddenness of a thunderbolt, burst one of the most angry and crashing storms of rain and hail ever heard. It beat like a deluge on the heavy glass roof of the hall, and the wind literally howled and roared. For a moment, (and no wonder) the nervous and sleeping Representatives were thrown into confusion. The slumberers awaked with fear, some started for the doors, some looked up with blanched cheeks and lips to the roof, and the little pages began to cry; it was a scene. But it was over almost as soon as the drowsied men were actually awake. They recovered themselves; the storm raged on, beating, dashing, and with loud noises at times. But the House went ahead with its business then, I think, as calmly and with as much deliberation as at any time in its career. Perhaps the shock did it good. (One is not without impression, after all, amid these members of Congress, of both the Houses, that if the flat routine of their duties should ever be broken in upon by some great emergency involving real danger, and calling for first-class personal qualities, those qualities would be found generally forthcoming, and from men not now credited with them.)

A YANKEE ANTIQUE ℘ MARCH 27, 1865 ℘ Sergeant Calvin F. Harlowe, Company C, 29th Massachusetts, 3d Brigade, 1st Division, Ninth Corps—a marked sample of heroism and death (some may say bravado, but I say *heroism*, of grandest, oldest order)—in the late attack by the rebel troops, and temporary capture by them, of Fort Steadman, at night. The fort was surprised at dead of night. Suddenly awakened from their sleep, and rushing from their tents, Harlowe, with others, found himself in the hands of the secesh—

they demanded his surrender—he answered, *Never while I live.* (Of course it was useless. The others surrendered; the odds were too great.) Again he was asked to yield, this time by a rebel captain. Though surrounded, and quite calm, he again refused, called sternly to his comrades to fight on, and himself attempted to do so. The rebel captain then shot him—but at the same instant he shot the captain. Both fell together mortally wounded. Harlowe died almost instantly. The rebels were driven out in a very short time. The body was buried next day, but soon taken up and sent home (Plymouth County, Mass.). Harlowe was only 22 years of age—was a tall, slim, dark-haired, blue-eyed young man—had come out originally with the 29th; and that is the way he met his death, after four years' campaign. He was in the Seven Days fight before Richmond, in second Bull Run, Antietam, first Fredericksburg, Vicksburg, Jackson, Wilderness, and the campaigns following—was as good a soldier as ever wore the blue, and every old officer in the regiment will bear that testimony. Though so young, and in a common rank, he had a spirit as resolute and brave as any hero in the books, ancient or modern—it was too great to say the words "I surrender"—and so he died. (When I think of such things, knowing them well, all the vast and complicated events of the war, on which history dwells and makes its volumes, fall aside, and for the moment at any rate I see nothing but young Calvin Harlowe's figure in the night, disdaining to surrender.)

WOUNDS AND DISEASES ᙍ The war is over, but the hospitals are fuller than ever, from former and current cases. A large majority of the wounds are in the arms and legs. But there is every kind of wound, in every part of the body. I should say of the sick, from my observation, that the prevailing maladies are typhoid fever and the camp fevers generally, diarrhea, catarrhal affections and bronchitis, rheumatism and pneumonia. These forms of sickness lead; all the rest follow. There are twice as many sick as there are wounded. The deaths range from seven to ten per cent of those under treatment.*

DEATH OF PRESIDENT LINCOLN ᙍ APRIL 16, '65 ᙍ I find in my notes of the time, this passage on the death of Abraham Lincoln: He leaves for America's history and biography, so far, not only its most dramatic reminiscence—he leaves, in my opinion, the greatest, best, most characteristic, artistic, moral personality. Not but that he had faults, and showed them in the Presidency; but honesty, goodness, shrewdness, conscience, and (a new virtue, unknown to other lands, and hardly yet really known here, but the foundation and tie of all, as the future will grandly develop), UNIONISM, in its truest and amplest sense, formed the hardpan of his character. These he sealed with his life. The tragic splendor of his death, purging, illuminating all, throws round his form, his head, an aureole that will remain and will grow brighter through time, while history lives, and love of country lasts. By many has this Union been helped; but if one name, one man, must be picked out, he, most of all, is the conservator of it, to the future. He was assassinated—but the Union is not assassinated—*ça ira!* One falls, and another falls. The soldier drops, sinks like a wave—but the ranks of the ocean eternally press on. Death does its work, obliterates a hundred, a thousand—President, general, captain, private—but the Nation is immortal.

SHERMAN'S ARMY'S JUBILATION—ITS SUDDEN STOPPAGE ᙍ When Sherman's armies (long after they left Atlanta) were marching through South and North Carolina—after leaving Savannah, the news of Lee's capitulation having been received—the men never moved a mile without from some part of the line sending up continued, inspiriting shouts. At intervals all day long sounded out the wild music of those peculiar army cries. They would be commenced by one regiment or brigade, immediately taken up by others, and at length whole corps and armies would join in these wild triumphant choruses. It was one of the characteristic expressions of the western troops, and became a habit, serving as a relief and outlet to the men—a vent for their feelings of victory, returning peace, etc. Morning, noon, and afternoon, spontaneous, for occasion or without occasion, these huge, strange cries, differing from any other, echoing through the open air for many a mile, expressing youth, joy, wildness, irrepressible strength, and the ideas of advance and conquest, sounded along the swamps and uplands of the South, floating to the skies. ("There never were men that kept in better spirits in danger or defeat—what then could they do in victory?"—said one of the 15th Corps to me, afterward.) This exuberance continued till the armies arrived at Raleigh. There the news of the President's murder was received. Then no more shouts or yells, for a week. All the marching was comparatively muffled. It was very significant—hardly a loud word or laugh in many of the regiments. A hush and silence pervaded all.

---

* In the U. S. Surgeon General's Office since, there is a formal record and treatment of 253,142 cases of wounds by government surgeons. What must have been the number unofficial, indirect—to say nothing of the Southern armies?

[41]

NO GOOD PORTRAIT OF LINCOLN ❧

Probably the reader has seen physiognomies (often old farmers, sea captains, and such) that, behind their homeliness, or even ugliness, held superior points so subtle, yet so palpable, making the real life of their faces almost as impossible to depict as a wild perfume or fruit taste, or a passionate tone of the living voice—and such was Lincoln's face, the peculiar color, the lines of it, the eyes, mouth, expression. Of technical beauty it had nothing—but to the eye of a great artist it furnished a rare study, a feast and fascination. The current portraits are all failures —most of them caricatures.

RELEASED UNION PRISONERS FROM SOUTH ❧

The released prisoners of war are now coming up from the Southern prisons. I have seen a number of them. The sight is worse than any sight of battlefields, or any collection of wounded, even the bloodiest. There was (as a sample) one large boatload, of several hundreds, brought about the 25th, to Annapolis; and out of the whole number only three individuals were able to walk from the boat. The rest were carried ashore and laid down in one place or another. Can those be *men*—those little livid brown, ash-streaked, monkey-looking dwarfs?—are they really not mummied, dwindled corpses? They lay there, most of them, quite still, but with a horrible look in their eyes and skinny lips (often with not enough flesh on the lips to cover their teeth). Probably no more appalling sight was ever seen on this earth. (There are deeds, crimes, that may be forgiven; but this is not among them. It steeps its perpetrators in blackest, escapeless, endless damnation. Over 50,000 have been compelled to die the death of starvation—reader, did you ever try to realize what *starvation* actually is?—in those prisons—and in a land of plenty.) An indescribable meanness, tyranny, aggravating course of insults, almost incredible—was evidently the rule of treatment through all the Southern military prisons. The dead there are not to be pitied as much as some of the living that come from there—if they can be called living—many of them are mentally imbecile, and will never recuperate.*

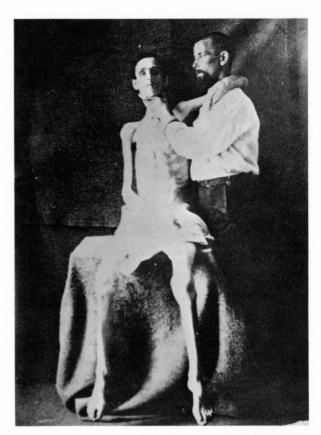

SOLDIERS RETURNED FROM RICHMOND PRISON

have not at least one dear relative or friend among these 60,000 whose sad fortune it was to end their service for the Union by lying down and dying for it in a Southern prison pen. The manner of their death, the horrors that clustered thickly around every moment of their existence, the loyal, unfaltering steadfastness with which they endured all that fate had brought them, has never been adequately told. It was not with them as with their comrades in the field, whose every act was performed in the presence of those whose duty it was to observe such matters and report them to the world. Hidden from the view of their friends in the North by the impenetrable veil which the military operations of the rebels drew around the so-called Confederacy, the people knew next to nothing of their career or their sufferings. Thousands died there less heeded even than the hundreds who perished on the battlefield. Grant did not lose as many men killed outright, in the terrible campaign from the Wilderness to the James River—43 days of desperate fighting—as died in July and August at Andersonville. Nearly twice as many died in that prison as fell from the day that Grant crossed the Rapidan, till he settled down in the trenches before Petersburg. More than four times as many Union dead lie under the solemn soughing pines about that forlorn little village in southern Georgia, than mark the course of Sherman from Chattanooga to Atlanta. The nation stands aghast at the expenditure of life which attended the two bloody campaigns of 1864, which virtually crushed the Confederacy, but no one remembers that more Union soldiers died in the rear of the rebel lines than were killed in the front of them. The great military events which stamped out the rebellion drew attention away from the sad drama which starvation and disease played in those gloomy pens in the far recesses of sombre Southern forests."

---

* *From a review of* Andersonville, A Story of Southern Military Prisons, *published serially in the* Toledo Blade, *in 1879, and afterward in book form:*

"There is a deep fascination in the subject of Andersonville—for that Golgotha, in which lie the whitening bones of 13,000 gallant young men, represents the dearest and costliest sacrifice of the war for the preservation of our national unity. It is a type, too, of its class. Its more than hundred hecatombs of dead represent several times that number of their brethren, for whom the prison gates of Belle Isle, Danville, Salisbury, Florence, Columbia, and Cahaba opened only in eternity. There are few families in the North who

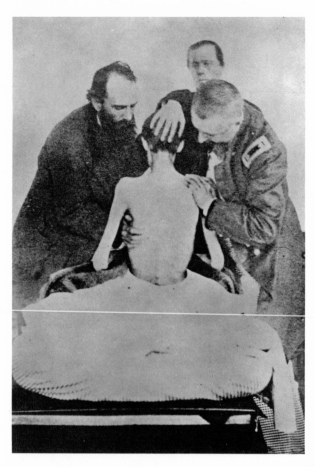

From a letter of "Johnny Bouquet," in N.Y. Tribune,
March 27, '81:

"I visited at Salisbury, N.C., the prison pen or the site of it, from which nearly 12,000 victims of Southern politicians were buried being confined in a pen without shelter, exposed to all the elements could do, to all the disease herding animals together could create, and to all the starvation and cruelty an incompetent and intense caitiff government could accomplish. From the conversation and almost from the recollection of the Northern people this place has dropped, but not so in the gossip of the Salisbury people, nearly all of whom say that the half was never told; that such was the nature of habitual outrage here that when Federal prisoners escaped the townspeople harbored them in their barns, afraid the vengeance of God would fall on them, to deliver even their enemies back to such cruelty. Said one old man at the Boyden House, who joined in the conversation one evening: 'There were often men buried out of that prison pen still alive. I have the testimony of a surgeon that he has seen them pulled out of the dead cart with their eyes open and taking notice, but too weak to lift a finger. There was not the least excuse for such treatment, as the Confederate government had seized every sawmill in the region, and could just as well have put up a shelter for these prisoners as not, wood being plentiful here. It will be hard to make any honest man in Salisbury say that there was the slightest necessity for those prisoners having to live in old tents, caves, and holes half-full of water. Representations were made to the Davis government against the officers in charge of it, but no attention was paid to them. Promotion was the punishment for cruelty there. The inmates were skeletons. Hell could have no terrors for any man who died there, except the inhuman keepers.' "

DEATH OF A PENNSYLVANIA SOLDIER

ॐ FRANK H. IRWIN, COMPANY E, 93D PENNSYLVANIA ॐ DIED MAY 1, '65 ॐ MY LETTER TO HIS MOTHER ॐ Dear Madam: No doubt you and Frank's friends have heard the sad fact of his death in hospital here, through his uncle, or the lady from Baltimore who took his things. (I have not seen them, only heard of them visiting Frank.) I will write you a few lines—as a casual friend that sat by his deathbed. Your son, Corporal Frank H. Irwin, was wounded near Fort Fisher, Virginia, March 25th, 1865—the wound was in the left knee, pretty bad. He was sent up to Washington, was received in Ward C, Armory Square Hospital, March 28th—the wound became worse, and on the 4th of April the leg was amputated a little above the knee—the operation was performed by Dr. Bliss, one of the best surgeons in the army —he did the whole operation himself—there was a good deal of bad matter gathered—the bullet was found in the knee. For a couple of weeks afterward he was doing pretty well. I visited and sat by him frequently, as he was fond of having me. The last ten or twelve days of April I saw that his case was critical. He previously had some fever, with cold spells. The last week in April he was much of the time flighty—but always mild and gentle. He died first of May. The actual cause of death was pyæmia (the absorption of the matter in the system instead of its discharge). Frank, as far as I saw, had everything requisite in surgical treatment, nursing, etc. He had watches much of the time. He was so good and well-behaved and affectionate; I myself liked him very much. I was in the habit of coming in afternoons and sitting by him, and soothing him, and he liked to have me—liked to put his arm out and lay his hand on my knee—would keep it so a long while. Toward the last he was more restless and flighty at night— often fancied himself with his regiment—by his talk sometimes seemed as if his feelings were hurt by being blamed by his officers for something he was entirely innocent of—said, "I never in my life was thought capable of such a thing, and never was." At other times he would fancy himself talking as it seemed to children or such like, his relatives I suppose, and giving them good advice; would talk to them a long while. All the time he was out of his head not one single bad word or idea escaped him. It was remarked that many a man's conversation in his senses was not half as good as Frank's delirium. He seemed quite willing to die—he had become very weak and had suffered a good deal, and was perfectly resigned, poor boy. I do not know his past life, but I feel as if it must have been good. At any rate what I saw of him here, under the most trying circumstances, with a painful wound, and among strangers, I can say that he behaved so brave, so composed, and so sweet and affectionate, it could not be surpassed. And now like many other noble and good men, after serving his country as a soldier, he has yielded up his young life at the very outset in her service. Such things are gloomy—yet there is a text, "God doeth all things well"—the meaning of which, after due time, appears to the soul. ๑ I thought perhaps a few words, though from a stranger, about your son, from one who was with him at the last, might be worth while—for I loved the young man, though I but saw him immediately to lose him. I am merely a friend visiting the hospitals occasionally to cheer the wounded and sick.   W. W.

THE ARMIES RETURNING ๑ MAY 7—SUNDAY ๑ Today as I was walking a mile or two south of Alexandria, I fell in with several large squads of the returning Western army (*Sherman's men*, as they called themselves), about a thousand in all, the largest portion of them half sick, some convalescents, on their way to a hospital camp. These fragmentary excerpts, with the unmistakable Western physiognomy and idioms, crawling along slowly—after a great campaign, blown this way, as it were, out of their latitude—I marked with curiosity, and talked with off and on for over an hour. Here and there was one very sick; but all were able to

THE GRAND REVIEW, MAY 1865. TWENTIETH ARMY CORPS OF GEORGIA

walk, except some of the last, who had given out, and were seated on the ground, faint and despondent. These I tried to cheer, told them the camp they were to reach was only a little way further over the hill, and so got them up and started, accompanying some of the worst a little way, and helping them, or putting them under the support of stronger comrades. ❧ MAY 21 ❧ Saw General Sheridan and his cavalry today; a strong, attractive sight; the men were mostly young (a few middle-aged), superb-looking fellows, brown, spare, keen, with well-worn clothing, many with pieces of waterproof cloth around their shoulders, hanging down. They dashed along pretty fast, in wide close ranks, all spattered with mud; no holiday soldiers; brigade after brigade. I could have watched for a week. Sheridan stood on a balcony, under a big tree, cooly smoking a cigar. His looks and manner impressed me favorably. ❧ MAY 22 ❧ Have been taking a walk along Pennsylvania Avenue and Seventh Street north. The city is full of soldiers, running around loose. Officers everywhere, of all grades. All have the weatherbeaten look of practical service. It is a sight I never tire of. All the armies are now here (or portions of them) for tomorrow's review. You see them swarming like bees everywhere.

THE GRAND REVIEW ❧ For two days now the broad spaces of Pennsylvania Avenue along to Treasury Hill, and so by detour around to the President's house, and so up to Georgetown, and across the aqueduct bridge, have been alive with a magnificent sight, the returning armies. In their wide ranks stretching clear across the Avenue, I watch them march or ride along, at a brisk pace, through two whole days—infantry, cavalry, artillery—some 200,000 men. Some days afterward one or two other corps; and then, still afterward, a good part of Sherman's immense army, brought up from Charleston, Savannah, etc.

WESTERN SOLDIERS ❧ MAY 26-7 ❧ The streets, the public buildings and grounds of Washington, still swarm with soldiers from Illinois, Indiana, Ohio, Missouri, Iowa, and all the Western states. I am continually meeting and talking with them. They often speak to me first, and always show great sociability, and glad to have a good interchange of chat. These Western soldiers are more slow in their movements, and in their intellectual quality also; have no extreme alertness. They are larger in size, have a more serious physiognomy, are continually looking at you as they pass in the street. They are largely animal, and handsomely so. During the war I have been at times with the Fourteenth, Fifteenth, Seventeenth, and Twentieth Corps. I always feel drawn toward the men, and like their personal contact when

we are crowded close together, as frequently these days in the streetcars. They all think the world of General Sherman; call him, "Old Bill" or sometimes "Uncle Billy."

A SOLDIER ON LINCOLN ❧ MAY 28 ❧ As I sat by the bedside of a sick Michigan soldier in hospital today, a convalescent from the adjoining bed rose and came to me, and presently we began talking. He was a middle-aged man, belonged to the 2d Virginia Regiment, but lived in Racine, Ohio, and had a family there. He spoke of President Lincoln, and said: "The war is over, and many are lost. And now we have lost the best, the fairest, the truest man in America. Take him altogether, he was the best man this country ever produced. It was quite a while I thought very different; but some time before the murder, that's the way I have seen it." There was deep earnestness in the soldier. (I found upon further talk he had known Mr. Lincoln personally, and quite closely, years before.) He was a veteran; was now in the fifth year of his service; was a cavalry man, and had been in a good deal of hard fighting.

TWO BROTHERS, ONE SOUTH, ONE NORTH ❧ MAY 28-9 ❧ I stayed tonight a long time by the bedside of a new patient, a young Baltimorean, aged about 19 years, W. S. P. (2d Maryland, Southern), very feeble, right leg amputated, can't sleep hardly at all—has taken a great deal of morphine, which as usual, is costing more than it comes to. Evidently very intelligent and well-bred—very affectionate—held on to my hand, and put it by his face, not willing to let me leave. As I was lingering, soothing him in his pain, he says to me suddenly, "I hardly think you know who I am—I don't wish to impose upon you—I am a rebel soldier." I said I did not know that, but it made no difference. Visiting him daily for about two weeks after that, while he lived (death had marked him, and he was quite alone), I loved him much, always kissed him, and he did me. In an adjoining ward I found his brother, an officer of rank, a Union soldier, a brave and religious man (Col. Clifton K. Prentiss, Sixth Maryland Infantry, Sixth Corps, wounded in one of the engagements at Petersburg, April 2—lingered, suffered much, died in Brooklyn, Aug. 20, '65). It was in the same battle both were hit. One was a strong Unionist, the other secesh; both fought on their respective sides, both badly wounded, and both brought together here after a separation of four years. Each died for his cause.

SOME SAD CASES YET ❧ MAY 31 ❧ James H. Williams, aged 21, 3d Virginia Cavalry—about as marked a case of a strong man brought low by a complication of diseases (laryngitis, fever, debility, and diarrhea) as I have ever seen—has superb physique, remains swarthy yet and flushed and red with fever—is altogether flighty—flesh of his great breast and arms tremulous, and pulse pounding away with treble quickness—lies a good deal of the time in a partial sleep, but with low muttering and groans—a sleep in which there is no rest. Powerful as he is, and so young, he will not be able to stand many more days of the strain and sapping heat of yesterday and today. His throat is in a bad way, tongue and lips parched. When I ask him how he feels, he is able just to articulate, "I feel pretty bad yet, old man," and looks at me with his great bright eyes. Father, John Williams, Millensport, Ohio. ❧ JUNE 9–10 ❧ I have been sitting late tonight by the bedside of a wounded captain, a special friend of mine, lying with a painful fracture of left leg in one of the hospitals, in a large ward partially vacant. The lights were put out, all but a little candle, far from where I sat. The full moon shone in through the windows, making long, slanting silvery patches on the floor. All was still; my friend too was silent, but could not sleep; so I sat there by him, slowly wafting the fan, and occupied with the musings that arose out of the scene, the long shadowy ward, the beautiful ghostly moonlight on the floor, the white beds, here and there an occupant with huddled form, the bedclothes thrown off. The hospitals have a number of cases of sunstroke and exhaustion by heat, from the late reviews. There are many such from the Sixth Corps, from the hot parade of day before yesterday. (Some of these shows cost the lives of scores of men.) ❧ SUNDAY,

SEPT. 10 ❧ Visited Douglas and Stanton Hospitals. They are quite full. Many of the cases are bad ones, lingering wounds, and old sickness. There is a more than usual look of despair on the countenances of many of the men; hope has left them. I went through the wards, talking as usual. There are several here from the Confederate Army whom I had seen in other hospitals, and they recognized me. Two were in a dying condition.

CALHOUN'S REAL MONUMENT ❧ In one of the hospital tents for special cases, as I sat today tending a new amputation, I heard a couple of neighboring soldiers talking to each other from their cots. One down with fever, but improving, had come up belated from Charleston not long before. The other was what we now call an "old veteran" (i.e., he was a Connecticut youth, probably of less than the age of twenty-five years, the four last of which he had spent in active service in the war in all parts of the country). The two were chatting of one thing and another. The fever soldier spoke of John C. Calhoun's monument, which he had seen, and was describing it. The veteran said: "I have seen Calhoun's monument. That you saw is not the real monument. But I have seen it. It is the desolated, ruined South; nearly the whole generation of young men between seventeen and thirty destroyed or maimed; all the old families used up—the rich impoverished, the plantations covered with weeds, the slaves unloosed and become the masters, and the name of Southerner blackened with every shame—all that is Calhoun's real monument."

HAREWOOD HOSPITAL, PAGES 46, 47, AND 48

HOSPITALS CLOSING ❧ OCTOBER 3 ❧ There are two Army hospitals now remaining. I went to the largest of these (Douglas) and spent the afternoon and evening. There are many sad cases, old wounds, incurable sickness, and some of the wounded from the March and April battles before Richmond. Few realize how sharp and bloody those closing battles were. Our men exposed themselves more than usual; pressed ahead without urging. Then the Southerners fought with extra desperation. Both sides knew that with the successful chasing of the rebel cabal from Richmond, and the occupation of that city by the national troops, the game was up. The dead and wounded were unusually many. Of the wounded the last lingering driblets have been brought to hospital here. I find many rebel wounded here, and have been extra busy today tending to the worst cases of them with the rest. ❧ OCT., NOV., AND DEC., '65—SUNDAYS ❧ Every Sunday of these months visited Harewood Hospital out in the woods, pleasant and recluse, some two and a half or three miles north of the Capitol. The situation is healthy, with broken ground, grassy slopes and patches of oak woods, the trees large and fine. It was one of the most extensive of the hospitals, now reduced to four or five partially occupied wards, the numerous others being vacant. In November, this became the last military hospital kept up by the government, all the others being closed. Cases of the worst and most incurable wounds, obstinate illness, and of poor fellows who have no homes to go to, are found here. ❧ DEC. 10—SUNDAY ❧ Again spending a good part of the day at Harewood. I write this about an hour before sundown. I have walked out for a few minutes to the edge of the woods to soothe myself with the hour and scene. It is a glorious, warm, golden-sunny, still afternoon. The only noise is from a crowd of cawing crows, on some trees three hundred yards distant. Clusters of gnats swimming and dancing in the air in all directions. The oak leaves are thick under the bare

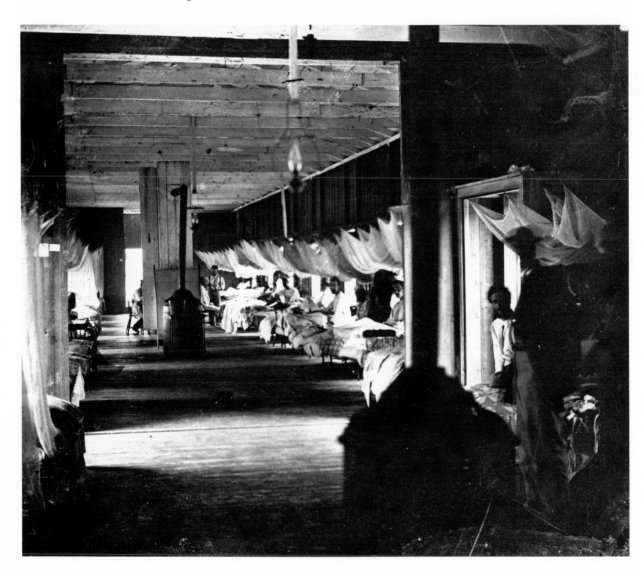

[47]

trees, and give a strong and delicious perfume. Inside the wards everything is gloomy. Death is there. As I entered, I was confronted by it the first thing; a corpse of a poor soldier, just dead, of typhoid fever. The attendants had just straightened the limbs, put coppers on the eyes, and were laying it out. ?◦ THE ROADS ◦? A great recreation, the past three years, has been in taking long walks out from Washington, five, seven, perhaps ten miles and back, generally with my friend Peter Doyle, who is as fond of it as I am. Fine moonlight nights, over the perfect military roads, hard and smooth—or Sundays—we had these delightful walks, never to be forgotten. The roads connecting Washington and the numerous forts around the city, made one useful result, at any rate, out of the war.

TYPICAL SOLDIERS ?◦ Even the typical soldiers I have been personally intimate with,—it seems to me if I were to make a list of them it would be like a city directory. Some few only have I mentioned in the foregoing pages—most are dead—a few yet living. There is Reuben Farwell, of Michigan (little "Mitch"); Benton H. Wilson, color-bearer, 185th New York; Wm. Stansberry; Manvill Winterstein, Ohio; Bethuel Smith; Capt. Simms, of 51st New York (killed at Petersburg mine explosion); Capt. Sam. Pooley and Lieut. Fred. McReady, same regt. Also, same regt., my brother, George W. Whitman—in active service all through, four years, re-enlisting twice—was promoted, step by step (several times immediately after battles), lieutenant, captain, major, and lieut. colonel—was in the actions at

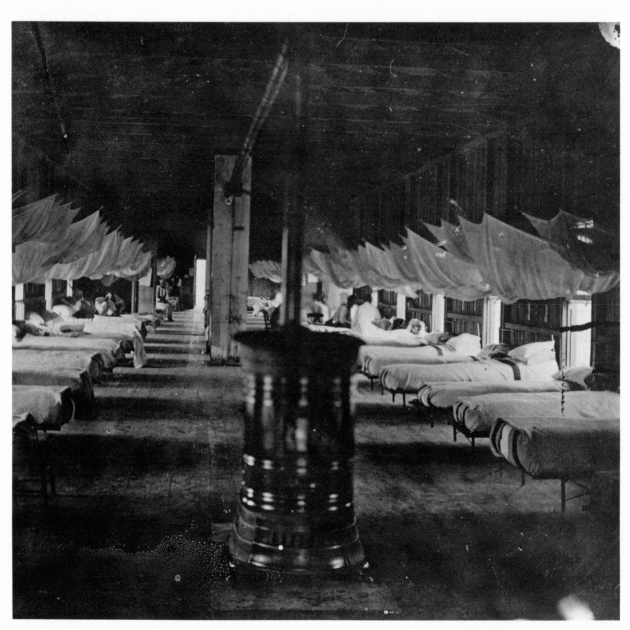

Roanoke, Newbern, 2d Bull Run, Chantilly, South Mountain, Antietam, Fredericksburg, Vicksburg, Jackson, the bloody conflicts of the Wilderness, and at Spotsylvania, Cold Harbor, and afterward around Petersburg; at one of these latter was taken prisoner, and passed four or five months in secesh military prisons, narrowly escaping with life, from a severe fever, from starvation and half-nakedness in the winter. (What a history that 51st New York had! Went out early—marched, fought everywhere—was in storms at sea, nearly wrecked—stormed forts—tramped hither and yon in Virginia, night and day, summer of '62—afterward Kentucky and Mississippi—re-enlisted—was in all the engagements and campaigns, as above.) I strengthen and comfort myself much with the certainty that the capacity for just such regiments (hundreds, thousands of them) is inexhaustible in the United States, and that there isn't a county nor a township in the republic—nor a street in any city—but could turn out, and, on occasion, would turn out, lots of just such typical soldiers, whenever wanted.

1

2

3

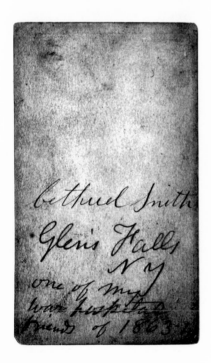

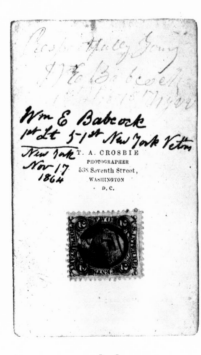

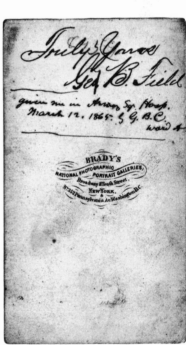

[49]

PAGE 49: 1. *Bethuel Smith, Glen's Falls, N.Y., one of my war hospital friends of 1863–4.*
2. *Wm. E. Babcock, 1st Lt., 51st New York Vet'rns, New York, Nov. 17, 1864.*
3. *Truly Yours, Geo. B. Field, given me in Armory Sq. Hosp., March 12, 1865 by G. B. F., Ward A.*

PAGE 50: 4. *To Walt Whitman, Respects of Anson Rider Junior.*

5. *Brooklyn City Hosp., Sept. '64, Edward W. Flower, Co. E, 8th Michigan Vol. (residence near Lansing, Mich.) lost right leg below knee.*

PAGE 51: 6. *Lt. James Watkins Mullery, Co. E., 15th New Jersey Vol., Vernon, Sussex Co., N.J., June 20, 1865.*
7. *Richard M. Ross, East Smithfield, Bradford Co., Penna., given me in Arm. Sq. Hosp. Ward A by R. M. R. soldier (sick with infl. rheum.) March 12, '65.*

PAGE 52: 8. *Walt! I am Will W. Wallace.*

SEVENTH NEW YORK STATE MILITIA, CAMP CAMERON, WASHINGTON, D.C., 1861.

4

5

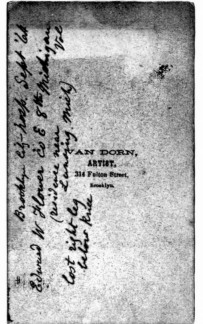

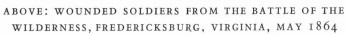

ABOVE: WOUNDED SOLDIERS FROM THE BATTLE OF THE
WILDERNESS, FREDERICKSBURG, VIRGINIA, MAY 1864

6

7

ABOVE: 1ST VOLUNTEER INFANTRY, MARCH 1865, WASHINGTON, D.C.   BELOW: R.I. INFANTRY

8

THIS PAGE: RHODE ISLAND INFANTRY

PAGES 54 AND 55: 7TH NEW YORK STATE MILITIA, CAMP CAMERON, WASHINGTON, D.C., 1861

THIS PAGE AND PAGE 60: 22ND NEW YORK STATE MILITIA, HARPER'S FERRY, VIRGINIA, 1861

ABOVE: LIEUTENANTS, 3RD PENNSYLVANIA CAVALRY   BELOW: GENERALS, 2ND ARMY CORPS

"CONVULSIVENESS" ⅋ As I have looked over the proof sheets of the preceding pages, I have once or twice feared that my diary would prove, at best, but a batch of convulsively written reminiscences. Well, be it so. They are but parts of the actual distraction, heat, smoke, and excitement of those times. The war itself, with the temper of society preceding it, can indeed be best described by that very word *convulsiveness*.

THREE YEARS SUMMED UP ⅋ During those three years in hospital, camp, or field, I made over six hundred visits or tours, and went, as I estimate, counting all, among from eighty thousand to a hundred thousand of the wounded and sick, as sustainer of spirit and body in some degree, in time of need. These visits varied from an hour or two to all day or night; for with dear or critical cases I generally watched all night. Sometimes I took up my quarters in the hospital, and slept or watched there several nights in succession. Those three years I consider the greatest privilege and satisfaction (with all their feverish excitements and physical deprivations and lamentable sights) and, of course, the most profound lesson of my life. I can say that in my ministerings I comprehended all, whoever came in my way, Northern or Southern, and slighted none. It aroused and brought out and decided undreamed-of depths of emotion. It has given me my most fervent views of the true *ensemble* and extent of the states. While I was with wounded and sick in thousands of cases from the New England states, and from New York, New Jersey, and Pennsylvania, and from Michigan, Wisconsin, Ohio, Indiana, Illinois, and all the Western states, I was with more or less from all the states, North and South, without exception. I was with many from the border states, especially from Maryland and Virginia, and found, during those lurid years 1862–63, far more Union Southerners, especially Tennesseans, than is supposed. I was with many rebel officers and men among our wounded, and gave them always what I had, and tried to cheer them the same as any. I was among the army teamsters considerably, and, indeed, always found myself drawn to them. Among the black soldiers, wounded or sick, and in the contraband camps, I also took my way whenever in their neighborhood, and did what I could for them.

CONTRABAND SLAVES, CULPEPER, VIRGINIA, NOVEMBER 1863

[58]

THE MILLION DEAD, TOO, SUMMED UP ❧ The dead in this war—there they lie, strewing the fields and woods and valleys and battlefields of the South—Virginia, the Peninsula—Malvern Hill and Fair Oaks—the banks of the Chickahominy—the terraces of Fredericksburg—Antietam bridge—the grisly ravines of Manassas—the bloody promenade of the Wilderness —the varieties of the *strayed* dead (the estimate of the War Department is 25,000 national soldiers killed in battle and never buried at all, 5,000 drowned—15,000 inhumed by strangers, or on the march in haste, in hitherto unfound localities—2,000 graves covered by sand and mud by Mississippi freshets, 3,000 carried away by caving-in of banks, etc.)—Gettysburg, the West, Southwest—Vicksburg—Chattanooga—the trenches of Petersburg—the numberless battles, camps, hospitals everywhere—the crop reaped by the mighty reapers, typhoid, dysentery, inflammations—and blackest and loathesomest of all, the dead and living burial pits, the prison pens of Andersonville, Salisbury, Belle-Isle, etc. (not Dante's pictured hell and all its woes, its degradations, filthy torments, excelled those prisons)—the dead, the dead, the dead—*our* dead—or South or North, ours all (all, all, all, finally dear to me)—or East or West— Atlantic coast or Mississippi valley—somewhere they crawled to die, alone, in bushes, low gullies, or on the sides of hills (there, in secluded spots, their skeletons, bleached bones, tufts of hair, buttons, fragments of clothing, are occasionally found yet)—our young men once so handsome and so joyous, taken from us—the son from the mother, the husband from the wife, the dear friend from the dear friend—the clusters of camp graves, in Georgia, the Carolinas, and in Tennessee—the single graves left in the woods or by the roadside (hundreds, thousands, obliterated)—the corpses floated down the rivers, and caught and lodged (dozens, scores, floated down the upper Potomac, after the cavalry engagements, the pursuit of Lee, following Gettysburg)—some lie at the bottom of the sea—the general million, and the special cemeteries in almost all the states—the infinite dead (the land entire saturated, perfumed with their impalpable ashes' exhalation in Nature's chemistry distilled, and shall be so forever, in every future grain of wheat and ear of corn, and every flower that grows, and

ANDERSONVILLE PRISON, GEORGIA, AUGUST 17, 1864

every breath we draw)—not only Northern dead leavening Southern soil—thousands, aye tens of thousands, of Southerners, crumble today in Northern earth. ?? And everywhere among these countless graves—everywhere in the many Soldier Cemeteries of the nation (there are now, I believe, over seventy of them)—as at the time in the vast trenches, the depositories of slain, Northern and Southern, after the great battles—not only where the scathing trail passed those years, but radiating since in all the peaceful quarters of the land—we see, and ages yet may see, on monuments and gravestones, singly or in masses, to thousands or tens of thousands, the significant word UNKNOWN. ?? (In some of the cemeteries nearly *all* the dead are unknown. At Salisbury, N.C., for instance, the known are only 85, while the unknown are 12,027, and 11,700 of these are buried in trenches. A national monument has been put up here, by order of Congress, to mark the spot—but what visible, material monument can ever fittingly commemorate that spot?)

THE REAL WAR WILL NEVER GET IN THE BOOKS ?? And so good-by to the war. I know not how it may have been, or may be, to others—to me the main interest I found (and still on recollection, find) in the rank and file of the armies, both sides, and in those specimens amid the hospitals, and even the dead on the field. To me the points illustrating the latent personal character and eligibilities of these states, in the two or three millions of American young and middle-aged men, North and South, embodied in those armies—and especially the one-third or one-fourth of their number stricken by wounds or disease at some time in the course of the contest—were of more significance even than the political interests involved. (As so much of a race depends on how it faces death, and how it stands personal anguish and sickness. As, in the glints of emotions under emergencies, and the indirect traits and asides in Plutarch, we get far profounder clues to the antique world than all its more formal history.) ?? Future years will never know the seething hell and the black infernal background of countless minor scenes and interiors (not the official surface courteousness of the generals, not the few great battles) of the Secession War; and it is best they should not—the real war will never get in the books. In the mushy influences of current times, too, the fervid atmosphere and typical events of those years are in danger of being totally forgotten. I have at night watched by the side of a sick man in the hospital, one who could not live many hours. I have seen his eyes flash and burn as he raised himself and recurred to the cruelties on his surrendered brother, and mutilations of the corpse afterward. (See, in the preceding pages, the inci-

dent at Upperville—the seventeen killed as in the description were left there on the ground. After they dropped dead, no one touched them—all were made sure of, however. The carcasses were left for the citizens to bury or not, as they chose.) ?? Such was the war. It was not a quadrille in a ballroom. Its interior history will not only never be written—its practicality, minutiæ of deeds and passions, will never be even suggested. The actual soldier of 1862-'65, North and South, with all his ways, his incredible dauntlessness, habits, practices, tastes, language, his fierce friendship, his appetite, rankness, his superb strength and animality, lawless gait, and a hundred unnamed lights and shades of camp, I say, will never be written—perhaps must not and should not be. ?? The preceding notes may furnish a few stray glimpses into that life, and into those lurid interiors, never to be fully conveyed to the future. The hospital part of the drama from '61 to '65 deserves indeed to be recorded. Of that many-threaded drama, with its sudden and strange surprises, its confounding of prophecies, its moments of despair, the dread of foreign interference, the interminable campaigns, the bloody battles, the mighty and cumbrous and green armies, the drafts and bounties—the immense money expenditure, like a heavy-pouring constant rain—with, over the whole land, the last three years of the struggle, an unending, universal mourning wail of women, parents, orphans—the marrow of the tragedy concentrated in those Army Hospitals (it seemed sometimes as if the whole interest of the land, North and South, was one vast central hospital, and all the rest of the affair but flanges)—those forming the untold and unwritten history of the war—infinitely greater (like life's) than the few scraps and distortions that are ever told or written. Think how much, and of importance, will be—how much, civic and military, has already been—buried in the grave, in eternal darkness.

22ND NEW YORK STATE MILITIA, HARPER'S FERRY, VIRGINIA, 1861.

AN INTERREGNUM PARAGRAPH ❧ Several years now elapse before I resume my diary. I continued at Washington working in the Attorney General's department through '66 and '67, and some time afterward. In February '73 I was stricken down by paralysis, gave up my desk, and migrated to Camden, New Jersey, where I lived during '74 and '75, quite unwell—but after that began to grow better; commenced going for weeks at a time, even for months, down in the country, to a charmingly recluse and rural spot along Timber Creek, twelve or thirteen miles from where it enters the Delaware River. Domiciled at the farmhouse of my friends, the Staffords, near by, I lived half the time along this creek and its adjacent fields and lanes. And it is to my life here that I, perhaps, owe partial recovery (a sort of second wind, or semirenewal of the lease of life) from the prostration of 1874–'75. If the notes of that outdoor life could only prove as glowing to you, reader dear, as the experience itself was to me! Doubtless in the course of the following, the fact of invalidism will crop out (I call myself a *half-paralytic* these days, and reverently bless the Lord it is no worse) between some of the lines—but I get my share of fun and healthy hours, and shall try to indicate them. (The trick is, I find, to tone your wants and tastes low down enough, and make much of negatives, and of mere daylight and the skies.)

NEW THEMES ENTERED UPON ❧ 1876–'77 ❧ I find the woods in mid-May and early June my best places for composition.* Seated on logs or stumps there, or resting on rails, nearly all the following memoranda have been jotted down. Wherever I go, indeed, winter or summer, city or country, alone at home or traveling, I must take notes (the ruling passion strong in age and disablement, and even the approach of—but I must not say it yet). Then underneath the following excerpta—crossing the t's and dotting the i's of certain moderate movements of late years—I am fain to fancy the foundations of quite a lesson learned. After you have exhausted what there is in business, politics, conviviality, love, and so on—have found that none of these finally satisfy, or

permanently wear—what remains? Nature remains: to bring out from their torpid recesses the affinities of a man or woman with the open air, the trees, fields, the changes of seasons—the sun by day and the stars of heaven by night. We will begin from these convictions. Literature flies so high and is so hotly spiced that our notes may seem hardly more than breaths of common air, or draughts of water to drink. But that is part of our lesson. ❧ Dear, soothing, healthy, restoration hours—after three confining years of paralysis—after the long strain of the war, and its wounds and death.

ENTERING A LONG FARM LANE ❧ As every man has his hobby-liking, mine is for a real farm lane fenced by old chestnut rails gray-green with dabs of moss and lichen, copious weeds and briers growing in spots athwart the heaps of stray-picked stones at the fence bases—irregular paths worn between, and horse and cow tracks—all characteristic accompaniments marking and scenting the neighborhood in their seasons—apple-tree blossoms in forward April—pigs, poultry, a field of August buckwheat, and in another the long flapping tassels of maize—and so to the pond, the expansion of the creek, the secluded-beautiful, with young and old trees, and such recesses and vistas!

TO THE SPRING AND BROOK ❧ So, still sauntering on, to the spring under the willows—musical as soft-clinking glasses—pouring a sizable stream, thick as my neck, pure and clear, out from its vent where the bank arches over like a great brown shaggy eyebrow or mouth-roof—gurgling, gurgling ceaselessly—meaning, saying something, of course (if one could only translate it)—always gurgling there, the whole year through—never giving out—oceans of mint, blackberries in summer—choice of light and shade—just the place for my July sun baths and water baths too—but mainly the inimitable soft sound-gurgles of it, as I sit there hot afternoons. How they and all grow into me, day after day—everything in keeping—the wild, just-palpable perfume, and the dapple of leaf shadows, and all the natural-medicinal, elemental-moral influences of the spot. ❧ Babble on, O brook, with that utterance of thine! I too will express what I have gathered in my days and progress, native, subterranean, past—and now thee. Spin and wind thy way—I with thee, a little while, at any rate. As I haunt thee so often, season by season, thou knowest, reckest not me (yet why be so certain? who can tell?)—but I will learn from thee, and dwell on thee—receive, copy, print from thee.

AN EARLY SUMMER REVEILLE ❧ Away then to loosen, to unstring the divine bow, so tense, so

---

* Without apology for the abrupt change of field and atmosphere—after what I have put in the preceding fifty or sixty pages—temporary episodes, thank heaven!—I restore my book to the bracing and buoyant equilibrium of concrete outdoor Nature, the only permanent reliance for sanity of book or human life.

Who knows (I have it in my fancy, my ambition) but the pages now ensuing may carry ray of sun, or smell of grass or corn, or call of bird, or gleam of stars by night, or snowflakes falling fresh and mystic, to denizen of heated city house, or tired workman or workwoman?—or maybe in sickroom or prison—to serve as cooling breeze, or Nature's aroma, to some fevered mouth or latent pulse.

[61]

long. Away, from curtain, carpet, sofa, book—from "society"—from city house, street, and modern improvements and luxuries—away to the primitive winding, aforementioned wooded creek, with its untrimmed bushes and turfy banks—away from ligatures, tight boots, buttons, and the whole cast-iron civilized life—from entourage of artificial store, machine, studio, office, parlor—from tailordom and fashion's clothes—from any clothes, perhaps, for the nonce, the summer heats advancing, there in those watery, shaded solitudes. Away, thou soul (let me pick thee out singly, reader dear, and talk in perfect freedom, negligently, confidentially) for one day and night at least, returning to the naked source-life of us all—to the breast of the great silent savage all-acceptive Mother. Alas! How many of us are so sodden—how many have wandered so far away, that return is almost impossible. ᴏᴇ But to my jottings, taking them as they come, from the heap, without particular selection. There is little consecutiveness in dates. They run any time within nearly five or six years. Each was carelessly penciled in the open air, at the time and place. The printers will learn this to some vexation perhaps, as much of their copy is from those hastily written first notes.

BIRDS MIGRATING AT MIDNIGHT ᴏᴇ Did you ever chance to hear the midnight flight of birds passing through the air and darkness overhead, in countless armies, changing their early or late summer habitat? It is something not to be forgotten. A friend called me up just after 12 last night to mark the peculiar noise of unusually immense flocks migrating north (rather late this year). In the silence, shadow, and delicious odor of the hour (the natural perfume belonging to the night alone), I thought it rare music. You could *hear* the characteristic motion—once or twice "the rush of mighty wings," but oftener a velvety rustle, long drawn out—sometimes quite near—with continual calls and chirps, and some song notes. It all lasted from 12 till after 3. Once in a while the species was plainly distinguishable; I could make out the bobolink, tanager, Wilson's thrush, white-crowned sparrow, and occasionally from high in the air came the notes of the plover.

BUMBLEBEES ᴏᴇ May-month—month of swarming, singing, mating birds—the bumblebee month—month of the flowering lilac (and then my own birth month). As I jot this paragraph, I am out just after sunrise, and down toward the creek. The lights, perfumes, melodies—the bluebirds, grassbirds, and robins, in every direction—the noisy, vocal, natural concert. For undertones, a neighboring woodpecker tapping his tree, and the distant clarion of chanticleer. Then the fresh earth smells—the colors, the delicate drabs and thin blues of the perspective. The bright green of the grass has received an added tinge from the last two days' mildness and moisture. How the sun silently mounts in the broad clear sky, on his day's journey! How the warm beams bathe all, and come streaming kissingly and almost hot on my face. ᴏᴇ A while since the croaking of the pond frogs and the first white of the dogwood blossoms. Now the golden dandelions in endless profusion, spotting the ground everywhere. The white cherry and pear blows—the wild violets, with their blue eyes looking up and saluting my feet, as I saunter the wood edge—the rosy blush of budding apple trees—the light-clear emerald hue of the wheatfields—the darker green of the rye—a warm elasticity pervading the air—the cedar bushes profusely decked with their little brown apples—the summer fully awakening—the convocation of black birds, garrulous flocks of them, gathering on some tree, and making the hour and place noisy as I sit near. ᴏᴇ LATER ᴏᴇ Nature marches in procession, in sections, like the corps of an army. All have done much for me, and still do. But for the last two days it has been the great wild bee, the humblebee, or "bumble," as the children call him. As I walk, or hobble, from the farmhouse down to the creek, I traverse the before-mentioned lane, fenced by old rails, with many splits, splinters, breaks, holes, etc., the choice habitat of those crooning, hairy insects. Up and down and by and between these rails, they swarm and dart and fly in countless myriads. As I wend slowly along, I am often accompanied with a moving cloud of them. They play a leading part in my morning, mid-day, or sunset rambles, and often dominate the landscape in a way I never before thought of—fill the long lane, not by scores or hundreds only, but by thousands. Large and vivacious and swift, with wonderful momentum and a loud swelling perpetual hum, varied now and then by something almost like a shriek, they dart to and fro, in rapid flashes, chasing each other, and (little things as they are) conveying to me a new and pronounced sense of strength, beauty, vitality, and movement. Are they in their mating season? Or what is the meaning of this plentitude, swiftness, eagerness, display? As I walked, I thought I was followed by a particular swarm, but upon observation I saw that it was a rapid succession of changing swarms, one after another. ᴏᴇ As I write, I am seated under a big wild cherry tree—the warm day tempered by partial clouds and a fresh breeze, neither too heavy nor light—and here I sit long and long, enveloped in the deep musical drone of these bees, flitting, balancing, darting to and fro about me by hundreds—big fellows with light yellow jackets, great glistening swelling bodies, stumpy heads and gauzy wings—humming their perpetual rich mellow boom. (Is there not a hint in it for a musical composition, of which it should be the background? some bumblebee symphony?) How it all nourishes, lulls me, in the way most needed; the open air, the rye fields, the apple orchards. The last two days have been faultless in sun, breeze, temperature, and everything; never two more perfect days, and I have enjoyed them wonderfully. My health is somewhat better, and my spirit at peace. (Yet the anniversary of the saddest loss and sorrow of my life is close at hand.) ᵒᵛ Another jotting, another perfect day: forenoon, from 7 to 9, two hours enveloped in sound of bumblebees and bird music. Down in the apple trees and in a neighboring cedar were three or four russet-backed thrushes, each singing his best, and roulading in ways I never heard surpassed. Two hours I abandon myself to hearing them, and indolently absorbing the scene. Almost every bird I notice has a special time in the year— sometimes limited to a few days—when it sings its best; and now is the period of these russet-backs. Meanwhile, up and down the lane, the darting, droning, musical bumblebees. A great swarm again for my entourage as I return home, moving along with me as before. ᵒᵛ As I write this, two or three weeks later, I am sitting near the brook under a tulip tree, 70 feet high, thick with the fresh verdure of its young maturity—a beautiful object —every branch, every leaf perfect. From top to bottom, seeking the sweet juice in the blossoms, it swarms with myriads of these wild bees, whose loud and steady humming makes an undertone to the whole, and to my mood and the hour. All of which I will bring to a close by extracting the following verses from Henry A. Beers's little volume: *As I lay yonder in tall grass*

A drunken bumblebee went past
Delirious with honey toddy.
The golden sash about his body
Scarce kept it in his swollen belly
Distent with honeysuckle jelly.
Rose liquor and the sweetpea wine
Had filled his soul with song divine;
Deep had he drunk the warm night through,
His hairy thighs were wet with dew.
Full many an antic he had played
While the world went round through sleep and shade.
Oft had he lit with thirsty lip
Some flower cup's nectared sweets to sip,
When on smooth petals he would slip,
Or over tangled stamens trip,
And headlong in the pollen rolled,
Crawl out quite dusted o'er with gold;
Or else his heavy feet would stumble
Against some bud, and down he'd tumble
Amongst the grass; there lie and grumble
In low, soft bass—poor maudlin bumble!

CEDAR APPLES ᵒᵛ As I journeyed today in a light wagon ten or twelve miles through the country, nothing pleased me more, in their homely beauty and novelty (I had either never seen the little things to such advantage, or had never noticed them before) than that peculiar fruit, with its profuse clear-yellow dangles of inch-long silk or yarn, in boundless profusion spotting the dark-green cedar bushes—contrasting well with their bronze tufts—the flossy shreds covering the knobs all over, like a shock of wild hair on elfin pates. On my ramble afterward down by the creek I plucked one from its bush, and shall keep it. These cedar apples last only a little while, however, and soon crumble and fade.

SUMMER SIGHTS AND INDOLENCES ᵒᵛ JUNE 10TH ᵒᵛ As I write, 5:30 P.M., here by the creek, nothing can exceed the quiet splendor and freshness around me. We had a heavy shower, with brief thunder and lightning, in the middle of the day; and since, overhead, one of those not uncommon yet indescribable skies (in quality, not details or forms) of limpid blue, with rolling silver-fringed clouds, and a pure dazzling sun. For underlay, trees in fullness of tender foliage—liquid, reedy, long-drawn notes of birds—based by the fretful mewing of a querulous catbird, and the pleasant chippering shriek of two kingfishers. I have been watching the latter the last half-hour, on their regular evening frolic over and in the stream; evidently a spree of the liveliest kind. They pursue each other, whirling and wheeling around, with many a jocund downward dip, splashing the spray in jets of diamonds—and then off they swoop, with slanting wings and graceful flight, sometimes so near me I can plainly see their dark gray feather-bodies and milk-white necks.

SUNDOWN PERFUME—QUAIL NOTES —THE HERMIT THRUSH ᵒᵛ JUNE 19TH, 4 TO 6:30 P.M. ᵒᵛ Sitting alone by the creek—solitude here, but the scene bright and vivid enough—the sun shining, and quite a fresh wind blowing (some heavy showers last night), the grass and trees looking their best—the clair-obscure of different greens, shadows, half-shadows, and the dappling glimpses of the water, through recesses—the wild flageolet note of a quail near by—the just-heard fretting of some hylas down there in the pond —crows cawing in the distance—a drove of young hogs rooting in soft ground near the oak under which I sit— some come sniffing near me, and then scamper away, with grunts. And still the clear notes of the quail—the quiver of leaf shadows over the paper as I write—the sky aloft, with white clouds, and the sun well declining to the west—the swift darting of many sand swallows coming and going, their holes in a neighboring marlbank—the odor of the cedar and oak, so palpable, as evening approaches—perfume, color, the bronze-and-gold of nearly ripened wheat—clover fields, with honey scent—the well-up maize, with long and rustling leaves —the great patches of thriving potatoes, dusky green, flecked all over with white blossoms—the old, warty, venerable oak above me—and ever, mixed with the dual notes of the quail, the soughing of the wind through some near-by pines. ৶ As I rise for return, I linger long to a delicious song epilogue (is it the hermit thrush?) from some bushy recess off there in the swamp, repeated leisurely and pensively over and over again. This, to the circle-gambols of the swallows flying by dozens in concentric rings in the last rays of sunset, like flashes of some airy wheel.

A JULY AFTERNOON BY THE POND ৶
The fervent heat, but so much more endurable in this pure air—the white and pink pond-blossoms, with great heart-shaped leaves; the glassy waters of the creek, the banks, with dense bushery, and the picturesque beeches and shade and turf; the tremulous, reedy call of some bird from recesses, breaking the warm, indolent, half-voluptuous silence; an occasional wasp, hornet, honey-bee or bumble (they hover near my hands or face, yet annoy me not, nor I them, as they appear to examine, find nothing, and away they go)—the vast space of the sky overhead so clear, and the buzzard up there sailing his slow whirl in majestic spirals and discs; just over the surface of the pond, two large slate-colored dragonflies, with wings of lace, circling and darting and occasionally balancing themselves quite still, their wings quivering all the time (are they not showing off for my amusement?)—the pond itself, with the sword-shaped calamus; the water snakes—occasionally a flitting black-bird, with red dabs on his shoulders, as he darts slantingly by—the sounds that bring out the solitude, warmth, light, and shade—the quawk of some pond duck (the crickets and grasshoppers are mute in the noon heat, but I hear the song of the first cicadas)—then at some distance the rattle and whir of a reaping machine as the horses draw it on a rapid walk through a rye field on the opposite side of the creek (what was the yellow or light-brown bird, large as a young hen, with short neck and long-stretched legs I just saw, in flapping and awkward flight over there through the trees?)—the prevailing delicate, yet palpable, spicy, grassy, clovery perfume to my nostrils; and over all, encircling all, to my sight and soul, the free space of the sky, transparent and blue—and hovering there in the west, a mass of white-gray fleecy clouds the sailors call "shoals of mackerel"—the sky, with silver swirls like locks of tossed hair, spreading, expanding—a vast voiceless, formless simulacrum—yet

maybe the most real reality and formulator of every-thing—who knows?

LOCUSTS AND KATYDIDS ৶ AUG. 22 ৶
Reedy monotones of locust, or sounds of katydid—I hear the latter at night, and the other both day and night, I thought the morning and evening warble of birds de-lightful, but I find I can listen to these strange insects with just as much pleasure. A single locust is now heard near noon from a tree two hundred feet off, as I write—a long whirring, continued, quite loud noise graded in distinct whirls, or swinging circles, increasing in strength and rapidity up to a certain point, and then a fluttering, quietly tapering fall. Each strain is continued from one to two minutes. The locust song is very appropriate to the scene—gushes, has meaning, is masculine, is like some fine old wine, not sweet, but far better than sweet. ৶ But the katydid—how shall I describe its piquant utterances? One sings from a willow tree just outside my open bedroom window, twenty yards distant; every clear night for a fortnight past has soothed me to sleep. I rode through a piece of woods for a hundred rods the other evening, and heard the katydids by myriads— very curious for once; but I like better my single neigh-bor on the tree. ৶ Let me say more about the song of the locust, even to repetition: a long, chromatic, tremu-lous crescendo, like a brass disk whirling round and round, emitting wave after wave of notes, beginning with a certain moderate beat or measure, rapidly in-creasing in speed and emphasis, reaching a point of great energy and significance, and then quickly and gracefully dropping down and out. Not the melody of the singing bird—far from it; the common musician might think without melody, but surely having to the finer ear a harmony of its own; monotonous—but what a swing there is in that brassy drone, round and round, cymbaline —or like the whirling of brass quoits.

THE LESSON OF A TREE ৶ SEPT. 1 ৶ I should not take either the biggest or the most picturesque tree to illustrate it. Here is one of my favorites now before me, a fine yellow poplar, quite straight, perhaps 90 feet high, and four thick at the butt. How strong, vital, en-during! How dumbly eloquent! What suggestions of imperturbability and *being*, as against the human trait of mere *seeming*. Then the qualities, almost emotional, pal-pably artistic, heroic, of a tree; so innocent and harmless, yet so savage. It *is*, yet says nothing. How it rebukes by its tough and equable serenity all weathers, this gusty-tempered little whiffet, man, that runs indoors at a mite of rain or snow. Science (or rather halfway science) scoffs at reminiscence of dryad and hamadryad, and of trees speaking. But, if they don't, they do as well as most speaking, writing, poetry, sermons—or rather they do a great deal better. I should say indeed that those old dryad reminiscences are quite as true as any, and profounder than most reminiscences we get. ("Cut this out," as the quack mediciners say, and keep by you.) Go and sit in a grove or woods, with one or more of those voiceless companions, and read the foregoing, and think. ⁊ One lesson from affiliating a tree—perhaps the greatest moral lesson anyhow from earth, rocks, animals—is that same lesson of inherency, of *what is*, without the least regard to what the looker-on (the critic) supposes or says, or whether he likes or dislikes. What worse—what more general malady pervades each and all of us, our literature, education, attitude toward each other (even toward ourselves) than a morbid trouble about *seems* (generally temporarily seems too), and no trouble at all, or hardly any, about the sane, slow-growing, perennial, real parts of character, books, friendship, marriage—humanity's invisible foundations and hold-together? (As the all-basis, the nerve, the great-sympathetic, the plenum within humanity, giving stamp to everything, is necessarily invisible.) ⁊ AUG. 4, 6 P.M. ⁊ Lights and shades and rare effects on tree foliage and grass—transparent greens, grays, etc. all in sunset pomp and dazzle. The clear beams are now thrown in many new places, on the quilted, seamed, bronze-drab, lower tree trunks, shadowed except at this hour—now flooding their young and old columnar ruggedness with strong light, unfolding to my sense new amazing features of silent, shaggy charm, the solid bark, the expression of harmless impassiveness, with many a bulge and gnarl unrecked before. In the revealings of such light, such exceptional hour, such mood, one does not wonder at the old story fables (indeed, why fables?) of people falling into lovesickness with trees, seized ecstatic with the mystic realism of the resistless silent strength in them—*strength*, which after all is perhaps the last, completest, highest beauty.

TREES I AM FAMILIAR WITH HERE
Oaks (many kinds—one sturdy old
    fellow, vital, green, bushy, five
    feet thick at the butt, I sit under
    every day)
Cedars, plenty
Tulip trees (*Liriodendron*, is of the
    magnolia family—I have seen it
    in Michigan and southern Illinois,
    140 feet high and 8 feet thick at the
    butt*; does not transplant well;
    best raised from seeds—the lumbermen call it yellow poplar)
Sycamores
Gum trees, both sweet and sour

Beeches
Black walnuts
Sassafras
Willows
Catalpas
Persimmons
Mountain ash
Hickories
Maples, many kinds
Locusts
Birches
Dogwood
Pine
The Elm
Chestnut
Linden
Aspen
Spruce
Hornbeam
Laurel
Holly

AUTUMN SIDE-BITS ⁊ SEPT. 20 ⁊ Under an old black oak, glossy and green, exhaling aroma—amid a grove the Albic druids might have chosen—enveloped in the warmth and light of the noonday sun, and swarms of flitting insects—with the harsh cawing of many crows a hundred rods away—here I sit in solitude, absorbing, enjoying all. The corn, stacked in its cone-shaped stacks, russet-colored and sere—a large field spotted thick with scarlet-gold pumpkins—an adjoining one of cabbages, showing well in their green and pearl, mottled by much light and shade—melon patches, with their bulging ovals, and great silver-streaked, ruffled, broad-edged leaves—and many an autumn sight and sound beside—the distant scream of a flock of guinea hens—and poured over all the September breeze, with pensive cadence through the treetops. ⁊ ANOTHER DAY ⁊ The ground in all directions strewed with debris from a storm. Timber Creek, as I slowly pace its banks, has ebbed low, and

* There is a tulip poplar within sight of Woodstown, which is twenty feet around, three feet from the ground, four feet across about eighteen feet up the trunk, which is broken off about three or four feet higher up. On the south side an arm has shot out from which rise two stems, each to about ninety-one or ninety-two feet from the ground. Twenty-five (or more) years since, the cavity in the butt was large enough for, and nine men at one time, ate dinner therein. It is supposed twelve to fifteen men could now, at one time, stand within its trunk. The severe winds of 1877 and 1878 did not seem to damage it, and the two stems send out yearly many blossoms, scenting the air immediately about it with their sweet perfume. It is entirely unprotected by other trees, on a hill. —*Woodstown, N.J., Register, April 15, '79.*

[65]

shows reaction from the turbulent swell of the late equinoctial. As I look around, I take account of stock—weeds and shrubs, knolls, paths, occasional stumps, some with smoothed tops (several I use as seats of rest, from place to place, and from one I am now jotting these lines)—frequent wild flowers, little white, star-shaped things, or the cardinal red of the lobelia, or the cherry-ball seeds of the perennial rose, or the many-threaded vines winding up and around trunks of trees. ❧ OCT. 1, 2, AND 3 ❧ Down every day in the solitude of the creek. A serene autumn sun and westerly breeze today (3d) as I sit here, the water surface prettily moving in wind ripples before me. On a stout old beech at the edge, decayed and slanting, almost fallen to the stream, yet with life and leaves in its mossy limbs, a gray squirrel, exploring, runs up and down, flirts his tail, leaps to the ground, sits on his haunches upright as he sees me (a Darwinian hint?), and then races up the tree again. ❧ OCT. 4 ❧ Cloudy and coolish; signs of incipient winter. Yet pleasant here, the leaves thick-falling, the ground brown with them already; rich coloring, yellows of all hues, pale and dark green, shades from lightest to richest red—all set in and toned down by the prevailing brown of the earth and gray of the sky. So, winter is coming, and I yet in my sickness. I sit here amid all these fair sights and vital influences, and abandon myself to that thought, with its wandering trains of speculation.

THE SKY—DAYS AND NIGHTS—HAPPINESS ❧ OCT. 20 ❧ A clear, crispy day—dry and breezy air, full of oxygen. Out of the sane, silent, beauteous miracles that envelop and fuse me—trees, water, grass, sunlight, and early frost—the one I am looking at most today is the sky. It has that delicate, transparent blue, peculiar to autumn, and the only clouds are little or larger white ones, giving their still and spiritual motion to the great concave. All through the earlier day (say from 7 to 11) it keeps a pure, yet vivid blue. But as noon approaches the color gets lighter, quite gray for two or three hours—then still paler for a spell, till sundown—which last I watch dazzling through the interstices of a knoll of big trees—darts of fire and a gorgeous show of light yellow, liver color, and red, with a vast silver glaze askant on the water—the transparent shadows, shafts, sparkle, and vivid colors beyond all the paintings ever made. ❧ I don't know what or how, but it seems to me mostly owing to these skies (every now and then I think, while I have of course seen them every day of my life, I never really saw the skies before), I have had this autumn some wondrously contented hours—may I not say perfectly happy ones? As I've read, Byron just before his death told a friend that he had known but three happy hours during his whole existence. Then there is the old

German legend of the king's bell, to the same point. While I was out there by the wood, that beautiful sunset through the trees, I thought of Byron's and the bell story, and the notion started in me that I was having a happy hour. (Though perhaps my best moments I never jot down; when they come I cannot afford to break the charm by inditing memoranda. I just abandon myself to the mood, and let it float on, carrying me in its placid ecstasy.) ❧ What is happiness, anyhow? Is this one of its hours, or the like of it?—so impalpable—a mere breath, an evanescent tinge? I am not sure—so let me give myself the benefit of the doubt. Hast Thou, pellucid, in Thy azure depths, medicine for case like mine? (Ah, the physical shatter and troubled spirit of me the last three years.) And dost Thou subtly, mystically now drip it through the air invisibly upon me? ❧ NIGHT OF OCT. 28 ❧ The heavens unusually transparent—the stars out by myriads—the great path of the Milky Way, with its branch, only seen of very clear nights—Jupiter, setting in the west, looks like a huge haphazard splash, and has a little star for companion.

Clothed in his white garments,
Into the round and clear arena slowly entered the Brahmin,
Holding a little child by the hand,
Like the moon with the planet Jupiter in a cloudless night-sky
—Old Hindu Poem

❧ EARLY IN NOVEMBER ❧ At its farther end the lane already described opens into a broad grassy upland field of over twenty acres, slightly sloping to the south. Here I am accustomed to walk for sky views and effects, either morning or sundown. Today from this field my soul is calmed and expanded beyond description, the whole forenoon by the clear blue arching over all, cloudless, nothing particular, only sky and daylight. Their soothing accompaniments, autumn leaves, the cool dry air, the faint aroma—crows cawing in the distance—two great buzzards wheeling gracefully and slowly far up there—the occasional murmur of the wind, sometimes quite gently, then threatening through the trees—a gang of farm laborers loading cornstalks in a field in sight, and the patient horses waiting.

COLORS—A CONTRAST ❧ Such a play of colors and lights, different seasons, different hours of the day—the lines of the far horizon where the faint-tinged edge of the landscape loses itself in the sky. As I slowly hobble up the lane toward day-close, an incomparable sunset shooting in molten sapphire and gold, shaft after shaft, through the ranks of the long-leaved corn, between me and the west. ❧ ANOTHER DAY ❧ The rich dark green of the tulip trees and the oaks, the gray of the swamp willows, the dull hues of the sycamores and black walnuts, the emerald of the cedars (after rain), and the light yellow of the beeches.

NOVEMBER 8, '76 ᐤ The forenoon leaden and cloudy, not cold or wet, but indicating both. As I hobble down here and sit by the silent pond, how different from the excitement amid which, in the cities, millions of people are now waiting news of yesterday's Presidential election, or receiving and discussing the result—in this secluded place uncared-for, unknown.

CROWS AND CROWS ᐤ NOV. 14 ᐤ As I sit here by the creek, resting after my walk, a warm languor bathes me from the sun. No sound but a cawing of crows, and no motion but their black flying figures from overhead, reflected in the mirror of the pond below. Indeed a principal feature of the scene today is these crows, their incessant cawing, far or near, and their countless flocks and processions moving from place to place, and at times almost darkening the air with their myriads. As I sit a moment writing this by the bank, I see the black, clear-cut reflection of them far below, flying through the watery looking glass, by ones, twos, or long strings. All last night I heard the noises from their great roost in a neighboring wood.

A WINTER DAY ON THE SEABEACH ᐤ One bright December midday lately I spent down on the New Jersey seashore, reaching it by a little more than an hour's railroad trip over the old Camden and Atlantic. I had started betimes, fortified by nice strong coffee and a good breakfast (cooked by the hands I love, my dear sister Lou's—how much better it makes the victuals taste, and then assimilate, strengthen you, perhaps make the whole day comfortable afterward). Five or six miles at the last, our track entered a broad region of salt grass meadows, intersected by lagoons, and cut up everywhere by watery runs. The sedgy perfume, delightful to my nostrils, reminded me of "the mash" and South Bay of my native island. I could have journeyed contentedly till night through these flat and odorous sea prairies. From half-past 11 till 2 I was nearly all the time along the beach, or in sight of the ocean, listening to its hoarse murmur and inhaling the bracing and welcome breezes. First, a rapid five-mile drive over the hard sand—our carriage wheels hardly made dents in it. Then after dinner (as there was nearly two hours to spare) I walked off in another direction (hardly met or saw a person) and, taking possession of what appeared to have been the reception room of an old bathhouse range, had a broad expanse of view all to myself—quaint, refreshing, unimpeded—a dry area of sedge and Indian grass immediately

before and around me—space, simple, unornamented space. Distant vessels, and the far-off, just visible trailing smoke of an inward-bound steamer; more plainly, ships, brigs, schooners, in sight, most of them with every sail set to the firm and steady wind. ᐤ The attractions, fascinations there are in sea and shore! How one dwells on their simplicity, even vacuity! What is it in us, aroused by those indirections and directions? That spread of waves and gray-white beach, salt, monotonous, senseless—such an entire absence of art, books, talk, elegance —so indescribably comforting, even this winter day— grim, yet so delicate-looking, so spiritual—striking emotional, impalpable depths, subtler than all the poems, paintings, music I have ever read, seen, heard. (Yet let me be fair, perhaps it is because I have read those poems and heard that music.)

SEASHORE FANCIES ᐤ Even as a boy, I had the fancy, the wish, to write a piece, perhaps a poem, about the seashore—that suggesting, dividing line, contact, junction, the solid marrying the liquid—that curious, lurking something (as doubtless every objective form finally becomes to the subjective spirit) which means far more than its mere first sight, grand as that is—blending the real and ideal, and each made portion of the other. Hours, days, in my Long Island youth and early manhood, I haunted the shores of Rockaway or Coney Island, or away east to the Hamptons or Montauk. Once, at the latter place (by the old lighthouse, nothing but sea-tossings in sight in every direction as far as the eye could reach), I remember well, I felt that I must one day write a book expressing this liquid, mystic theme. Afterward, I recollect, how it came to me that instead of any special lyrical or epical or literary attempt, the seashore should be an invisible *influence*, a pervading gauge and tally for me, in my composition. (Let me give a hint here to young writers. I am not sure but I have unwittingly followed out the same rule with other powers besides sea and shores—avoiding them, in the way of any dead set at poetizing them, as too big for formal handling—quite satisfied if I could indirectly show that we have met and fused, even if only once, but enough— that we have really absorbed each other and understand each other.) ᐤ There is a dream, a picture, that for years at intervals (sometimes quite long ones, but surely again, in time) has come noiselessly up before me, and I really believe, fiction as it is, has entered largely into my practical life—certainly into my writings, and shaped and colored them. It is nothing more or less than a stretch of interminable white-brown sand, hard and smooth and broad, with the ocean perpetually, grandly, rolling in upon it, with slow-measured sweep, with rustle and hiss and foam, and many a thump as of low bass drums. This scene, this picture, I say, has risen before me at times for years. Sometimes I wake at night and can hear and see it plainly.

IN MEMORY OF THOMAS PAINE ֎ SPO-KEN AT LINCOLN HALL, PHILADELPHIA, SUNDAY, JAN. 28, '77, FOR 140TH ANNIVERSARY OF T. P.'S BIRTHDAY ֎ Some thirty-five years ago, in New York City, at Tammany Hall, of which place I was then a frequenter, I happened to become quite well acquainted with Thomas Paine's perhaps most intimate chum, and certainly his later years' very frequent companion, a remarkably fine old man, Col. Fellows, who may yet be remembered by some stray relics of that period and spot. If you will allow me, I will first give a description of the Colonel himself. He was tall, of military bearing, aged about 78 I should think, hair white as snow, clean-shaved on the face, dressed very neatly, a tailcoat of blue cloth with metal buttons, buff vest, pantaloons of drab color, and his neck, breast, and wrists showing the whitest of linen. Under all circumstances, fine manners; a good but not profuse talker, his wits still fully about him, balanced and live and undimmed as ever. He kept pretty fair health, though so old. For employment—for he was poor—he had a post as constable of some of the upper courts. I used to think him very picturesque on the fringe of a crowd holding a tall staff, with his erect form, and his superb, bare, thick-haired, closely cropped white head. The judges and young lawyers, with whom he was ever a favorite, and the subject of respect, used to call him Aristides. It was the general opinion among them that if manly rectitude and the instincts of absolute justice remained vital anywhere about New York City Hall, or Tammany, they were to be found in Col. Fellows. He liked young men, and enjoyed to leisurely talk with them over a social glass of toddy, after his day's work (he on these occasions never drank but one glass); and it was at reiterated meetings of this kind in old Tammany's back parlor of those days that he told me much about Thomas Paine. At one of our interviews he gave me a minute account of Paine's sickness and death. In short, from those talks, I was and am satisfied that my old friend, with his marked advantages, had mentally, morally, and emotionally gauged the author of *Common Sense*, and besides giving me a good portrait of his appearance and manners, had taken the true measure of his interior character. ֎ Paine's practical demeanor, and much of his theoretical belief, was a mixture of the French and English schools of a century ago, and the best of both. Like most old-fashioned people, he drank a glass or two every day, but was no tippler, nor intemperate, let alone being a drunkard. He lived simply and economically, but quite well—was always cheery and

courteous, perhaps occasionally a little blunt, having very positive opinions upon politics, religion, and so forth. That he labored well and wisely for the states in the trying period of their parturition, and in the seeds of their character, there seems to me no question. I dare not say how much of what our Union is owning and enjoying today—its independence—its ardent belief in, and substantial practice of, radical human rights—and the severance of its government from all ecclesiastical and superstitious dominion—I dare not say how much of all this is owing to Thomas Paine, but I am inclined to think a good portion of it decidedly is. ֎ But I was not going either into an analysis or eulogium of the man. I wanted to carry you back a generation or two, and give you by indirection a moment's glance—and also to ventilate a very earnest and I believe authentic opinion, nay conviction, of that time, the fruit of the interviews I have mentioned, and of questioning and cross-questioning, clenched by my best information since, that Thomas Paine had a noble personality, as exhibited in presence, face, voice, dress, manner, and what may be called his atmosphere and magnetism, especially the later years of his life. I am sure of it. Of the foul and foolish fictions yet told about the circumstances of his decease, the absolute fact is that as he lived a good life, after its kind, he died calmly and philosophically, as became him. He served the embryo Union with most precious service—a service that every man, woman and child in our thirty-eight states is to some extent receiving the benefit of today—and I for one here cheerfully, reverently throw my pebble on the cairn of his memory. As we all know, the season demands—or rather, will it ever be out of season? —that America learn to better dwell on her choicest possession, the legacy of her good and faithful men—that she well preserve their fame, if unquestioned—or, if need be, that she fail not to dissipate what clouds have intruded on that fame, and burnish it newer, truer, and brighter, continually.

A TWO-HOURS' ICE-SAIL ֎ FEB. 3, '77 ֎ From 4 to 6 P.M. crossing the Delaware (back again at my Camden home), unable to make our landing, through the ice; our boat stanch and strong and skillfully piloted, but old and sulky, and poorly minding her helm. (*Power*, so important in poetry and war, is also first point of all in a winter steamboat, with long stretches of ice packs to tackle.) For over two hours we bumped and beat about, the invisible ebb, sluggish but irresistible, often carrying us long distances against our will. In the first tinge of dusk, as I looked around, I thought there could not be presented a more chilling, arctic, grim-extended, depressing scene. Everything was yet plainly visible; for miles north and south, ice, ice, ice, mostly broken, but some big cakes, and no clear water in sight. The shores, piers, surfaces, roofs, shipping, mantled with snow. A faint winter vapor hung a fitting accompaniment around and over the endless whitish spread, and gave it just a tinge of steel and brown. ༀ FEB. 6 ༀ As I cross home in the 6 P.M. boat again, the transparent shadows are filled everywhere with leisurely falling, slightly slanting, curiously sparse, but very large flakes of snow. On the shores, near and far, the glow of just-lit gas clusters at intervals. The ice, sometimes in hummocks, sometimes floating fields, through which our boat goes crunching. The light permeated by that peculiar evening haze, right after sunset, which sometimes renders quite distant objects so distinctly.

SPRING OVERTURES—RECREATIONS ༀ FEB. 10 ༀ The first chirping, almost singing, of a bird today. Then I noticed a couple of honeybees spirting and humming about the open window in the sun. ༀ FEB. 11 ༀ In the soft rose and pale gold of the declining light, this beautiful evening, I heard the first hum and preparation of awakening spring—very faint—whether in the earth or roots, or starting of insects, I know not—but it was audible, as I leaned on a rail (I am down in my country quarters awhile) and looked long at the western horizon. Turning to the east, Sirius, as the shadows deepened, came forth in dazzling splendor. And great Orion; and a little to the northeast the Big Dipper, standing on end. ༀ FEB. 20 ༀ A solitary and pleasant sundown hour at the pond, exercising arms, chest, my whole body, by a tough oak sapling thick as my wrist, twelve feet high—pulling and pushing, inspiring the good air. After I wrestle with the tree awhile, I can feel its young sap and virtue welling up out of the ground and tingling through me from crown to toe, like health's wine. Then for addition and variety I launch forth in my vocalism; shout declamatory pieces, sentiments, sorrow, anger, etc., from the stock poets or plays —or inflate my lungs and sing the wild tunes and refrains I heard of the blacks down south, or patriotic songs I learned in the army. I make the echoes ring, I tell you! As the twilight fell, in a pause of these ebullitions, an owl somewhere the other side of the creek sounded *too-oo-oo-oo-oo*, soft and pensive (and I fancied a little sarcastic) repeated four or five times. Either to applaud the Negro songs—or perhaps an ironical comment on the sorrow, anger, or style of the stock poets.

ONE OF THE HUMAN KINKS ༀ How is it that in all the serenity and lonesomeness of solitude, away off here amid the hush of the forest, alone, or as I have found in prairie wilds, or mountain stillness, one is never entirely without the instinct of looking around (I

never am, and others tell me the same of themselves, confidentially) for somebody to appear, or start up out of the earth, or from behind some tree or rock? Is it a lingering, inherited remains of man's primitive wariness, from the wild animals or from his savage ancestry far back? It is not at all nervousness or fear. Seems as if something unknown were possibly lurking in those bushes, or solitary places. Nay, it is quite certain there is —some vital unseen presence.

AN AFTERNOON SCENE ༀ FEB. 22 ༀ Last night and today rainy and thick, till midafternoon, when the wind chopped round, the clouds swiftly drew off like curtains, the clear appeared, and with it the fairest, grandest, most wondrous rainbow I ever saw, all complete, very vivid at its earth ends, spreading vast effusions of illuminated haze, violet, yellow, drab green, in all directions overhead, through which the sun beamed—an indescribable utterance of color and light, so gorgeous yet so soft, such as I had never witnessed before. Then its continuance: a full hour passed before the last of those earth ends disappeared. The sky behind was all spread in translucent blue, with many little white clouds and edges. To these a sunset, filling, dominating the esthetic and soul senses, sumptuously, tenderly, full. I end this note by the pond, just light enough to see, through the evening shadows, the western reflections in its water-mirror surface, with inverted figures of trees. I hear now and then the *flup* of a pike leaping out and rippling the water.

THE GATES OPENING ༀ APRIL 6 ༀ Palpable spring indeed, or the indications of it. I am sitting in bright sunshine, at the edge of the creek, the surface just rippled by the wind. All is solitude, morning freshness, negligence. For companions my two kingfishers sailing, winding, darting, dipping, sometimes capriciously separate, then flying together. I hear their guttural twittering again and again; for awhile nothing but that peculiar sound. As noon approaches other birds warm up. The reedy notes of the robin, and a musical passage of two parts, one a clear delicious gurgle, with several other birds I cannot place. To which is joined (yes, I just hear it) one low purr at intervals from some impatient hylas at the pond edge. The sibilant murmur of a pretty stiff breeze now and then through the trees. Then a poor little dead leaf, long frostbound, whirls from somewhere up aloft in one wild escaped freedom spree in space and sunlight, and then dashes down to the waters, which hold it closely and soon drown it out of sight. The bushes and trees are yet bare, but the beeches have their wrinkled yellow leaves of last season's foliage largely left, frequent cedars and pines yet green, and the grass not without proofs of coming fullness. And over all a wonderfully fine dome of clear blue, the play of light coming and going, and great fleeces of white clouds swimming so silently.

THE COMMON EARTH, THE SOIL &

The soil, too—let others pen-and-ink the sea, the air (as I sometimes try)—but now I feel to choose the common soil for theme—naught else. The brown soil here (just between winter-close and opening spring and vegetation)—the rain shower at night, and the fresh smell next morning—the red worms wriggling out of the ground—the dead leaves, the incipient grass, and the latent life underneath—the effort to start something—already in sheltered spots some little flowers—the distant emerald show of winter wheat and the rye fields—the yet naked trees, with clear interstices, giving prospects hidden in summer—the tough fallow and the plow team, and the stout boy whistling to his horses for encouragement—and there the dark fat earth in long slanting stripes upturned.

BIRDS AND BIRDS AND BIRDS & A LITTLE LATER—BRIGHT WEATHER &

An unusual melodiousness, these days (last of April and first of May) from the blackbirds; indeed all sorts of birds, darting, whistling, hopping, or perched on trees. Never before have I seen, heard, or been in the midst of, and got so flooded and saturated with them and their performances, as this current month. Such oceans, such successions of them. Let me make a list of those I find here:

Black birds (plenty)	Meadowlarks (plenty)
Ring Doves	Catbirds (plenty)
Owls	Cuckoos
Woodpeckers	Pond snipes (plenty)
Kingbirds	Cheewinks
Crows (plenty)	Quawks
Wrens	Ground robins
Kingfishers	Ravens
Quails	Gray snipes
Turkey buzzards	Eagles
Hen hawks	Highholes
Yellowbirds	Herons
Thrushes	Tits
Reedbirds	Wood pigeons

Early came the—

Bluebirds	Meadowlark
Killdeer	White-bellied swallow
Plover	Sandpiper
Robin	Wilson's thrush
Woodcock	Flicker

FULL-STARRED NIGHTS & MAY 21 &

Back in Camden. Again commencing one of those unusually transparent, full-starred, blue-black nights, as if to show that however lush and pompous the day may be, there is something left in the not-day that can outvie it. The rarest, finest sample of long-drawn-out clear-obscure, from sundown to 9 o'clock. I went down to the Delaware, and crossed and crossed. Venus like blazing silver well up in the west. The large, pale thin crescent of the new moon, half an hour high, sinking languidly under a bar-sinister of cloud, and then emerging. Arcturus right overhead. A faint fragrant sea odor wafted up from the south. The gloaming, the tempered coolness, with every feature of the scene, indescribably soothing and tonic—one of those hours that give hints to the soul, impossible to put in a statement. (Ah, where would be any food for spirituality without night and the stars?) The vacant spaciousness of the air, and the veiled blue of the heavens, seemed miracles enough. & As the night advanced it changed its spirit and garments to ampler stateliness. I was almost conscious of a definite presence, Nature silently near. The great constellation of the Water Serpent stretched its coils over more than half the heavens. The Swan with outspread wings was flying down the Milky Way. The northern Crown, the Eagle, Lyra, all up there in their places. From the whole dome shot down points of light, rapport with me, through the clear blue-black. All the usual sense of motion, all animal life, seemed discarded, seemed a fiction; a curious power, like the placid rest of Egyptian gods, took possession, none the less potent for being impalpable. Earlier I had seen many bats, balancing in the luminous twilight, darting their black forms hither and yon over the river; but now they altogether disappeared. The evening star and the moon had gone. Alertness and peace lay calmly couching together through the fluid universal shadows. & AUG. 26 & Bright has the day been, and my spirits an equal *forzando*. Then comes the night, different, inexpressibly pensive, with its own tender and tempered splendor. Venus lingers in the west with a voluptuous dazzle unshown hitherto this summer. Mars rises early, and the red sulky moon, two days past her full; Jupiter at night's meridian, and the long curling-slanted Scorpion stretching full view in the south, Antares-necked. Mars walks the heavens lord-paramount now; all through this month I go out after supper and watch for him; sometimes getting up at midnight to take another look at his unparalleled luster. (I see lately an astronomer has made out through the new Washington telescope that Mars has certainly one moon, perhaps two.) Pale and distant, but near in the heavens, Saturn precedes him.

MULLEINS AND MULLEINS ஃ Large, placid mulleins, as summer advances, velvety in texture, of a light greenish-drab color, growing everywhere in the fields—at first earth's big rosettes in their broad-leaved low cluster-plants, eight, ten, twenty leaves to a plant—plentiful on the fallow twenty-acre lot, at the end of the lane, and especially by the ridge sides of the fences—then close to the ground, but soon springing up—leaves as broad as my hand, and the lower ones twice as long—so fresh and dewy in the morning—stalks now four or five, even seven or eight feet high. The farmers, I find, think the mullein a mean unworthy weed, but I have grown to a fondness for it. Every object has its lesson, enclosing the suggestion of everything else—and lately I sometimes think all is concentrated for me in these hardy, yellow-flowered weeds. As I come down the lane early in the morning, I pause before their soft wool-like fleece and stem and broad leaves, glittering with countless diamonds. Annually for three summers now, they and I have silently returned together; at such long intervals I stand or sit among them, musing—and woven with the rest, of so many hours and moods of partial rehabilitation—of my sane or sick spirit, here as near at peace as it can be.

DISTANT SOUNDS ஃ The axe of the wood-cutter, the measured thud of a single threshing flail, the crowing of chanticleer in the barnyard (with invariable responses from other barnyards), and the lowing of cattle—but most of all, or far or near, the wind—through the high treetops, or through low bushes, laving one's face and hands so gently, this balmy-bright noon, the coolest for a long time (Sept. 2)—I will not call it *sighing*, for to me it is always a firm, sane, cheery expression, though a monotone, giving many varieties, or swift or slow, or dense or delicate. The wind in the patch of pine woods off there—how sibilant! Or at sea, I can imagine it this moment, tossing the waves, with spurts of foam flying far, and the free whistle, and the scent of the salt—and that vast paradox somehow with all its action and restlessness conveying a sense of eternal rest. ஃ OTHER ADJUNCTS ஃ But the sun and moon here and these times. As never more wonderful by day, the gorgeous orb imperial, so vast, so ardently, lovingly hot—so never a more glorious moon of nights, especially the last three or four. The great planets too—Mars never before so flaming bright, so flashing large, with slight yellow tinge (the astronomers say—is it true?—nearer to us than any time the past century)—and well up, Lord Jupiter (a little while since close by the moon)—and in the west, after the sun sinks, voluptuous Venus, now languid and shorn of her beams, as if from some divine excess.

A SUN-BATH—NAKEDNESS ஃ SUNDAY, AUG. 27 ஃ Another day quite free from marked prostration and pain. It seems indeed as if peace and nutriment from heaven subtly filter into me as I slowly hobble down these country lanes and across fields, in the good air—as I sit here in solitude with Nature—open, voiceless, mystic, far removed, yet palpable, eloquent Nature. I merge myself in the scene, in the perfect day. Hovering over the clear brook water, I am soothed by its soft gurgle in one place, and the hoarser murmurs of its three-foot fall in another. Come, ye disconsolate, in whom any latent eligibility is left—come get the sure virtues of creek shore, and wood and field. Two months (July and August, '77) have I absorbed them, and they begin to make a new man of me. Every day, seclusion—every day at least two or three hours of freedom, bathing, no talk, no bonds, no dress, no books, no *manners*. ஃ Shall I tell you, reader, to what I attribute my already much-restored health? That I have been almost two years, off and on, without drugs and medicines, and daily in the open air. Last summer I found a particularly secluded little dell off one side by my creek, originally a large dug-out marl pit, now abandoned, filled with bushes, trees, grass, a group of willows, a straggling bank, and a spring of delicious water running right through the middle of it, with two or three little cascades. Here I retreated every hot day, and follow it up this summer. Here I realize the meaning of that old fellow who said he was seldom less alone than when alone. Never before did I get so close to Nature; never before did she come so close to me. By old habit, I penciled down from time to time, almost automatically, moods, sights, hours, tints, and outlines, on the spot. Let me specially record the satisfaction of this current forenoon, so serene and primitive, so conventionally exceptional, natural. ஃ An hour or so after breakfast I wended my way down to the recesses of the aforesaid dell, which I and certain thrushes, catbirds, etc., had all to ourselves. A light southwest wind was blowing through the tree-tops. It was just the place and time for my Adamic air bath and flesh brushing from head to foot. So hanging clothes on a rail near by, keeping old broadbrim straw on head and easy shoes on feet, haven't I had a good time the last two hours! First with the stiff-elastic bristles rasping arms, breast, sides, till they turned scarlet—then partially bathing in the clear waters of the running brook—taking everything very leisurely, with many rests and pauses—stepping about barefooted every few minutes now and then in some neighboring black ooze, for unctuous mud bath to my feet—a brief second and third rinsing in the crystal running waters—rubbing with the fragrant towel—slow negligent promenades on the turf up and down in the sun, varied with occa-

[71]

sional rests, and further frictions of the bristle brush—sometimes carrying my portable chair with me from place to place, as my range is quite extensive here, nearly a hundred rods, feeling quite secure from intrusion (and that indeed I am not at all nervous about, if it accidentally happens). ⁊ As I walked slowly over the grass, the sun shone out enough to show the shadow moving with me. Somehow I seemed to get identity with each and every thing around me, in its condition. Nature was naked, and I was also. It was too lazy, soothing, and joyous-equable to speculate about. Yet I might have thought somehow in this vein: Perhaps the inner, never-lost rapport we hold with earth, light, air, trees, etc., is not to be realized through eyes and mind only, but through the whole corporeal body, which I will not have blinded or bandaged any more than the eyes. Sweet, sane, still nakedness in Nature!—ah, if poor, sick, prurient humanity in cities might really know you once more! Is not nakedness then indecent? No, not inherently. It is your thought, your sophistication, your fear, your respectability, that is indecent. There come moods when these clothes of ours are not only too irksome to wear, but are themselves indecent. Perhaps indeed he or she to whom the free exhilarating ecstasy of nakedness in Nature has never been eligible (and how many thousands there are!) has not really known what purity is—nor what faith or art or health really is. (Probably the whole curriculum of first-class philosophy, beauty, heroism, form, illustrated by the old Hellenic race—the highest height and deepest depth known to civilization in those departments—came from their natural and religious idea of Nakedness.) ⁊ Many such hours, from time to time, the last two summers—I attribute my partial rehabilitation largely to them. Some good people may think it a feeble or half-cracked way of spending one's time and thinking. Maybe it is.

THE OAKS AND I ⁊ SEPT. 5, '77 ⁊ I write this, 11 A.M., sheltered under a dense oak by the bank, where I have taken refuge from a sudden rain. I came down here (we had sulky drizzles all the morning, but an hour ago a lull) for the before-mentioned daily and simple exercise I am fond of—to pull on that young hickory sapling out there—to sway and yield to its tough-limber upright stem—haply to get into my old sinews some of its elastic fiber and clear sap. I stand on the turf and take these health pulls moderately and at intervals for nearly an hour, inhaling great draughts of fresh air. Wandering by the creek, I have three or four naturally favorable spots where I rest—besides a chair I lug with me and use for more deliberate occasions. At other spots convenient I have selected, besides the hickory just named, strong and limber boughs of beech or holly, in easy-reaching

distance, for my natural gymnasia, for arms, chest, trunk muscles. I can soon feel the sap and sinew rising through me, like mercury to heat. I hold on boughs or slender trees caressingly there in the sun and shade, wrestle with their innocent stalwartness—and *know* the virtue thereof passes from them into me. (Or maybe we interchange—maybe the trees are more aware of it all than I ever thought.) ⁊ But now pleasantly imprisoned here under the big oak—the rain dripping, and the sky covered with leaden clouds—nothing but the pond on one side, and the other a spread of grass, spotted with the milky blossoms of the wild carrot—the sound of an ax wielded at some distant woodpile—yet in this dull scene (as most folks would call it) why am I so (almost) happy here and alone? Why would any intrusion, even from people I like, spoil the charm? But am I alone? Doubtless there comes a time—perhaps it has come to me—when one feels through his whole being, and pronouncedly the emotional part, that identity between himself subjectively and Nature objectively which Schelling and Fichte are so fond of pressing. How it is I know not, but I often realize a presence here—in clear moods I am certain of it, and neither chemistry nor reasoning nor esthetics will give the least explanation. All the past two summers it has been strengthening and nourishing my sick body and soul, as never before. Thanks, invisible physician, for thy silent delicious medicine, thy day and night, thy waters and thy airs, the banks, the grass, the trees, and e'en the weeds!

A QUINTET ⁊ While I have been kept by the rain under the shelter of my great oak (perfectly dry and comfortable, to the rattle of the drops all around), I have penciled off the mood of the hour in a little quintet, which I will give you:

> At vacancy with Nature,
> Acceptive and at ease,
> Distilling the present hour,
> Whatever, wherever it is,
> And over the past, oblivion.

⁊ Can you get hold of it, reader dear? And how do you like it, anyhow?

THE FIRST FROST—MEMS. ⁊ Where I was stopping I saw the first palpable frost, on my sunrise walk, October 6; all over the yet-green spread a light blue-gray veil, giving a new show to the entire landscape. I had but little time to notice it, for the sun rose cloudless and mellow-warm, and as I returned along the lane it had turned to glittering patches of wet. As I walk I notice the bursting pods of wild cotton (Indian hemp they call it here), with flossy-silky contents and dark red-brown seeds—a startled rabbit—I pull a handful of the balsamic life everlasting and stuff it down in my trousers-pocket for scent.

THREE YOUNG MEN'S DEATHS ᴁ DECEMBER 20 ᴁ Somehow I got thinking today of young men's deaths—not at all sadly or sentimentally, but gravely, realistically, perhaps a little artistically. Let me give the following three cases from budgets of personal memoranda, which I have been turning over, alone in my room, and resuming and dwelling on, this rainy afternoon. Who is there to whom the theme does not come home? Then I don't know how it may be to others, but to me not only is there nothing gloomy or depressing in such cases—on the contrary, as reminiscences, I find them soothing, bracing, tonic. ᴁ ERASTUS HASKELL—(I just transcribe verbatim from a letter written by myself in one of the Army hospitals, 16 years ago, during the Secession War.) WASHINGTON, JULY 28, 1863 ᴁ Dear M.,—I am writing this in the hospital, sitting by the side of a soldier, I do not expect to last many hours. His fate has been a hard one—he seems to be only about 19 or 20—Erastus Haskell, Company K, 141st N.Y.—has been out about a year, and sick or half-sick more than half that time—has been down on the peninsula—was detailed to go in the band as fifer boy. While sick, the surgeon told him to keep up with the rest (probably worked and marched too long). He is a shy, and seems to me a very sensible boy—has fine manners—never complains—was sick down on the peninsula in an old storehouse—typhoid fever. The first week this July was brought up here—journey very bad, no accommodations, no nourishment, nothing but hard jolting, and exposure enough to make a well man sick (these fearful journeys do the job for many)—arrived here July 11th—a silent dark-skinned Spanish-looking youth, with large very dark blue eyes, peculiar looking. Doctor F. here made light of his sickness—said he would recover soon, etc.; but I thought very different, and told F. so repeatedly (I came near quarreling with him about it from the first)—but he laughed, and would not listen to me. About four days ago, I told Doctor he would in my opinion lose the boy without doubt—but F. again laughed at me. The next day he changed his opinion—I brought the head surgeon of the post—he said the boy would probably die, but they would make a hard fight for him. ᴁ The last two days he has been lying panting for breath—a pitiful sight. I have been with him some every day or night since he arrived. He suffers a great deal with the heat—says little or nothing—is flighty the last three days, at times—knows me always, however—calls me "Walter" (sometimes calls the name over and over and over again, musingly, abstractedly, to himself). His father lives at Breesport, Chemung County,

N.Y., is a mechanic with large family—is a steady, religious man; his mother too is living. I have written to them, and shall write again today—Erastus has not received a word from home for months. ᴁ As I sit here writing to you, M., I wish you could see the whole scene. This young man lies within reach of me, flat on his back, his hands clasped across his breast, his thick black hair cut close; he is dozing, breathing hard, every breath a spasm—it looks so cruel. He is a noble youngster—I consider him past all hope. Often there is no one with him for a long while. I am here as much as possible. ᴁ WILLIAM ALCOTT, FIREMAN. CAMDEN, NOV., 1874 ᴁ Last Monday afternoon his widow, mother, relatives, mates of the Fire Department, and his other friends (I was one, only lately it is true, but our love grew fast and close, the days and nights of those eight weeks by the chair of rapid decline, and the bed of death), gathered to the funeral of this young man, who had grown up, and was well known here. With nothing special, perhaps, to record, I would give a word or two to his memory. He seemed to me not an inappropriate specimen, in character and elements, of that bulk of the average good American race that ebbs and flows perennially beneath this scum of eructations on the surface. Always very quiet in manner, neat in person and dress, good-tempered—punctual and industrious at his work, till he could work no longer—he just lived his steady, square, unobtrusive life, in its own humble sphere, doubtless unconscious of itself. (Though I think there were currents of emotion and intellect undeveloped beneath, far deeper than his acquaintances ever suspected—or than he himself ever did.) He was no talker. His troubles, when he had any, he kept to himself. As there was nothing querulous about him in life, he made no complaints during his last sickness. He was one of those persons that while his associates never thought of attributing any particular talent or grace to him, yet all insensibly, really, liked Billy Alcott. ᴁ I, too, loved him. At last, after being with him quite a good deal—after hours and days of panting for breath, much of the time unconscious (for though the consumption that had been lurking in his system, once thoroughly started, made rapid progress, there was still great vitality in him, and indeed for four or five days he lay dying, before the close)—late on Wednesday night, Nov. 4th, where we surrounded his bed in silence, there came a lull—a longer drawn breath, a pause, a faint sigh—another—a weaker breath, another sigh—a pause again and just a tremble—and the face of the poor wasted young man (he was just 26) fell gently over, in death, on my hand, on the pillow. ᴁ CHARLES CASWELL ᴁ (I extract the following, verbatim, from a letter to me dated September 29, from my friend John Burroughs, at Esopus-on-Hudson,

New York State.)—S. was away when your picture came, attending his sick brother, Charles—who has since died—an event that has saddened me much. Charlie was younger than S., and a most attractive young fellow. He worked at my father's, and had done so for two years. He was about the best specimen of a young country farmhand I ever knew. You would have loved him. He was like one of your poems. With his great strength, his blond hair, his cheerfulness and contentment, his universal good will, and his silent manly ways, he was a youth hard to match. He was murdered by an old doctor. He had typhoid fever, and the old fool bled him twice. He lived to wear out the fever, but had not strength to rally. He was out of his head nearly all the time. In the morning, as he died in the afternoon, S. was standing over him, when Charlie put his arms around S.'s neck, and pulled his face down and kissed him. S. said he knew then the end was near. (S. stuck to him day and night to the last.) When I was home in August, Charlie was cradling on the hill, and it was a picture to see him walk through the grain. All work seemed play to him. He had no vices, any more than Nature has, and was beloved by all who knew him. ৵ I have written thus to you about him, for such young men belong to you; he was of your kind. I wish you could have known him. He had the sweetness of a child, and the strength and courage and readiness of a young Viking. His mother and father are poor; they have a rough, hard farm. His mother works in the field with her husband when the work presses. She has had twelve children.

FEBRUARY DAYS ৵ FEBRUARY 7, 1878 ৵ Glistening sun today, with slight haze, warm enough, and yet tart, as I sit here in the open air, down in my country retreat, under an old cedar. For two hours I have been idly wandering around the woods and pond, lugging my chair, picking out choice spots to sit awhile —then up and slowly on again. All is peace here. Of course, none of the summer noises or vitality; today hardly even the winter ones. I amuse myself by exercising my voice in recitations, and in ringing the changes on all the vocal and alphabetical sounds. Not even an echo; only the cawing of a solitary crow, flying at some distance. The pond is one bright, flat spread, without a ripple—a vast Claude Lorrain glass, in which I study the sky, the light, the leafless trees, and an occasional crow, with flapping wings, flying overhead. The brown fields have a few white patches of snow left. ৵FEB. 9 ৵ After an hour's ramble, now retreating, resting, sitting close by the pond, in a warm nook, writing this, sheltered from the breeze, just before noon. The *emotional* aspects and influences of Nature! I, too, like the rest, feel

these modern tendencies (from all the prevailing intellections, literature, and poems) to turn everything to pathos, ennui, morbidity, dissatisfaction, death. Yet how clear it is to me that those are not the born results, influences of Nature at all, but of one's own distorted, sick or silly soul. Here, amid this wild, free scene, how healthy, how joyous, how clean and vigorous and sweet! ৵ MIDAFTERNOON ৵ One of my nooks is south of the barn, and here I am sitting now, on a log, still basking in the sun, shielded from the wind. Near me are the cattle, feeding on cornstalks. Occasionally a cow or the young bull (how handsome and bold he is!) scratches and munches the far end of the log on which I sit. The fresh milky odor is quite perceptible, also the perfume of hay from the barn. The perpetual rustle of dry cornstalks, the low sough of the wind round the barn gables, the grunting of pigs, the distant whistle of a locomotive, and occasional crowing of chanticleers, are the sounds. ৵ FEB. 19 ৵ Cold and sharp last night— clear and not much wind—the full moon shining, and a fine spread of constellations and little and big stars— Sirius very bright, rising early, preceded by many-orbed Orion, glittering, vast, sworded, and chasing with his dog. The earth hard frozen, and a stiff glare of ice over the pond. Attracted by the calm splendor of the night, I attempted a short walk, but was driven back by the cold. Too severe for me also at 9 o'clock, when I came out this morning, so I turned back again. But now, near noon, I have walked down the lane, basking all the way in the sun (this farm has a pleasant southerly exposure), and here I am, seated under the lee of a bank, close by the water. There are bluebirds already flying about, and I hear much chirping and twittering and two or three real songs, sustained quite awhile, in the midday brilliance and warmth. (There! That is a true carol, coming out boldly and repeatedly, as if the singer meant it.) Then as the noon strengthens, the reedy trill of the robin —to my ear the most cheering of bird notes. At intervals, like bars and breaks (out of the low murmur that in any scene, however quiet, is never entirely absent to a delicate ear), the occasional crunch and cracking of the ice glare congealed over the creek, as it gives way to the sunbeams—sometimes with a low sigh—sometimes with indignant, obstinate tug and snort. ৵ (Robert Burns says in one of his letters: "There is scarcely any earthly object gives me more—I do not know if I should call it pleasure—but something which exalts me—something which enraptures me—than to walk in the sheltered side of a wood in a cloudy winter day, and hear the stormy wind howling among the trees, and raving over the plain. It is my best season of devotion." Some of his most characteristic poems were composed in such scenes and seasons.)

A MEADOWLARK ⁊ MARCH 16 ⁊ Fine, clear, dazzling morning, the sun an hour high, the air just tart enough. What a stamp in advance my whole day receives from the song of that meadowlark perched on a fence-stake twenty rods distant! Two or three liquid-simple notes, repeated at intervals, full of careless happiness and hope. With its peculiar shimmering-slow progress and rapid-noiseless action of the wings, it flies on a ways, lights on another stake, and so on to another, shimmering and singing many minutes.

SUNDOWN LIGHTS ⁊ MAY 6, 5 P.M. ⁊ This is the hour for strange effects in light and shade—enough to make a colorist go delirious—long spokes of molten silver sent horizontally through the trees (now in their brightest tenderest green), each leaf and branch of endless foliage a lit-up miracle, then lying all prone on the youthful-ripe, interminable grass, and giving the blades not only aggregate but individual splendor, in ways unknown to any other hour. I have particular spots where I get these effects in their perfection. One broad splash lies on the water, with many a rippling twinkle, offset by the rapidly deepening black-green murky-transparent shadows behind, and at intervals all along the banks. These, with great shafts of horizontal fire thrown among the trees and along the grass as the sun lowers, give effects more and more peculiar, more and more superb, unearthly, rich, and dazzling.

THOUGHTS UNDER AN OAK—A DREAM ⁊ JUNE 2 ⁊ This is the fourth day of a dark northeast storm, wind and rain. Day before yesterday was my birthday. I have now entered on my 60th year. Every day of the storm, protected by overshoes and a waterproof blanket, I regularly come down to the pond, and ensconce myself under the lee of the great oak; I am here now writing these lines. The dark smoke-colored clouds roll in furious silence athwart the sky; the soft green leaves dangle all round me; the wind steadily keeps up its hoarse, soothing music over my head—Nature's mighty whisper. Seated here in solitude I have been musing over my life—connecting events. dates, as links of a chain, neither sadly nor cheerily, but somehow, today here under the oak, in the rain, in an unusually matter-of-fact spirit. ⁊ But my great oak—sturdy, vital, green—five feet thick at the butt: I sit a great deal near or under him. Then the tuilp tree near by —the Apollo of the woods—tall and graceful, yet robust and sinewy, inimitable in hang of foliage and throwing-out of limb; as if the beauteous, vital, leafy creature could walk, if it only would. (I had a sort of dream-trance the other day, in which I saw my favorite trees step out and promenade up, down and around, very

curiously—with a whisper from one, leaning down as he passed me, "*We do all this on the present occasion, exceptionally, just for you.*")

CLOVER AND HAY PERFUME ⁊ JULY 3D, 4TH, 5TH ⁊ Clear, hot, favorable weather—has been a good summer—the growth of clover and grass now generally mowed. The familiar delicious perfume fills the barns and lanes. As you go along you see the fields of grayish white slightly tinged with yellow, the loosely stacked grain, the slow-moving wagons passing, and farmers in the fields with stout boys pitching and loading the sheaves. The corn is about beginning to tassel. All over the middle and southern states the spear-shaped battalia, multitudinous, curving, flaunting—long, glossy, dark-green plumes for the great horseman, earth. I hear the cheery notes of my old acquaintance Tommy Quail; but too late for the whippoorwill (though I heard one solitary lingerer night before last). I watch the broad majestic flight of a turkey buzzard, sometimes high up, sometimes low enough to see the lines of his form, even his spread quills, in relief against the sky. Once or twice lately I have seen an eagle here at early candlelight flying low.

AN UNKNOWN ⁊ JUNE 15 ⁊ Today I noticed a new large bird, size of a nearly grown hen—a haughty, white-bodied, dark-winged hawk—I suppose a hawk from his bill and general look—only he had a clear, loud, quite musical, sort of bell-like call, which he repeated again and again, at intervals, from a lofty dead treetop, overhanging the water. Sat there a long time, and I on the opposite bank watching him. Then he darted down, skimming pretty close to the stream—rose slowly, a magnificent sight, and sailed with steady, wide-spread wings, no flapping at all, up and down the pond two or three times, near me, in circles in clear sight, as if for my delectation. Once he came quite close over my head; I saw plainly his hooked bill and hard, restless eyes.

BIRD-WHISTLING ⁊ How much music (wild, simple, savage, doubtless, but so tart-sweet) there is in mere whistling. It is four-fifths of the utterance of birds. There are all sorts and styles. For the last half-hour, now, while I have been sitting here, some feathered fellow away off in the bushes has been repeating over and over again what I may call a kind of throbbing whistle. And now a bird about the robin size has just appeared, all mulberry red, flitting among the bushes—head, wings, body, deep red, not very bright—no song, as I have heard. *4 o'clock*: There is a real concert going on around me—a dozen different birds pitching in with a will.

There have been occasional rains, and the growths all show its vivifying influences. As I finish this, seated on a log close by the pond edge, much chirping and trilling in the distance, and a feathered recluse in the woods near by is singing deliciously—not many notes, but full of music of almost human sympathy—continuing for a long, long while.

HORSEMINT ❧ AUG. 22 ❧ Not a human being, and hardly the evidence of one, in sight. After my brief semidaily bath, I sit here for a bit, the brook musically brawling, to the chromatic tones of a fretful catbird somewhere off in the bushes. On my walk hither two hours since, through fields and the old lane, I stopped to view, now the sky, now the mile-off woods on the hill, and now the apple orchards. What a contrast from New York's or Philadelphia's streets! Everywhere great patches of dingy-blossomed horsemint wafting a spicy odor through the air (especially evenings). Everywhere the flowering boneset, and the rose-bloom of the wild bean.

THREE OF US ❧ JULY 14 ❧ My two kingfishers still haunt the pond. In the bright sun and breeze and perfect temperature of today, noon, I am sitting here by one of the gurgling brooks, dipping a French water-pen in the limpid crystal, and using it to write these lines, again watching the feathered twain as they fly and sport athwart the water, so close, almost touching into its surface. Indeed, there seem to be three of us. For nearly an hour I indolently look and join them while they dart and turn and take their airy gambols, sometimes far up the creek, disappearing for a few moments, and then surely returning again, and performing most of their flight within sight of me, as if they knew I appreciated and absorbed their vitality, spirituality, faithfulness, and the rapid, vanishing, delicate lines of moving yet quiet electricity they draw for me across the spread of the grass, the trees, and the blue sky. While the brook babbles, babbles, and the shadows of the boughs dapple in the sunshine around me, and the cool west-by-nor'west wind faintly soughs in the thick bushes and treetops. ❧ Among the objects of beauty and interest now beginning to appear quite plentifully in this secluded spot, I notice the humming-bird, the dragonfly with its wings of slate-colored gauze, and many varieties of beautiful and plain butterflies, idly flapping among the plants and wild posies. The mullein has shot up out of its nest of broad leaves, to a tall stalk towering sometimes five or six feet high, now studded with knobs of golden blossoms. The milkweed (I see a great gorgeous creature of gamboge and black lighting on one as I write) is in flower, with its delicate red fringe; and there are profuse

clusters of a feathery blossom waving in the wind on taper stems. I see lots of these and much else in every direction, as I saunter or sit. For the last half-hour a bird has persistently kept up a simple, sweet, melodious song, from the bushes. (I have a positive conviction that some of these birds sing, and others fly and flirt about here, for my especial benefit.)

DEATH OF WILLIAM CULLEN BRYANT ❧ NEW YORK CITY ❧ Came on from West Philadelphia, June 13, in the 2 P.M. train to Jersey City, and so across and to my friends, Mr. and Mrs. J. H. J., and their large house, large family (and large hearts), amid which I feel at home, at peace—away up on Fifth Avenue, near Eighty-sixth Street, quiet, breezy, overlooking the dense woody fringe of the park—plenty of space and sky, birds chirping, and air comparatively fresh and odorless. Two hours before starting, saw the announcement of William Cullen Bryant's funeral, and felt a strong desire to attend. I had known Mr. Bryant over thirty years ago, and he had been markedly kind to me. Off and on, along that time for years as they passed, we met and chatted together. I thought him very sociable in his way, and a man to become attached to. We were both walkers, and when I worked in Brooklyn he several times came over, middle of afternoons, and we took rambles miles long, till dark, out toward Bedford or Flatbush, in company. On these occasions he gave me clear accounts of scenes in Europe—the cities, looks, architecture, art, especially Italy—where he had traveled a good deal. ❧ JUNE 14—THE FUNERAL ❧ And so the good, stainless, noble old citizen and poet lies in the closed coffin there—and this is his funeral. A solemn, impressive, simple scene, to spirit and senses. The remarkable gathering of gray heads, celebrities—the finely rendered anthem, and other music—the church, dim even now at approaching noon, in its light from the mellow-stained windows—the pronounced eulogy on the bard who loved Nature so fondly, and sang so well her shows and seasons—ending with these appropriate well-known lines:

I gazed upon the glorious sky,
  And the green mountains round,
And thought that when I came to lie
  At rest within the ground,
'Twere pleasant that in flowery June,
When brooks send up a joyous tune,
  And groves a cheerful sound,
The sexton's hand, my grave to make,
The rich green mountain turf should break.

[76]

JAUNT UP THE HUDSON ☙ JUNE 20TH ☙ On the *Mary Powell*, enjoyed everything beyond precedent. The delicious, tender summer day, just warm enough—the constantly changing but ever beautiful panorama on both sides of the river (went up near a hundred miles)—the high straight walls of the stony Palisades—beautiful Yonkers, and beautiful Irvington—the never-ending hills, mostly in rounded lines, swathed with verdure—the distant turns, like great shoulders in blue veils—the frequent gray and brown of the tall-rising rocks—the river itself, now narrowing, now expanding—the white sails of the many sloops, yachts, etc., some near, some in the distance—the rapid succession of handsome villages and cities (our boat is a swift traveler, and makes few stops)—the Race—picturesque West Point, and indeed all along—the costly and often turreted mansions forever showing in some cheery light color, through the woods—make up the scene.

HAPPINESS AND RASPBERRIES ☙ JUNE 21 ☙ Here I am, on the west bank of the Hudson, 80 miles north of New York, near Esopus, at the handsome, roomy, honeysuckle-and-rose-embowered cottage of John Burroughs. The place, the perfect June days and nights (leaning toward crisp and cool), the hospitality of J. and Mrs. B., the air, the fruit (especially my favorite dish, currants and raspberries, mixed, sugared, fresh and ripe from the bushes—I pick 'em myself)—the room I occupy at night, the perfect bed, the window giving an ample view of the Hudson and the opposite shores, so wonderful toward sunset, and the rolling music of the R.R. trains, far over there—the peaceful rest—the early Venus-heralded dawn—the noiseless splash of sunrise, the light and warmth indescribably glorious, in which (soon as the sun is well up) I have a capital rubbing and rasping with the flesh brush—with an extra scour on the back by Al. J., who is here with us—all inspiriting my invalid frame with new life, for the day. Then, after some whiffs of morning air, the delicious coffee of Mrs. B., with the cream, strawberries, and many substantials, for breakfast.

A SPECIMEN TRAMP FAMILY ☙ JUNE 22 ☙ This afternoon we went out (J. B., Al., and I) on quite a drive around the country. The scenery, the perpetual stone fences (some venerable old fellows, dark-spotted with lichens)—the many fine locust trees—the runs of brawling water, often over descents of rock—these, and lots else. It is lucky the roads are first-rate here (as they are), for it is up- or downhill everywhere, and sometimes steep enough. B. has a tiptop horse, strong, young, and both gentle and fast. There is a great deal of waste land and hills on the river edge of Ulster County, with a wonderful luxuriance of wild flowers and bushes—and it seems to me I never saw more vitality of trees—eloquent hemlocks, plenty of locusts and fine maples, and the Balm of Gilead, giving out aroma. In the fields and along the roadsides unusual crops of the tall-stemmed wild daisy, white as milk and yellow as gold. ☙ We passed quite a number of tramps, singly or in couples—one squad, a family in a rickety one-horse wagon, with some baskets evidently their work and trade—the man seated on a low board, in front, driving—the gauntish woman by his side, with a baby well bundled in her arms, its little red feet and lower legs sticking out right toward us as we passed—and in the wagon behind we saw two (or three) crouching little children. It was a queer, taking, rather sad picture. If I had been alone and on foot, I should have stopped and held confab. But on our return nearly two hours afterward, we found them a ways further along the same road, in a lonesome open spot, hauled aside, unhitched, and evidently going to camp for the night. The freed horse was not far off, quietly cropping the grass. The man was busy at the wagon, the boy had gathered some dry wood, and was making a fire—and as we went a little further we met the woman afoot. I could not see her face, in its great sunbonnet, but somehow her figure and gait told misery, terror, destitution. She had the rag-bundled, half-starved infant still in her arms, and in her hands held two or three baskets, which she had evidently taken to the next house for sale. A little barefoot five-year-old girl-child, with fine eyes, trotted behind her, clutching her gown. We stopped, asking about the baskets, which we bought. As we paid the money, she kept her face hidden in the recesses of her bonnet. Then as we started, and stopped again, Al. (whose sympathies were evidently aroused) went back to the camping group to get another basket. He caught a look of her face, and talked with her a little. Eyes, voice, and manner were those of a corpse, animated by electricity. She was quite young—the man she was traveling with, middle-aged. Poor woman—what story was it, out of her fortunes, to account for that inexpressibly scared way, those glassy eyes, and that hollow voice?

MANHATTAN FROM THE BAY ☙ JUNE 25 ☙ Returned to New York last night. Out today on the waters for a sail in the wide bay, southeast of Staten Island—a rough, tossing ride, and a free sight—the long stretch of Sandy Hook, the highlands of Navesink, and the many vessels outward and inward bound. We came up through the midst of all, in the full sun. I especially enjoyed the last hour or two. A moderate sea breeze had set in; yet over the city, and the waters adjacent, was a thin haze, concealing nothing, only adding to the beauty. From my point of view, as I write amid the soft breeze, with a sea temperature, surely nothing on earth of its kind can go beyond this show. To the left the North River with its far vista—nearer, three or four warships, anchored peacefully—the Jersey side, the banks of Weehawken, the Palisades, and the gradually receding blue, lost in the distance—to the right the East River—the mast-hemmed shores—the grand obelisk-like towers of the bridge, one on either side, in haze, yet plainly defined, giant brothers twain, throwing free, graceful, interlinking loops high across the tumbled tumultuous current below (the tide is just changing to its ebb)—the broad water-spread everywhere crowded —no, not crowded, but thick as stars in the sky—with all sorts and sizes of sail and steam vessels, plying ferry-boats, arriving and departing coasters, great ocean Dons, iron-black, modern, magnificent in size and power, filled with their incalculable value of human life and precious merchandise—with here and there, above all, those daring, careening things of grace and wonder, those white and shaded swift-darting fish-birds (I wonder if shore or sea elsewhere can outvie them), ever with their slanting spars, and fierce, pure, hawklike beauty and motion—first-class New York sloop or schooner yachts, sailing, this fine day, the free sea in a good wind. And rising out of the midst, tall-topped, ship-hemmed, modern, American, yet strangely oriental, V-shaped Manhattan, with its compact mass, its spires, its cloud-touching edifices grouped at the center—the green of the trees, and all the white, brown, and gray of the architecture well blended, as I see it, under a miracle of limpid sky, delicious light of heaven above, and June haze on the surface below.

HUMAN AND HEROIC NEW YORK ᵃ The general subjective view of New York and Brooklyn (will not the time hasten when the two shall be municipally united in one, and named Manhattan?)—what I may call the human interior and exterior of these great seething oceanic populations, as I get it in this visit, is to me best of all. After an absence of many years (I went away at the outbreak of the Secession War, and have never been back to stay since), again I resume with curiosity the crowds, the streets I knew so well, Broadway, the ferries, the west side of the city, democratic Bowery—human appearances and manners as seen in all these, and along the wharves, and in the perpetual travel of the horsecars, or the crowded excursion steamers, or in Wall and Nassau Streets by day—in the places of amusement at night—bubbling and whirling and moving like its own environment of waters—endless humanity in all phases—Brooklyn also—taken in for the

last three weeks. No need to specify minutely—enough to say that (making all allowances for the shadows and side-streaks of a million-headed city) the brief total of the impressions, the human qualities, of these vast cities is to me comforting, even heroic, beyond statement. Alertness, generally fine physique, clear eyes that look straight at you, a singular combination of reticence and self-possession, with good nature and friendliness—a prevailing range of according manners, taste, and intellect, surely beyond any elsewhere upon earth—and a palpable outcropping of that personal comradeship I look forward to as the subtlest, strongest future hold of this many-itemed Union—are not only constantly visible here in these mighty channels of men, but they form the rule and average. Today, I should say—defiant of cynics and pessimists, and with a full knowledge of all their exceptions—an appreciative and perceptive study of the current humanity of New York gives the directest proof yet of successful democracy, and of the solution of that paradox, the eligibility of the free and fully developed individual with the paramount aggregate. In old age, lame and sick, pondering for years on many a doubt and danger for this republic of ours—fully aware of all that can be said on the other side—I find in this visit to New York, and the daily contact and rapport with its myriad people, on the scale of the oceans and tides, the best, most effective medicine my soul has yet partaken— the grandest physical habitat and surroundings of land and water the globe affords—namely, Manhattan Island and Brooklyn, which the future shall join in one city— city of superb democracy, amid superb surroundings.

HOURS FOR THE SOUL ᵃ JULY 22D, 1878 ᵃ Living down in the country again. A wonderful conjunction of all that goes to make those sometime miracle hours after sunset—so near and yet so far. Perfect, or nearly perfect days, I notice, are not so very uncommon; but the combinations that make perfect nights are few, even in a lifetime. We have one of those perfections tonight. Sunset left things pretty clear; the larger stars were visible soon as the shades allowed. A while after 8, three or four great black clouds suddenly rose, seemingly from different points, and sweeping with broad swirls of wind but no thunder, underspread the orbs from view everywhere, and indicated a violent heat storm. But without storm, clouds, blackness, and all, sped and vanished as suddenly as they had risen; and from a little after 9 till 11 the atmosphere and the whole show above were in that state of exceptional clearness and glory just alluded to. In the northwest turned the Great Dipper with its pointers round the Cynosure. A little south of east the constellation of the Scorpion was fully up, with red Antares glowing in its neck; while dominating, majestic Jupiter swam, an hour and a half risen, in the east (no moon till after 11). A large part of the sky seemed just laid in great splashes of phosphorus. You could look deeper in, farther through, than usual; the orbs thick as heads of wheat in a field. Not that there was a special brilliancy either—nothing near as sharp as I have seen of keen winter nights, but a curious general luminousness throughout to sight, sense, and soul. The latter had much to do with it. (I am convinced there are hours of Nature, especially of the atmosphere, mornings and evenings, addressed to the soul. Night transcends, for that purpose, what the proudest day can do.) Now, indeed, if never before, the heavens declared the glory of God. It was to the full the sky of the Bible, of Arabia, of the prophets, and of the oldest poems. There, in abstraction and stillness (I had gone off by myself to absorb the scene, to have the spell unbroken), the copiousness, the removedness, vitality, loose-clear-crowdedness, of that stellar concave spreading overhead, softly absorbed into me, rising so free, interminably high, stretching east, west, north, south—and I, though but a point in the center below, embodying all. ℘ As if for the first time, indeed, creation noiselessly sank into and through me its placid and untellable lesson, beyond—O, so infinitely beyond!—anything from arts, books, sermons, or from science, old or new. The spirit's hour—religion's hour —the visible suggestion of God in space and time—now once definitely indicated, if never again. The untold pointed at—the heavens all paved with it. The Milky Way, as if some superhuman symphony, some ode of universal vagueness, disdaining syllable and sound— a flashing glance of Deity, addressed to the soul. All silently—the indescribable night and stars—far off and silently. ℘ THE DAWN—JULY 23 ℘ This morning, between one and two hours before sunrise, a spectacle wrought on the same background, yet of quite different beauty and meaning. The moon well up in the heavens, and past her half, is shining brightly—the air and sky of that cynical-clear, Minervalike quality, virgin cool— not the weight of sentiment or mystery, or passion's ecstasy indefinable—not the religious sense, the varied All, distilled and sublimated into one, of the night just described. Every star now clearcut, showing for just what it is, there in the colorless ether. The character of the heralded morning, ineffably sweet and fresh and limpid, but for the esthetic sense alone, and for purity without sentiment. I have itemized the night—but dare I attempt the cloudless dawn? (What subtle tie is this between one's soul and the break of day? Alike, and yet no two nights or morning shows ever exactly alike.) Preceded by an immense star, almost unearthly in its effusion of white splendor, with two or three long unequal spoke-rays of diamond radiance, shedding down

through the fresh morning air below—an hour of this, and then the sunrise. ℘ THE EAST ℘ What a subject for a poem! Indeed, where else a more pregnant, more splendid one? Where one more idealistic-real, more subtle, more sensuous-delicate? The East, answering all lands, all ages, peoples; touching all senses, here, immediate, now—and yet so indescribably far off—such retrospect! The East—long stretching—so losing itself —the Orient, the gardens of Asia, the womb of history and song—forth-issuing all those strange, dim cavalcades—

Florid with blood, pensive, rapt with musing, hot with passion,
Sultry with perfume, with ample and flowing garments,
With sunburnt visage, intense soul and glittering eyes.

℘ Always the East—old, how incalculably old! And yet here the same—ours yet, fresh as a rose, to every morning, every life, today—and always will be. ℘ SEPT. 17 ℘ Another presentation—same theme—just before sunrise again (a favorite hour with me). The clear gray sky, a faint glow in the dull liver-color of the east, the cool fresh odor and the moisture—the cattle and horses off there grazing in the fields—the star Venus again, two hours high. For sounds, the chirping of crickets in the grass, the clarion of Chanticleer, and the distant cawing of an early crow. Quietly over the dense fringe of cedars and pines rises that dazzling, red, transparent disk of flame, and the low sheets of white vapor roll and roll into dissolution. ℘ THE MOON—MAY 18 ℘ I went to bed early last night, but found myself waked shortly after 12, and, turning awhile sleepless and mentally feverish, I rose, dressed myself, sallied forth, and walked down the lane. The full moon, some three or four hours up—a sprinkle of light and less-light clouds just lazily moving —Jupiter an hour high in the east, and here and there throughout the heavens a random star appearing and disappearing. So, beautifully veiled and varied—the air, with that early-summer perfume, not at all damp or raw—at times Luna languidly emerging in richest brightness for minutes, and then partially enveloped again. Far off a whippoorwill plied his notes incessantly. It was that silent time between 1 and 3. ℘ The rare nocturnal scene, how soon it soothed and pacified me! Is there not something about the moon, some relation or reminder, which no poem or literature has yet caught? (In very old and primitive ballads I have come across lines or asides that suggest it.) After a while the clouds mostly cleared, and as the moon swam on, she carried, shimmering and shifting, delicate color effects of pellucid green and tawny vapor. Let me conclude this part with an extract (some writer in the *Tribune*, May 16, 1878): *No one ever gets tired of the moon. Goddess that she is by dower of her eternal beauty, she is a true woman by her tact —knows the charm of being seldom seen, of coming by surprise and staying but a little while; never wears the same dress two nights running, nor all night the same way; commends herself to the matter-of-fact people by her usefulness, and makes her uselessness adored by poets, artists, and all lovers in all lands; lends herself to every symbolism and to every emblem; is Diana's bow and Venus's mirror and Mary's throne; is a sickle, a scarf, an eyebrow, his face or her face, as looked at by her or by him; is the madman's hell, the poet's heaven, the baby's toy, the philosopher's study; and while her admirers follow her footsteps, and hang on her lovely looks, she knows how to keep her woman's secret—her other side—unguessed and unguessable.* ෨ FURTHERMORE—FEBRUARY 19, 1880 ෨ Just before 10 P.M. cold and entirely clear again, the show overhead, bearing southwest, of wonderful and crowded magnificence. The moon in her third quarter —the clusters of the Hyades and Pleiades, with the planet Mars between—in full crossing sprawl in the sky the great Egyptian X (Sirius, Procyon, and the main stars in the constellations of the Ship, the Dove, and of Orion); just north of east Boötes, and in his knee Arcturus, an hour high, mounting the heaven, ambitiously large and sparkling, as if he meant to challenge with Sirius the stellar supremacy. ෨ With the sentiment of the stars and moon such nights I get all the free margins and indefiniteness of music or poetry, fused in geometry's utmost exactness.

STRAW-COLORED AND OTHER PSYCHES
෨ AUG. 4 ෨ A pretty sight! Where I sit in the shade—a warm day, the sun shining from cloudless skies, the forenoon well advanced—I look over a ten-acre field of luxuriant clover hay (the second crop)—the livid-ripe red blossoms and dabs of August brown thickly spotting the prevailing dark green. Over all flutter myriads of light yellow butterflies, mostly skimming along the surface, dipping and oscillating, giving a curious animation to the scene. The beautiful, spiritual insects! Straw-colored Psyches! Occasionally one of them leaves his mates and mounts, perhaps spirally, perhaps in a straight line in the air, fluttering up, up, till literally out of sight. In the lane as I came along just now I noticed one spot, ten feet square or so, where more than a hundred had collected, holding a revel, a gyration dance, or butterfly good-time, winding and circling, down and across, but always keeping within the limits. The little creatures have come out all of a sudden the last few days, and are now very plentiful. As I sit outdoors, or walk, I hardly look around without somewhere seeing two (always two) fluttering through the air in amorous dalliance. Then their inimitable color, their fragility, peculiar motion—and that strange, frequent way of one leaving the crowd and mounting up, up in the free ether, and apparently never returning. As I look over the field, these yellow-wings everywhere mildly sparkling, many snowy blossoms of the wild carrot gracefully bending on their tall and taper stems—while for sounds, the distant guttural screech of a flock of guinea hens comes shrilly yet somehow musically to my ears. And now a faint growl of heat thunder in the north—and ever the low rising and falling wind-purr from the tops of the maples and willows. ෨ AUG. 20 ෨ Butterflies and butterflies (taking the place of the bumblebees of three months since, who have quite disappeared) continue to flit to and fro, all sorts, white, yellow, brown, purple— now and then some gorgeous fellow flashing lazily by on wings like artists' palettes dabbed with every color. Over the breast of the pond I notice many white ones, crossing, pursuing their idle capricious flight. Near where I sit grows a tall-stemmed weed topped with a profusion of rich scarlet blossoms, on which the snowy insects alight and dally, sometimes four or five of them at a time. By and by a hummingbird visits the same, and I watch him coming and going, daintily balancing and shimmering about. These white butterflies give new beautiful contrasts to the pure greens of the August foliage (we have had some copious rains lately) and over the glistening bronze of the pond surface. You can tame even such insects; I have one big and handsome moth down here, knows and comes to me, likes me to hold him up on my extended hand. ෨ ANOTHER DAY, LATER. ෨ A grand twelve-acre field of ripe cabbages with their prevailing hue of malachite green, and floating-flying over and among them in all directions myriads of these same white butterflies. As I came up the lane today I saw a living globe of the same, two to three feet in diameter, many scores clustered together and rolling along in the air, adhering to their ball shape, six or eight feet above the ground.

A NIGHT REMEMBRANCE ෨ AUG. 25, 9– 10 A.M. ෨ I sit by the edge of the pond, everything quiet, the broad polished surface spread before me—the blue of the heavens and the white clouds returned from it—and flitting across, now and then, the reflection of some flying bird. Last night I was down here with a friend till after midnight; everything a miracle of splendor—the glory of the stars, and the completely rounded moon—the passing clouds, silver and luminous-tawny —now and then masses of vapory illuminated scud— and silently by my side my dear friend. The shades of the trees, and patches of moonlight on the grass—the softly blowing breeze, and just-palpable odor of the neighboring ripening corn—the indolent and spiritual night, inexpressibly rich, tender, suggestive—something altogether to filter through one's soul, and nourish and feed and soothe the memory long afterward.

WILD FLOWERS ❧ This has been and is yet a great season for wild flowers; oceans of them line the roads through the woods, border the edges of the water-runlets, grow all along the old fences, and are scattered in profusion over the fields. An eight-petaled blossom of gold-yellow, clear and bright, with a brown tuft in the middle, nearly as large as a silver half-dollar, is very common; yesterday on a long drive I noticed it thickly lining the borders of the brooks everywhere. Then there is a beautiful weed covered with blue flowers (the blue of the old Chinese teacups treasured by our grandaunts) I am continually stopping to admire—a little larger than a dime, and very plentiful. White, however, is the prevailing color. The wild carrot I have spoken of, also the fragrant life everlasting. But there are all hues and beauties, especially on the frequent tracts of half-open scrub oak and dwarf cedar hereabout—wild asters of all colors. Notwithstanding the frost-touch the hardy little chaps maintain themselves in all their bloom. The tree leaves, too, some of them are beginning to turn yellow or drab or dull green. The deep wine color of the sumacs and gum trees is already visible, and the straw color of the dogwood and beech. Let me give the names of some of these perennial blossoms and friendly weeds I have made acquaintance with hereabout one season or another in my walks:

wild azalea	dandelions
wild honeysuckle	yarrow
wild roses	coreopsis
goldenrod	wild pea
larkspur	woodbine
early crocus	elderberry
sweet flag (great patches of it)	pokeweed
creeper, trumpet flower	sunflower
scented marjoram	chamomile
snakeroot	violets
Solomon's-seal	clematis
sweet balm	bloodroot
mint (great plenty)	swamp magnolia
wild geranium	milkweed
wild heliotrope	wild daisy (plenty)
burdock	wild chrysanthemum

A CIVILITY TOO LONG NEGLECTED ❧ The foregoing reminds me of something. As the individualities I would mainly portray have certainly been slighted by folks who make pictures, volumes, poems out of them—as a faint testimonial of my own gratitude for many hours of peace and comfort in half-sickness (and not by any means sure but they will somehow get wind of the compliment), I hereby dedicate the last half of these Specimen Days to the

bees	water snakes
blackbirds	crows
dragonflies	millers
pond turtles	mosquitoes
mulleins, tansy, peppermint	butterflies
	wasps and hornets
moths (great and little, some splendid fellows)	catbirds (and all other birds)
glowworms (swarming millions of them, indescribably strange and beautiful at night over the pond and creek)	cedars
	tulip trees (and all other trees) and to the spots and memories of those days, and of the creek

DELAWARE RIVER—DAYS AND NIGHTS ❧ APRIL 5, 1879 ❧ With the return of spring to the skies, airs, waters of the Delaware, return the seagulls. I never tire of watching their broad and easy flight, in spirals, or as they oscillate with slow unflapping wings, or look down with curved beak, or dipping to the water after food. The crows, plenty enough all through the winter, have vanished with the ice. Not one of them now to be seen. The steamboats have again come forth —bustling up, handsome, freshly painted, for summer work—the *Columbia*, the *Edwin Forrest* (the *Republic* not yet out), the *Reybold*, the *Nelly White*, the *Twilight*, the *Ariel*, the *Warner*, the *Perry*, the *Taggart*, the *Jersey Blue* —even the hulky old *Trenton*—not forgetting those saucy little bullpups of the current, the steam tugs. ❧ But let me bunch and catalog the affair—the river itself, all the way from the sea—Cape Island on one side and Henlopen Light on the other—up the broad bay north, and so to Philadelphia, and on farther to Trenton; the sights I am most familiar with (as I live a good part of the time in Camden, I view matters from that outlook)— the great, arrogant, black, full-freighted ocean steamers, inward or outward bound—the ample width here between the two cities, intersected by Windmill Island— an occasional man-of-war, sometimes a foreigner, at anchor, with her guns and portholes, and the boats, and the brown-faced sailors, and the regular oar-strokes, and the gay crowds of "visiting day"—the frequent large and handsome three-masted schooners (a favorite style of marine build, hereabout of late years), some of them new and very jaunty, with their white-gray sails and yellow pine spars—the sloops dashing along in a fair wind (I see one now, coming up, under broad canvas, her gaff-topsail shining in the sun, high and picturesque —what a thing of beauty amid the sky and waters!)— the crowded wharf-slips along the city—the flags of different nationalities, the sturdy English cross on its ground of blood, the French tricolor, the banner of the great North German empire, and the Italian and the

Spanish colors—sometimes, of an afternoon, the whole scene enlivened by a fleet of yachts, in a half calm, lazily returning from a race down at Gloucester; the neat, rakish, revenue steamer *Hamilton* in midstream, with her perpendicular stripes flaunting aft—and, turning the eyes north, the long ribands of fleecy white steam, or dingy black smoke, stretching far, fan-shaped, slanting diagonally across from the Kensington or Richmond shores, in the west-by-southwest wind.

SCENES ON FERRY AND RIVER—LAST WINTER'S NIGHTS ᘒ Then the Camden ferry. What exhilaration, change, people, business, by day. What soothing, silent, wondrous hours, at night, crossing on the boat, most all to myself—pacing the deck, alone, forward or aft. What communion with the waters, the air, the exquisite *chiaroscuro*—the sky and stars, that speak no word, nothing to the intellect, yet so eloquent, so communicative to the soul. And the ferrymen —little they know how much they have been to me, day and night—how many spells of listlessness, ennui, debility, they and their hardy ways have dispelled. And the pilots—Captains Hand, Walton, and Giverson by day, and Captain Olive at night; Eugene Crosby, with his strong young arm so often supporting, circling, convoying me over the gaps of the bridge, through impediments, safely aboard. Indeed all my ferry friends—Captain Frazee, the superintendent; Lindell, Hiskey, Fred Rauch, Price, Watson, and a dozen more. And the ferry itself, with its queer scenes—sometimes children suddenly born in the waiting-houses (an actual fact—and more than once)—sometimes a masquerade party, going over at night, with a band of music, dancing and whirling like mad on the broad deck, in their fantastic dresses; sometimes the astronomer, Mr. Whitall (who posts me up in points about the stars by a living lesson there and then, and answering every question)—sometimes a prolific family group, eight, nine, ten, even twelve! (Yesterday, as I crossed, a mother, father, and eight children, waiting in the ferryhouse, bound westward somewhere.) ᘒ I have mentioned the crows. I always watch them from the boats. They play quite a part in the winter scenes on the river, by day. Their black splatches are seen in relief against the snow and ice everywhere at that season—sometimes flying and flapping—sometimes on little or larger cakes, sailing up or down the stream. One day the river was mostly clear— only a single long ridge of broken ice making a narrow stripe by itself, running along down the current for over a mile, quite rapidly. On this white stripe the crows were congregated, hundreds of them—a funny procession ("half mourning" was the comment of some one). ᘒ Then the reception room, for passengers waiting—

life illustrated thoroughly. Take a March picture I jotted there two or three weeks since. Afternoon, about 3:30 o'clock it begins to snow. There has been a matinee performance at the theater—from 4:15 to 5 comes a stream of homeward-bound ladies. I never knew the spacious room to present a gayer, more lively scene—handsome, well-dressed Jersey women and girls, scores of them, streaming in for nearly an hour—the bright eyes and glowing faces, coming in from the air—a sprinkling of snow on bonnets or dresses as they enter—the five or ten minutes' waiting—the chatting and laughing— (women can have capital times among themselves, with plenty of wit, lunches, jovial abandon)—Lizzie, the pleasant-mannered waiting-room woman—for sound, the bell taps and steam signals of the departing boats with their rhythmic break and undertone—the domestic pictures, mothers with bevies of daughters (a charming sight)—children, countrymen—the railroad men in their blue clothes and caps—all the various characters of city and country represented or suggested. Then outside some belated passenger frantically running, jumping after the boat. Towards six o'clock the human stream gradually thickening—now a pressure of vehicles, drays, piled railroad crates—now a drove of cattle, making quite an excitement, the drovers with heavy sticks, belaboring the steaming sides of the frightened brutes. Inside the reception room, business bargains, flirting, love-making, *éclaircissements*, proposals—pleasant, sober-faced Phil coming in with his burden of afternoon papers—or Jo, or Charley (who jumped in the dock last week, and saved a stout lady from drowning), to replenish the stove, after clearing it with a long crowbar poker. ᘒ Besides all this "comedy human," the river affords nutriment of a higher order. Here are some of my memoranda of the past winter, just as penciled down on the spot. ᘒ A JANUARY NIGHT ᘒ Fine trips across the wide Delaware tonight. Tide pretty high, and a strong ebb. River, a little after 8, full of ice, mostly broken, but some large cakes making our strong-timbered steamboat hum and quiver as she strikes them. In the clear moonlight they spread, strange, unearthly, silvery, faintly glistening, as far as I can see. Bumping, trembling, sometimes hissing like a thousand snakes, the tide procession, as we wend with or through it, affording a grand undertone, in keeping with the scene. Overhead, the splendor indescribable; yet something haughty, almost supercilious, in the night. Never did I realize more latent sentiment, almost *passion*, in those silent interminable stars up there. One can understand, such a night, why, from the days of the Pharaohs or Job, the dome of heaven, sprinkled with planets, has supplied the subtlest, deepest criticism on human pride, glory, ambition. ᘒ ANOTHER WINTER NIGHT ᘒ I don't know anything more *filling* than to be on the wide, firm deck of a powerful boat, a clear, cool, extra-moonlight night, crushing proudly and resistlessly through this thick, marbly, glistening ice. The whole river is now spread with it—some immense cakes. There is such weirdness about the scene—partly the quality of the light, with its tinge of blue, the lunar twilight—only the large stars holding their own in the radiance of the moon. Temperature sharp, comfortable for motion, dry, full of oxygen. But the sense of power—the steady, scornful, imperious urge of our strong new engine, as she plows her way through the big and little cakes. ✌ ANOTHER ✌ For two hours I crossed and recrossed, merely for pleasure—for a still excitement. Both sky and river went through several changes. The first for awhile held two vast fan-shaped echelons of light clouds, through which the moon waded, now radiating, carrying with her an aureole of tawny transparent brown, and now flooding the whole vast with clear vapory light green, through which, as through an illuminated veil, she moved with measured womanly motion. Then, another trip, the heavens would be absolutely clear, and Luna in all her effulgence. The Big Dipper in the north, with the double star in the handle much plainer than common. Then the sheeny track of light in the water, dancing and rippling. Such transformations; such pictures and poems, inimitable. ✌ ANOTHER ✌ I am studying the stars, under advantages, as I cross tonight. (It is late in February, and again extra clear.) High toward the west, the Pleiades, tremulous with delicate sparkle, in the soft heavens. Aldebaran, leading the V-shaped Hyades—and overhead Capella and her kids. Most majestic of all, in full display in the high south, Orion, vast-spread, roomy, chief histrion of the stage, with his shiny yellow rosette on his shoulder, and his three Kings—and a little to the east, Sirius, calmly arrogant, most wondrous single star. Going late ashore (I couldn't give up the beauty and soothingness of the night), as I stayed around, or slowly wandered, I heard the echoing calls of the railroad men in the West Jersey depot yard, shifting and switching trains, engines etc.; amid the general silence otherwise, and something in the acoustic quality of the air, musical, emotional effects, never thought of before. I lingered long and long, listening to them. ✌ NIGHT OF MARCH, 18 '79 ✌ One of the calm, pleasantly cool, exquisitely clear and cloudless, early spring nights—the atmosphere again that rare vitreous blue-black welcomed by astronomers. Just at 8, evening, the scene overhead of certainly solemnest beauty, never surpassed. Venus nearly down in the west, of a size and luster as if trying to outshow herself, before departing. Teeming, maternal orb—I take you again to myself. I am reminded of that spring preceding Abraham Lincoln's murder,

when I, restlessly haunting the Potomac banks around Washington city, watched you, off there, aloof, moody as myself:

As we walked up and down in the dark blue so mystic,
As we walked in silence the transparent shadowy night,
As I saw you had something to tell, as you bent to me night
   after night,
As you droop from the sky low down, as if to my side (while
   the other stars all looked on,)
As we wandered together the solemn night.

✌ With departing Venus, large to the last, and shining even to the edge of the horizon, the vast dome presents at this moment, such a spectacle! Mercury was visible just after sunset—a rare sight. Arcturus is now risen, just north of east. In calm glory all the stars of Orion hold the place of honor, in meridian, to the south—with the Dog Star a little to the left. And now, just rising, Spica, late, low, and slightly veiled. Castor, Regulus, and the rest all shining unusually clear (no Mars or Jupiter or moon till morning). On the edges of the river, many lamps twinkling—with two or three huge chimneys, a couple of miles up, belching forth molten, steady flames, volcanolike, illuminating all around—and sometimes an electric or calcium, its Dante-Inferno gleams, in far shafts, terrible, ghastly-powerful. Of later May nights, crossing, I like to watch the fishermen's little buoy lights —so pretty, so dreamy—like corpse candles—undulating delicate and lonesome on the surface of the shadowy waters, floating with the current.

THE FIRST SPRING DAY ON CHESTNUT STREET ✌ Winter, relaxing its hold, has already allowed us a foretaste of spring. As I write, yesterday afternoon's softness and brightness (after the morning fog, which gave it a better setting, by contrast) showed Chestnut Street—say between Broad and Fourth—to more advantage in its various asides, and all its stores, and gay-dressed crowds generally, than for three months past. I took a walk there between one and two. Doubtless, there were plenty of hard-up folks along the pavements, but nine-tenths of the myriad-moving human panorama to all appearance seemed flush, well fed, and fully provided. At all events it was good to be on Chestnut Street yesterday. The peddlers on the sidewalk ("sleeve-buttons, three for five cents"), the handsome little fellow with canary-bird whistles—the cane men, toy men, toothpick men—the old women squatted in a heap on the cold stone flags, with her basket of matches, pins, and tape—the young Negro mother, sitting, begging, with her two little coffee-colored twins on her lap —the beauty of the crammed conservatory of rare flowers, flaunting reds, yellows, snowy lilies, incredible orchids, at the Baldwin mansion near Twelfth Street—

the show of fine poultry, beef, fish, at the restaurants—the china stores, with glass and statuettes—the luscious tropical fruits—the streetcars plodding along, with their tintinnabulating bells—the fat, cab-looking, rapidly driven one-horse vehicles of the Post Office, squeezed full of coming or going letter carriers, so healthy and handsome and manly-looking, in their gray uniforms—the costly books, pictures, curiosities, in the windows—the gigantic policemen at most of the corners—will all be readily remembered and recognized as features of this principal avenue of Philadelphia. Chestnut Street, I have discovered, is not without individuality and its own points, even when compared with the great promenade streets of other cities. I have never been in Europe, but acquired years' familiar experience with New York's (perhaps the world's) great thoroughfare, Broadway, and possess to some extent a personal and saunterer's knowledge of St. Charles Street in New Orleans, Tremont Street in Boston, and the broad trottoirs of Pennsylvania Avenue in Washington. Of course it is a pity that Chestnut were not two or three times wider; but the street, any fine day, shows vividness, motion, variety, not easily to be surpassed. (Sparkling eyes, human faces, magnetism, well-dressed women, ambulating to and fro—with lots of fine things in the windows—are they not about the same, the civilized world over?)

> How fast the flitting figures come!
> The mild, the fierce, the stony face;
> Some bright with thoughtless smiles—and some
> Where secret tears have left their trace.

&v A few days ago one of the six-story clothing stores along here had the space inside its plate-glass show window partitioned into a little corral, and littered deeply with rich clover and hay (I could smell the odor outside), on which reposed two magnificent fat sheep, full-sized but young—the handsomest creatures of the kind I ever saw. I stopped long and long, with the crowd, to view them—one lying down chewing the cud, and one standing up, looking out, with dense-fringed patient eyes. Their wool, of a clear tawny color, with streaks of glistening black—altogether a queer sight amidst that crowded promenade of dandies, dollars, and dry goods.

UP THE HUDSON TO ULSTER COUNTY

&v APRIL 23 &v Off to New York on a little tour and visit. Leaving the hospitable, homelike quarters of my valued friends, Mr. and Mrs. J. H. Johnston—took the 4 P.M. boat, bound up the Hudson, 100 miles or so. Sunset and evening fine. Especially enjoyed the hour after we passed Cozzen's Landing—the night lit by the crescent moon and Venus, now swimming in tender glory, and now hid by the high rocks and hills of the western shore, which we hugged close. (Where I spend the next

ten days is in Ulster County and its neighborhood, with frequent morning and evening drives, observations of the river, and short rambles.) &v APRIL 24—NOON &v A little more and the sun would be oppressive. The bees are out gathering their bread from willows and other trees. I watch them returning, darting through the air or lighting on the hives, their thighs covered with the yellow forage. A solitary robin sings near. I sit in my shirtsleeves and gaze from an open bay window on the indolent scene—the thin haze, the Fishkill hills in the distance—off on the river, a sloop with slanting mainsail, and two or three little shadboats. Over on the railroad opposite, long freight trains, sometimes weighted by cylinder tanks of petroleum, thirty, forty, fifty cars in a string, panting and rumbling along in full view, but the sound softened by distance.

DAYS AT J. B.'S—TURF FIRES—SPRING

SONGS &v APRIL 26 &v At sunrise, the pure clear sound of the meadowlark. An hour later, some notes, few and simple, yet delicious and perfect, from the bush sparrow—toward noon the reedy trill of the robin. Today is the fairest, sweetest yet—penetrating warmth—a lovely veil in the air, partly heat vapor and partly from the turf fires everywhere in patches on the farms. A group of soft maples near by silently bursts out in crimson tips, buzzing all day with busy bees. The white sails of sloops and schooners glide up or down the river; and long trains of cars, with ponderous roll, or faint bell notes, almost constantly on the opposite shore. The earliest wild flowers in the woods and fields, spicy arbutus, blue liverwort, frail anemone, and the pretty white blossoms of the bloodroot. I launch out in slow rambles, discovering them. As I go along the roads I like to see the farmers' fires in patches, burning the dry brush, turf, debris. How the smoke crawls along, flat to the ground, slanting, slowly rising, reaching away, and at last dissipating! I like its acrid smell—whiffs just reaching me—welcomer than French perfume. &v The birds are plenty; of any sort, or of two or three sorts, curiously, not a sign, till suddenly some warm, gushing, sunny April (or even March) day—lo! there they are, from twig to twig, or fence to fence, flirting, singing, some mating, preparing to build. But most of them *en passant* —a fortnight, a month in these parts, and then away. As in all phases, Nature keeps up her vital, copious, eternal procession. Still, plenty of the birds hang around all or most of the season—now their love time, and era of nest building. I find flying over the river, crows, gulls, and hawks. I hear the afternoon shriek of the latter, darting about, preparing to nest. The oriole will soon be heard here, and the twanging *meoeow* of the catbird; also the kingbird, cuckoo, and the warblers. All along, there are

[84]

three peculiarly characteristic spring songs—the meadowlark's, so sweet, so alert and remonstrating (as if he said, "don't you see?" or, "can't you understand?")—the cheery, mellow, human tones of the robin (I have been trying for years to get a brief term, or phrase, that would identify and describe that robin call)—and the amorous whistle of the highhole. Insects are out plentifully at midday. ತಿ APRIL 29 ತಿ As we drove lingering along the road we heard, just after sundown, the song of the wood thrush. We stopped without a word, and listened long. The delicious notes—a sweet, artless, voluntary, simple anthem, as from the flute stops of some organ, wafted through the twilight—echoing well to us from the perpendicular high rock where, in some thick young trees' recesses at the base, sat the bird—filled our senses, our souls.

MEETING A HERMIT ತಿ I found in one of my rambles up the hills a real hermit, living in a lonesome spot, hard to get at, rocky, the view fine, with a little patch of land two rods square. A man of youngish middle age, city born and raised, had been to school, had traveled in Europe and California. I first met him once or twice on the road, and passed the time of day, with some small talk, then; the third time, he asked me to go along a bit and rest in his hut (an almost unprecedented compliment, as I heard from others afterward). He was of Quaker stock, I think; talked with ease and moderate freedom, but did not unbosom his life, or story, or tragedy, or whatever it was.

AN ULSTER COUNTY WATERFALL ತಿ I jot this mem. in a wild scene of woods and hills, where we have come to visit a waterfall. I never saw finer or more copious hemlocks, many of them large, some old and hoary. Such a sentiment to them, secretive, shaggy—what I call weatherbeaten and let-alone—a rich underlay of ferns, yew sprouts and mosses, beginning to be spotted with the early summer wild flowers. Enveloping all, the monotone and liquid gurgle from the hoarse, impetuous, copious fall—the greenish-tawny, darkly transparent waters, plunging with velocity down the rocks, with patches of milk-white foam—a stream of hurrying amber, thirty feet wide, risen far back in the hills and woods, now rushing with volume—every hundred rods a fall, and sometimes three or four in that distance. A primitive forest, druidical, solitary, and savage—not ten visitors a year—broken rocks everywhere—shade overhead, thick underfoot with leaves—a just palpable wild and delicate aroma.

WALTER DUMONT AND HIS MEDAL ತಿ As I sauntered along the high road yesterday, I stopped to watch a man near by, plowing a rough, stony field with a yoke of oxen. Usually there is much geeing and hawing, excitement, and continual noise and expletives about a job of this kind. But I noticed how different, how easy and wordless, yet firm and sufficient, the work of this young plowman. His name was Walter Dumont, a farmer and son of a farmer, working for their living. Three years ago, when the steamer *Sunnyside* was wrecked of a bitter icy night on the west bank here, Walter went out in his boat—was the first man on hand with assistance—made a way through the ice to shore, connected a line, performed work of first-class readiness, daring, danger, and saved numerous lives. Some weeks after, one evening when he was up at Esopus, among the usual loafing crowd at the country store and Post Office, there arrived the gift of an unexpected official gold medal for the quiet hero. The impromptu presentation was made to him on the spot, but he blushed, hesitated as he took it, and had nothing to say.

HUDSON RIVER SIGHTS ತಿ It was a happy thought to build the Hudson River Railroad right along the shore. The grade is already made by nature; you are sure of ventilation one side—and you are in nobody's way. I see, hear, the locomotives and cars, rumbling, roaring, flaming, smoking, constantly, away off there, night and day—less than a mile distant, and in full view by day. I like both sight and sound. Express trains thunder and lighten along; of freight trains, most of them very long, there cannot be less than a hundred a day. At night, far down, you see the headlight approaching, coming steadily on like a meteor. The river at night has its special character-beauties. The shad fishermen go forth in their boats and pay out their nets—one sitting forward, rowing, and one standing up aft, dropping it properly—marking the line with little floats bearing candles, conveying, as they glide over the water, an indescribable sentiment and doubled brightness. I like to watch the tows at night, too, with their twinkling lamps, and hear the husky panting of the steamers; or catch the sloops' and schooners' shadowy forms, like phantoms, white, silent, indefinite, out there. Then the Hudson of a clear moonlight night. ತಿ But there is one sight the very grandest. Sometimes in the fiercest driving storm of wind, rain, hail or snow, a great eagle will appear over the river, now soaring with steady and now overbended wings—always confronting the gale, or perhaps cleaving into, or at times literally *sitting* upon it. It is like reading some first-class natural tragedy or epic, or hearing martial trumpets. The splendid bird enjoys the hubbub—is adjusted and equal to it—finishes it so artistically. His pinions just oscillating—the position of his head and neck—his resistless, occasionally varied flight—now

[85]

a swirl, now an upward movement—the black clouds driving—the angry wash below—the hiss of rain, the wind's piping (perhaps the ice colliding, grunting)—he tacking or jibing—now, as it were, for a change, abandoning himself to the gale, moving with it with such velocity—and now, resuming control, he comes up against it, lord of the situation and the storm—lord, amid it, of power and savage joy. ᴆ Sometimes (as at present writing), middle of sunny afternoon, the old *Vanderbilt* steamer stalking ahead—I plainly hear her rhythmic, slushing paddles—drawing by long hawsers an immense and varied following string ("an old sow and pigs," the river folk call it). First comes a big barge, with a house built on it, and spars towering over the roof; then canal boats, a lengthened, clustering train, fastened and linked together—the one in the middle, with high staff, flaunting a broad and gaudy flag—others with the almost invariable lines of new-washed clothes, drying; two sloops and a schooner aside the tow—little wind, and that adverse—with three long, dark, empty barges bringing up the rear. People are on the boats: men lounging, women in sunbonnets, children, stovepipes with streaming smoke.

TWO CITY AREAS, CERTAIN HOURS ᴆ

NEW YORK, MAY 24, '79 ᴆ Perhaps no quarters of this city (I have returned again for a while) make more brilliant, animated, crowded, spectacular human presentations these fine May afternoons than the two I am now going to describe from personal observation. First: that area comprising Fourteenth Street (especially the short range between Broadway and Fifth Avenue) with Union Square, its adjacencies, and so retrostretching down Broadway for half a mile. All the walks here are wide, and the spaces ample and free—now flooded with liquid gold from the last two hours of powerful sunshine. The whole area at 5 o'clock, the days of my observations, must have contained from thirty to forty thousand finely dressed people, all in motion, plenty of them good-looking, many beautiful women, often youths and children, the latter in groups with their nurses—the trottoirs everywhere close-spread, thick-tangled (yet no collision, no trouble), with masses of bright color, action, and tasty toilets (surely the women dress better than ever before, and the men do too). As if New York would show these afternoons what it can do in its humanity, its choicest physique and physiognomy, and its countless prodigality of locomotion, dry goods, glitter, magnetism, and happiness. ᴆ Second: also from 5 to 7 P.M. the stretch of Fifth Avenue, all the way from the Central Park exits at Fifty-ninth Street, down to Fourteenth, especially along the high grade by Fortieth Street, and down the hill. A Mississippi of horses and

rich vehicles, not by dozens and scores, but hundreds and thousands—the broad avenue filled and crammed with them—a moving, sparkling, hurrying crush, for more than two miles. (I wonder they don't get blocked, but I believe they never do.) Altogether it is to me the marvel sight of New York. I like to get in one of the Fifth Avenue stages and ride up, stemming the swift-moving procession. I doubt if London or Paris or any city in the world can show such a carriage carnival as I have seen here five or six times these beautiful May afternoons.

CENTRAL PARK WALKS AND TALKS ᴆ

MAY 16 TO 22 ᴆ I visit Central Park now almost every day, sitting, or slowly rambling, or riding around. The whole place presents its very best appearance this current month—the full flush of the trees, the plentiful white and pink of the flowering shrubs, the emerald green of the grass spreading everywhere, yellow-dotted still with dandelions—the specialty of the plentiful gray rocks, peculiar to these grounds, cropping out, miles and miles—and over all the beauty and purity, three days out of four, of our summer skies. As I sit, placidly, early afternoon, off against Ninetieth Street, the policeman, C. C., a well-formed, sandy-complexioned young fellow, comes over and stands near me. We grow quite friendly and chatty forthwith. He is a New Yorker born and raised, and in answer to my questions tells me about the life of a New York park policeman (while he talks, keeping his eyes and ears vigilantly open, occasionally pausing and moving where he can get full views of the vistas of the road, up and down, and the spaces around). The pay is $2.40 a day (seven days to a week)—the men come on and work eight hours straight ahead, which is all that is required of them out of the twenty-four. The position has more risks than one might suppose—for instance if a team or horse runs away (which happens daily), each man is expected not only to be prompt, but to waive safety and stop wildest nags or nag (*do it*, and don't be thinking of your bones or face)—give the alarm whistle too, so that other guards may repeat, and the vehicles up and down the tracks be warned. Injuries to the men are continually happening. There is much alertness and quiet strength. (Few appreciate, I have often thought, the Ulyssean capacity, derring-do, quick readiness in emergencies, practicality, unwitting devotion and heroism, among our American young men and working people—the firemen, the railroad employees, the steamer and ferry men, the police, the conductors and drivers—the whole splendid average of native stock, city and country.) It is good work, though; and upon the whole, the Park force members like it. They see life, and the excitement keeps them up. There is not so much difficulty as might be supposed from tramps, roughs, or in keeping people "off the grass." The worst trouble of the regular Park employee is from malarial fever, chills, and the like.

A FINE AFTERNOON, 4 TO 6 ⁊ Ten thousand vehicles careering through the park this perfect afternoon. Such a show! And I have seen all—watched it narrowly, and at my leisure. Private barouches, cabs, and coupés, some fine horseflesh—lapdogs, footmen, fashions, foreigners, cockades on hats, crests on panels—the full oceanic tide of New York's wealth and "gentility." It was an impressive, rich, interminable circus on a grand scale, full of action and color in the beauty of the day, under the clear sun and moderate breeze. Family groups, couples, single drivers—of course, dresses generally elegant—much "style" (yet perhaps little or nothing, even in that direction, that fully justified itself). Through the windows of two or three of the richest carriages I saw faces almost corpselike, so ashy and listless. Indeed the whole affair exhibited less of sterling America, either in spirit or countenance, than I had counted on from such a select mass spectacle. I suppose, as a proof of limitless wealth, leisure, and the aforesaid "gentility," it was tremendous. Yet what I saw those hours (I took two other occasions, two other afternoons to watch the same scene) confirms a thought that haunts me every additional glimpse I get of our toploftical general or rather exceptional phases of wealth and fashion in this country—namely, that they are ill at ease, much too conscious, cased in too many cerements, and far from happy—that there is nothing in them which we who are poor and plain need at all envy, and that instead of the perennial smell of the grass and woods and shores, their typical redolence is of soaps and essences, very rare maybe, but suggesting the barber shop—something that turns stale and musty in a few hours anyhow. ⁊ Perhaps the show on the horseback road was prettiest. Many groups (threes a favorite number), some couples, some singly—many ladies—frequently horses or parties dashing along on a full run—fine riding the rule—a few really first-class animals. As the afternoon waned, the wheeled carriages grew less, but the saddle-riders seemed to increase. They lingered long—and I saw some charming forms and faces.

DEPARTING OF THE BIG STEAMERS ⁊ MAY 15 ⁊ A three-hours' bay trip from 12 to 3 this afternoon, accompanying the *City of Brussels* down as far as the Narrows, in behalf of some Europe-bound friends, to give them a good send-off. Our spirited little tug, the *Seth Low*, kept close to the great black *Brussels*, sometimes one side, sometimes the other, always up to

her, or even pressing ahead (like the blooded pony accompanying the royal elephant). The whole affair, from the first, was an animated, quick-passing, characteristic New York scene; the large, good-looking, well-dressed crowd on the wharf end—men and women come to see their friends depart, and bid them Godspeed—the ship's sides swarming with passengers—groups of bronze-faced sailors, with uniformed officers at their posts—the quiet directions, as she quickly unfastens and moves out, prompt to a minute—the emotional faces, adieus, and fluttering handkerchiefs, and many smiles and some tears on the wharf—the answering faces, smiles, tears, and fluttering handkerchiefs from the ship (what can be subtler and finer than this play of faces on such occasions in these responding crowds?—what go more to one's heart?)—the proud, steady, noiseless cleaving of the grand oceaner down the bay—we speeding by her side a few miles, and then turning, wheeling, amid a babel of wild hurrahs, shouted partings, earsplitting steam whistles, kissing of hands, and waving of handkerchiefs. ⁊ This departing of the big steamers, noons or afternoons —there is no better medicine when one is listless or vapory. I am fond of going down Wednesdays and Saturdays—their more special days—to watch them and the crowds on the wharves, the arriving passengers, the general bustle and activity, the eager looks from the faces, the clear-toned voices (a traveled foreigner, a musician, told me the other day she thinks an American crowd has the finest voices in the world), the whole look of the great, shapely black ships themselves, and their groups and lined sides—in the setting of our bay with the blue sky overhead. Two days after the above I saw the *Britannic*, the *Donau*, the *Helvetia*, and the *Schiedam* steam out, all off for Europe—a magnificent sight.

TWO HOURS ON THE MINNESOTA ⁊ From 7 to 9, aboard the United States school ship *Minnesota*, lying up the North River. Captain Luce sent his gig for us about sundown, to the foot of Twenty-third Street, and received us aboard with officerlike hospitality and sailor heartiness. There are several hundred youths on the *Minnesota* to be trained for efficiently manning the government Navy. I like the idea much; and, so far as I have seen tonight, I like the way it is carried out on this huge vessel. Below, on the gun deck, were gathered nearly a hundred of the boys, to give us some of their singing exercises, with a melodeon accompaniment played by one of their number. They sang with a will. The best part, however, was the sight of the young fellows themselves. I went over among them before the singing began, and talked a few minutes informally. They are from all the states; I asked for the Southerners, but could only find one, a lad from Baltimore. In age, apparently, they range from about fourteen years to nineteen or twenty. They are all of American birth, and have to pass a rigid medical examination; well-grown youths, good flesh, bright eyes, looking straight at you, healthy, intelligent, not a slouch among them, nor a menial—in every one the promise of a man. I have been to many public aggregations of young and old, and of schools and colleges, in my day, but I confess I have never been so near satisfied, so comforted (both from the fact of the school itself, and the splendid proof of our country, our composite race, and the sample promises of its good average capacities, its future) as in the collection from all parts of the United States on this Navy training ship. ("Are there going to be *any men* there?" was the dry and pregnant reply of Emerson to one who had been crowding him with the rich material statistics and possibilities of some western or Pacific region.) MAY 26 Aboard the *Minnesota* again. Lieut. Murphy kindly came for me in his boat. Enjoyed specially those brief trips to and fro—the sailors, tanned, strong, so bright and able-looking, pulling their oars in long side-swing, man-of-war style, as they rowed me across. I saw the boys in companies drilling with small arms; had a talk with Chaplain Rawson. At 11 o'clock all of us gathered to breakfast around a long table in the great wardroom —I among the rest—a genial, plentiful, hospitable affair every way—plenty to eat, and of the best; became acquainted with several new officers. This second visit, with its observations, talks (two or three at random with the boys), confirmed my first impressions.

MATURE SUMMER DAYS AND NIGHTS

AUG. 4 Forenoon—as I sit under the willow shade (have retreated down in the country again), a little bird is leisurely dousing and flirting himself amid the brook almost within reach of me. He evidently fears me not— takes me for some concomitant of the neighboring earthy banks, free bushery, and wild weeds. 6 P.M.—The last three days have been perfect ones for the season (four nights ago copious rains, with vehement thunder and lightning). I write this sitting by the creek watching my two kingfishers at their sundown sport. The strong, beautiful, joyous creatures! Their wings glisten in the slanted sunbeams as they circle and circle around, occasionally dipping and dashing the water, and making long stretches up and down the creek. Wherever I go over fields, through lanes, in by-places, blooms the white-flowering wild carrot, its delicate pat of snowflakes crowning its slender stem, gracefully oscillating in the breeze.

EXPOSITION BUILDING—NEW CITY HALL—RIVER TRIP PHILADELPHIA, AUG. 26

Last night and tonight of unsurpassed clearness, after two days' rain; moon splendor and star splendor. Being out toward the great Exposition Building, West Philadelphia, I saw it lit up, and thought I would go in. There was a ball, democratic but nice; plenty of young couples waltzing and quadrilling—music by a good string band. To the sight and hearing of these—to moderate strolls up and down the roomy spaces—to getting off aside, resting in an armchair and looking up a long while at the grand high roof with its graceful and multitudinous work of iron rods, angles, gray colors, plays of light and shade, receding into dim outlines—to absorbing (in the intervals of the string band) some capital voluntaries and rolling caprices from the big organ at the other end of the building—to sighting a shadowed figure or group or couple of lovers every now and then passing some near or farther aisle—I abandoned myself for over an hour. Returning home, riding down Market Street in an open summer car, something detained us between Fifteenth and Broad, and I got out to view better the new, three-fifths-built marble edifice, the City Hall, of magnificent proportions—a majestic and lovely show there in the moonlight—flooded all over, façades, myriad silver-white lines and carved heads and moldings, with the soft dazzle—silent, weird, beautiful—well, I know that never when finished will that magnificent pile impress one as it impressed me those fifteen minutes. Tonight, since, I have been long on the river. I watch the C-shaped Northern Crown (with the star Alshacca that blazed out so suddenly, alarmingly, one night a few years ago). The moon in her third quarter, and up nearly all night. And there, as I look eastward, my long-absent Pleiades, welcome again to sight. For an hour I enjoy the soothing and vital scene to the low splash of waves— new stars steadily, noiselessly rising in the east. As I cross the Delaware, one of the deck hands, F. R., tells me how a woman jumped overboard and was drowned a couple of hours since. It happened in mid-channel—she leaped from the forward part of the boat, which went over her. He saw her rise on the other side in the swift-running water, throw her arms and closed hands high up (white hands and bare forearms in the moonlight like a flash), and then she sank. (I found out afterward that this young fellow had promptly jumped in, swum after the poor creature, and made, though unsuccessfully, the bravest efforts to rescue her; but he didn't mention that part at all in telling me the story.)

SWALLOWS ON THE RIVER SEPT. 3

Cloudy and wet, and wind due east; air without palpable fog, but very heavy with moisture—welcome for a change. Forenoon, crossing the Delaware, I noticed unusual numbers of swallows in flight, circling, darting, graceful beyond description, close to the water. Thick, around the bows of the ferryboat as she lay tied in her slip, they flew; and as we went out I watched beyond the pierheads, and across the broad stream, their swift-winding loop-ribands of motion, down close to it, cutting and intersecting. Though I had seen swallows all my life, seemed as though I never before realized their peculiar beauty and character in the landscape. (Some time ago, for an hour, in a huge old country barn, watching these birds flying, recalled the 22d book of *The Odyssey*, where Ulysses slays the suitors, bringing things to *éclaircissement*, and Minerva, swallow-bodied, darts up through the spaces of the hall, sits high on a beam, looks complacently on the show of slaughter, and feels in her element, exulting, joyous.)

BEGIN A LONG JAUNT WEST ᴓ The following three or four months (Sept. to Dec. '79) I made quite a western journey, fetching up at Denver, Colorado, and penetrating the Rocky Mountain region enough to get a good notion of it all. Left West Philadelphia after 9 o'clock one night, middle of September, in a comfortable sleeper. Oblivious of the two or three hundred miles across Pennsylvania; at Pittsburgh in the morning to breakfast. Pretty good view of the city and Birmingham—fog and damp, smoke, coke furnaces, flames, discolored wooden houses, and vast collections of coal barges. Presently a bit of fine region, West Virginia, the Panhandle, and crossing the river, the Ohio. By day through the latter state—then Indiana—and so rocked to slumber for a second night, flying like lightning through Illinois.

IN THE SLEEPER ᴓ What a fierce, weird pleasure to lie in my berth at night in the luxurious palace car, drawn by the mighty Baldwin—embodying, and filling me, too, full of the swiftest motion and most resistless strength! It is late, perhaps midnight or after—distances joined like magic—as we speed through Harrisburg, Columbus, Indianapolis. The element of danger adds zest to it all. On we go, rumbling and flashing, with our loud whinnies thrown out from time to time, or trumpet blasts, into the darkness. Passing the homes of men, the farms, barns, cattle—the silent villages. And the car itself, the sleeper, with curtains drawn and lights turned down—in the berths the slumberers, many of them women and children—as on, on, on, we fly like lightning through the night—how strangely sound and sweet they sleep! (They say the French Voltaire in his time designated the grand opera and a ship of war the most signal illustrations of the growth of humanity's and art's advance beyond primitive barbarism. Perhaps if the witty philosopher were here these days, and went in the

same car with perfect bedding and feed from New York to San Francisco, he would shift his type and sample to one of our American sleepers.)

MISSOURI STATE ᴓ We should have made the run of 960 miles from Philadelphia to St. Louis in thirty-six hours, but we had a collision and bad locomotive smash about two-thirds of the way, which set us back. So merely stopping overnight that time in St. Louis, I sped on westward. As I crossed Missouri State the whole distance by the St. Louis and Kansas City Northern Railroad, a fine early autumn day, I thought my eyes had never looked on scenes of greater pastoral beauty. For over two hundred miles successive rolling prairies, agriculturally perfect viewed by Pennsylvania and New Jersey eyes, and dotted here and there with fine timber. Yet fine as the land is, it isn't the finest portion (there is a bed of impervious clay and hardpan beneath this section that holds water too firmly, "drowns the land in wet weather, and bakes it in dry," as a cynical farmer told me). South are some richer tracts, though perhaps the beauty spots of the state are the northwestern counties. Altogether, I am clear (now, and from what I have seen and learned since) that Missouri, in climate, soil, relative situation, wheat, grass, mines, railroads, and every important materialistic respect, stands in the front rank of the Union. Of Missouri averaged politically and socially I have heard all sorts of talk, some pretty severe—but I should have no fear myself of getting along safely and comfortably anywhere among the Missourians. They raise a good deal of tobacco. You see at this time quantities of the light greenish-gray leaves pulled and hanging out to dry on temporary frameworks or rows of sticks. Looks much like the mullein familiar to eastern eyes.

LAWRENCE AND TOPEKA, KANSAS ᴓ We thought of stopping in Kansas City, but when we got there we found a train ready and a crowd of hospitable Kansians to take us on to Lawrence, to which I proceeded. I shall not soon forget my good days in L., in company with Judge Usher and his sons (especially John and Linton), true westerners of the noblest type. Nor the similar days in Topeka. Nor the brotherly kindness of my R.R. friends there, and the city and state officials. Lawrence and Topeka are large, bustling, half-rural, handsome cities. I took two or three long drives about the latter, drawn by a spirited team over smooth roads.

THE PRAIRIES ᴓ AND AN UNDELIVERED SPEECH ᴓ At a large popular meeting at Topeka—the Kansas State Silver Wedding, fifteen or twenty thousand people—I had been erroneously billed to deliver a poem. As I seemed to be made much of, and wanted to be good-natured, I hastily penciled out the following little speech. Unfortunately (or fortunately) I had such a good time and rest, and talk and dinner, with the U. boys, that I let the hours slip away and didn't drive over to the meeting and speak my piece. But here it is just the same: *My friends, your bills announce me as giving a poem; but I have no poem—have composed none for this occasion. And I can honestly say I am now glad of it. Under these skies resplendent in September beauty—amid the peculiar landscape you are used to, but which is new to me— these interminable and stately prairies—in the freedom and vigor and sane enthusiasm of this perfect western air and autumn sunshine—it seems to me a poem would be almost an impertinence. But if you care to have a word from me, I should speak it about these very prairies; they impress me most, of all the objective shows I see or have seen on this, my first real visit to the West. As I have rolled rapidly hither for more than a thousand miles, through fair Ohio, through bread-raising Indiana and Illinois—through ample Missouri, that contains and raises everything; as I have partially explored your charming city during the last two days, and, standing on Oread Hill, by the University, have launched my view across broad expanses of living green, in every direction—I have again been most impressed, I say, and shall remain for the rest of my life most impressed, with that feature of the topography of your western central world—that vast Something, stretching out on its own unbounded scale, unconfined, which there is in these prairies, combining the real and ideal, and beautiful as dreams.* ❧ *I wonder indeed if the people of this continental inland West know how much of first-class art they have in these prairies—how original and all your own—how much of the influences of a character for your future humanity, broad, patriotic, heroic, and new? How entirely they tally on land the grandeur and superb monotony of the skies of heaven, and the ocean with its waters? How freeing, soothing, nourishing they are to the soul?* ❧ *Then is it not subtly they who have given us our leading modern Americans, Lincoln and Grant? —vast-spread, average men—their foregrounds of character altogether practical and real, yet (to those who have eyes to see) with finest backgrounds of the ideal, towering high as any. And do we not see, in them, foreshadowings of the future races that shall fill these prairies?* ❧ *Not but what the Yankee and Atlantic states, and every other part—Texas, and the states flanking the southeast and the Gulf of Mexico—the Pacific shore empire—the Territories and Lakes, and the Canada line (the day is not yet, but it will come, including Canada entire)—are equally and integrally and indissolubly this nation, the sine qua non of the human, political, and commercial New World. But this favored central area of (in round numbers) two thousand miles square seems fated to be the home both of what I would call America's distinctive ideas and distinctive realities.*

ON TO DENVER—A FRONTIER INCIDENT ❧ The jaunt of five or six hundred miles from Topeka to Denver took me through a variety of country, but all unmistakably prolific, western, American, and on the largest scale. For a long distance we follow the line of the Kansas River (I like better the old name, Kaw), a stretch of very rich, dark soil, famed for its wheat, and called the Golden Belt—then plains and plains, hour after hour—Ellsworth County, the center of the state—where I must stop a moment to tell a characteristic story of early days—scene, the very spot where I am passing—time, 1868. In a scrimmage at some public gathering in the town, A. had shot B. quite badly, but had not killed him. The sober men of Ellsworth conferred with one another and decided that A. deserved punishment. As they wished to set a good example and establish their reputation the reverse of a lynching town, they open an informal court and bring both men before them for deliberate trial. Soon as this trial begins the wounded man is led forward to give his testimony. Seeing his enemy in durance and unarmed, B. walks suddenly up in a fury and shoots A. through the head— shoots him dead. The court is instantly adjourned, and its unanimous members, without a word of debate, walk the murderer B. out, wounded as he is, and hang him. ❧ In due time we reach Denver, which city I fall in love with from the first, and have that feeling confirmed, the longer I stay there. One of my pleasantest days was a jaunt, via Platte Canyon, to Leadville.

AN HOUR ON KENOSHA SUMMIT ❧ Jottings from the Rocky Mountains, mostly penciled during a day's trip over the South Park R.R., returning from Leadville, and especially the hour we were detained (much to my satisfaction) at Kenosha Summit. As afternoon advances, novelties, far-reaching splendors, accumulate under the bright sun in this pure air. But I had better commence with the day. ❧ The confronting of Platte Canyon just at dawn, after a ten miles' ride in early darkness on the rail from Denver—the seasonable stoppage at the entrance of the canyon, and good breakfast of eggs, trout, and nice griddlecakes—then as we travel on, and get well in the gorge, all the wonders, beauty, savage power of the scene—the wild stream of water, from sources of snows, brawling continually in sight one side—the dazzling sun, and the morning lights on the rocks—such turns and grades in the track, squirming around corners, or up and down hills—far glimpses of a hundred peaks, titanic necklaces, stretching north and south—the huge rightly named Dome Rock—and as we dash along, others similar, simple, monolithic, elephantine.

AN EGOTISTICAL "FIND" 𐫱 "I have found the law of my own poems," was the unspoken but more and more decided feeling that came to me as I passed, hour after hour, amid all this grim yet joyous elemental abandon—this plenitude of material, entire absence of art, untrammeled play of primitive Nature—the chasm, the gorge, the crystal mountain stream, repeated scores, hundreds of miles—the broad handling and absolute uncrampedness—the fantastic forms, bathed in transparent browns, faint reds and grays, towering sometimes a thousand, sometimes two or three thousand feet high—at their tops now and then huge masses poised, and mixing with the clouds, with only their outlines, hazed in misty lilac, visible. ("In Nature's grandest shows," says an old Dutch writer, an ecclesiastic, "amid the ocean's depth, if so might be, or countless worlds rolling above at night, a man thinks of them, weighs all, not for themselves or the abstract, but with reference to his own personality, and how they may affect him or color his destinies.")

NEW SENSES—NEW JOYS 𐫱 We follow the stream of amber and bronze brawling along its bed, with its frequent cascades and snow-white foam. Through the canyon we fly—mountains not only each side, but seemingly, till we get near, right in front of us—every rood a new view flashing, and each flash defying description—on the almost perpendicular sides, clinging pines, cedars, spruces, crimson sumac bushes, spots of wild grass—but dominating all, those towering rocks, rocks, rocks, bathed in delicate varicolors, with the clear sky of autumn overhead. New senses, new joys, seem developed. Talk as you like, a typical Rocky Mountain canyon, or a limitless, sealike stretch of the great Kansas or Colorado plains, under favoring circumstances, tallies, perhaps expresses, certainly awakes, those grandest and subtlest element emotions in the human soul, that all the marble temples and sculptures from Phidias to Thorwaldsen—all paintings, poems, reminiscences, or even music, probably never can.

STEAM POWER, TELEGRAPHS, ETC. 𐫱 I get out on a ten minutes' stoppage at Deer Creek, to enjoy the unequaled combination of hill, stone, and wood. As we speed again, the yellow granite in the sunshine, with natural spires, minarets, castellated perches far aloft—then long stretches of straight-upright palisades, rhinoceros color—then gamboge and tinted chromos. Ever the best of my pleasures the cool-fresh Colorado atmosphere, yet sufficiently warm. Signs of man's restless advent and pioneerage, hard as Nature's face is—deserted dugouts by dozens in the side-hills—the scantling hut, the telegraph pole, the smoke of some impromptu chimney or outdoor fire—at intervals little settlements of log houses, or parties of surveyors or telegraph builders, with their comfortable tents. Once, a canvas office where you could send a message by electricity anywhere around the world! Yes, pronounced signs of the man of latest dates, dauntlessly grappling with these grisliest shows of the old cosmos. At several places steam sawmills, with their piles of logs and boards, and the pipes puffing. Occasionally Platte Canyon expanding into a grassy flat of a few acres. At one such place, toward the end, where we stop, and I get out to stretch my legs, as I look skyward, or rather mountaintopward, a huge hawk or eagle (a rare sight here) is idly soaring, balancing along the ether, now sinking low and coming quite near, and then up again in stately, languid circles—then higher, higher, slanting to the north, and gradually out of sight.

AMERICA'S BACKBONE 𐫱 I jot these lines literally at Kenosha Summit, where we return, afternoon, and take a long rest, 10,000 feet above sea level. At this immense height the South Park stretches fifty miles before me. Mountainous chains and peaks in every variety of perspective, every hue of vista, fringe the view, in nearer, or middle, or far-dim distance, or fade on the horizon. We have now reached, penetrated the Rockies (Hayden calls it the Front Range) for a hundred miles or so; and though these chains spread away in every direction, especially north and south, thousands and thousands farther, I have seen specimens of the utmost of them, and know henceforth at least what they are and what they look like. Not themselves alone, for they typify stretches and areas of half the globe—are, in fact, the vertebræ or backbone of our hemisphere. As the anatomists say a man is only a spine, topped, footed, breasted, and radiated, so the whole Western world is, in a sense, but an expansion of these mountains. In South America they are the Andes, in Central America and Mexico the Cordilleras, and in our states they go under different names—in California the Coast and Cascade ranges—thence more eastwardly the Sierra Nevadas—but mainly and more centrally here the Rocky Mountains proper, with many an elevation such as Lincoln's, Grey's, Harvard's, Yale's, Long's, and Pike's Peaks, all over 14,000 feet high. (East, the highest peaks of the Alleghanies, the Adirondacks, the Catskills, and the White Mountains, range from 2,000 to 5,500 feet—only Mount Washington, in the latter, 6,300 feet.)

THE PARKS 𐫱 In the midst of all here, lie such beautiful contrasts as the sunken basins of the North, Middle, and South Parks (the latter I am now on one side of, and overlooking), each the size of a large, level, almost quadrangular, grassy, western county, walled in by walls of hills, and each park the source of a river. The ones I specify are the largest in Colorado, but the whole of that state, and of Wyoming, Utah, Nevada, and western California, through their sierras and ravines, are copiously marked by similar spreads and openings, many of the small ones of paradisiac loveliness and perfection, with their offsets of mountains, streams, atmosphere, and hues beyond compare.

ART FEATURES ᐧ Talk, I say again, of going to Europe, of visiting the ruins of feudal castles, or Colosseum remains, or kings' palaces—when you can come *here*. The alternations one gets, too; after the Illinois and Kansas prairies of a thousand miles—smooth and easy areas of the corn and wheat of ten million democratic farms in the future—here start up in every conceivable presentation of shape, these nonutilitarian piles, coping the skies, emanating a beauty, terror, power, more than Dante or Angelo ever knew. Yes, I think the chyle of not only poetry and painting, but oratory, and even the metaphysics and music fit for the New World, before being finally assimilated, need first and feeding visits here. ᐧ MOUNTAIN STREAMS ᐧ The spiritual contrast and ethereality of the whole region consists largely to me in its never-absent peculiar streams—the snows of inaccessible upper areas melting and running down through the gorges continually. Nothing like the water of pastoral plains, or creeks with wooded banks and turf, or anything of the kind elsewhere. The shapes that element takes in the shows of the globe cannot be fully understood by an artist until he has studied these unique rivulets. ᐧ AERIAL EFFECTS ᐧ But perhaps as I gaze around me the rarest sight of all is in atmospheric hues. The prairies—as I crossed them in my journey hither—and these mountains and parks, seem to me to afford new lights and shades. Everywhere the aerial gradations and sky effects inimitable; nowhere else such perspectives, such transparent lilacs and grays. I can conceive of some superior landscape painter, some fine colorist, after sketching awhile out here, discarding all his previous work, delightful to stock exhibition amateurs, as muddy, raw, and artificial. Near one's eye ranges an infinite variety; high up, the bare whitey-brown, above timber line; in certain spots afar, patches of snow any time of year (no trees, no flowers, no birds, at those chilling altitudes). As I write I see the Snowy Range through the blue mist, beautiful and far off. I plainly see the patches of snow.

DENVER IMPRESSIONS ᐧ Through the long-lingering half-light of the most superb of evenings we returned to Denver, where I stayed several days leisurely exploring, receiving impressions, with which I may as well taper off this memorandum, itemizing what I saw there. The best was the men, three-fourths of them large, able, calm, alert, American. And cash! Why, they create it here. Out in the smelting works (the biggest and most improved ones, for the precious metals, in the world), I saw long rows of vats, pans, covered by bubbling-boiling water, and filled with pure silver, four or five inches thick, many thousand dollars' worth in a pan. The foreman who was showing me shoveled it carelessly up with a little wooden shovel, as one might toss beans. Then large silver bricks, worth $2,000 a brick, dozens of piles, twenty in a pile. In one place in the mountains, at a mining camp, I had a few days before seen rough bullion on the ground in the open air, like the confectioner's pyramids at some swell dinner in New York. (Such a sweet morsel to roll over with a poor author's pen and ink—and appropriate to slip in here—that the silver product of Colorado and Utah, with the gold product of California, New Mexico, Nevada, and Dakota, foots up an addition to the world's coin of considerably over a hundred millions every year.) ᐧ A city, this Denver, well laid out—Laramie Street, and 15th and 16th and Champa Streets, with others, particularly fine—some with tall storehouses of stone or iron, and windows of plate glass—all the streets with little canals of mountain water running along the sides—plenty of people, "business," modernness—yet not without a certain racy wild smack all its own. A place of fast horses (many mares with their colts), and I saw lots of big greyhounds for antelope hunting. Now and then groups of miners, some just come in, some starting out, very picturesque. ᐧ One of the papers here interviewed me, and reported me as saying offhand: "I have lived in or visited all the great cities on the Atlantic third of the republic—Boston, Brooklyn with its hills, New Orleans, Baltimore, stately Washington, broad Philadelphia, teeming Cincinnati and Chicago, and for thirty years in that wonder, washed by hurried and glittering tides, my own New York, not only the New World's but the world's city—but, newcomer to Denver as I am, and threading its streets, breathing its air, warmed by its sunshine, and having what there is of its human as well as aerial ozone flashed upon me now for only three or four days, I am very much like a man feels sometimes toward certain people he meets with, warms to, and hardly knows why. I, too, can hardly tell why, but as I entered the city in the slight haze of a late September afternoon, and have breathed its air, and slept well o' nights, and have roamed or rode leisurely, and watched the comers and goers at the hotels, and absorbed the climatic magnetism of this curiously attractive region, there has steadily grown upon me a feeling of affection for the spot, which, sudden as it is, has become so definite and strong that I must put it on record." ᏸᎤ So much for my feeling toward the Queen City of the plains and peaks, where she sits in her delicious rare atmosphere, over 5,000 feet above sea level, irrigated by mountain streams, one way looking east over the prairies for a thousand miles, and having the other, westward, in constant view by day, draped in their violet haze, mountaintops innumerable. Yes, I fell in love with Denver, and even felt a wish to spend my declining and dying days there.

I TURN SOUTH—AND THEN EAST AGAIN ᏸᎤ Leave Denver at 8 A.M. by the Rio Grande R.R. going south. Mountains constantly in sight in the apparently near distance, veiled slightly, but still clear and very grand—their cones, colors, sides, distinct against the sky—hundreds, it seemed thousands, interminable necklaces of them, their tops and slopes hazed more or less slightly in that blue-gray, under the autumn sun, for over a hundred miles—the most spiritual show of objective Nature I ever beheld, or ever thought possible. Occasionally the light strengthens, making a contrast of yellow-tinged silver on one side, with dark and shaded gray on the other. I took a long look at Pike's Peak, and was a little disappointed. (I suppose I had expected something stunning.) Our view over plains to the left stretches amply, with corrals here and there, the frequent cactus and wild sage, and herds of cattle feeding. Thus about 120 miles to Pueblo. At that town we board the comfortable and well-equipped Atchison, Topeka and Sante Fe R.R., now striking east.

UNFULFILLED WANTS—THE ARKANSAS RIVER ᏸᎤ I had wanted to go to the Yellowstone River region—wanted specially to see the National Park, and the geysers and the "hoo-doo" or goblin land of that country; indeed, hesitated a little at Pueblo, the turning point—wanted to thread the Veta Pass—wanted to go over the Santa Fe Trail away southwestward to New Mexico—but turned and set my face eastward—leaving behind me whetting glimpse-tastes of southeastern Colorado, Pueblo, Bald Mountain, the Spanish peaks, Sangre de Cristos, Mile Shoe Curve (which my veteran friend on the locomotive told me was "the boss railroad curve of the universe"), Fort Garland on the plains, Veta, and the three great peaks of the Sierra Blancas. ᏸᎤ The Arkansas River plays quite a part in the whole of this region—I see it, or its high-cut rocky northern shore, for miles, and cross and recross it frequently, as it winds and squirms like a snake. The plains vary here even more than usual—sometimes a long sterile stretch of scores of miles—then green, fertile, and grassy an equal length. Some very large herds of sheep.

(One wants new words in writing about these plains, and all the inland American West—the terms, *far*, *large*, *vast*, etc., are insufficient.)

A SILENT LITTLE FOLLOWER—THE CO-REOPSIS ᏸᎤ Here I must say a word about a little follower, present even now before my eyes. I have been accompanied on my whole journey from Barnegat to Pike's Peak by a pleasant floricultural friend, or rather millions of friends—nothing more or less than a hardy little yellow five-petaled September and October wild flower, growing I think everywhere in the middle and northern United States. I had seen it on the Hudson and over Long Island, and along the banks of the Delaware and through New Jersey (as years ago up the Connecticut, and one fall by Lake Champlain). This trip it followed me regularly, with its slender stem and eyes of gold, from Cape May to the Kaw valley, and so through the canyon and to these plains. In Missouri I saw immense fields all bright with it. Toward western Illinois I woke up one morning in the sleeper and the first thing when I drew the curtain of my berth and looked out was its pretty countenance and bending neck. ᏸᎤ SEPT. 25TH ᏸᎤ Early morning—still going east after we leave Sterling, Kansas, where I stopped a day and night. The sun up about half an hour; nothing can be fresher or more beautiful than this time, this region. I see quite a field of my yellow flower in full bloom. At intervals dots of nice two-story houses, as we ride swiftly by. Over the immense area, flat as a floor, visible for twenty miles in every direction in the clear air, a prevalence of autumn-drab and reddish-tawny herbage—sparse stacks of hay and enclosures, breaking the landscape—as we rumble by, flocks of prairie hens starting up. Between Sterling and Florence a fine country. (Remembrances to E. L., my old-young soldier friend of war times, and his wife and boy at S.)

THE PRAIRIES AND GREAT PLAINS IN POETRY ᏸᎤ AFTER TRAVELING ILLINOIS, MISSOURI, KANSAS, AND COLORADO ᏸᎤ Grand as the thought that doubtless the child is already born who will see a hundred millions of people, the most prosperous and advanced of the world, inhabiting these prairies, the Great Plains, and the valley of the Mississippi, I could not help thinking it would be grander still to see all those inimitable American areas fused in the alembic of a perfect poem, or other esthetic work, entirely western, fresh, and limitless—altogether our own, without a trace or taste of Europe's soil, reminiscence, technical letter, or spirit. My days and nights, as I travel here—what an exhilaration!—not the air alone, and the sense of vastness, but every local sight and feature. Everywhere something characteristic—the cactuses, pinks, buffalo grass, wild sage—the receding perspective, and the far circle-line of the horizon all times of day, especially forenoon—the clear, pure, cool, rarefied nutriment for the lungs, previously quite unknown—the black patches and streaks left by surface conflagrations—the deep-plowed furrow of the fireguard—the slanting snow-racks built all along to shield the railroad from winter drifts—the prairie dogs and the herds of antelope—the curious "dry rivers"—occasionally a dugout or corral—Fort Riley and Fort Wallace—those towns of the northern plains (like ships on the sea). Eagle Tail, Coyote, Cheyenne, Agate, Monotony, Kit Carson—with ever the anthill and the buffalo wallow—ever the herds of cattle and the cowboys ("cow punchers"), to me a strangely interesting class, bright-eyed as hawks, with their swarthy complexions and their broad-brimmed hats—apparently always on horseback, with loose arms slightly raised and swinging as they ride.

THE SPANISH PEAKS—EVENING ON THE PLAINS ℘ Between Pueblo and Bent's Fort, southward, in a clear afternoon sun spell, I catch exceptionally good glimpses of the Spanish Peaks. We are in southeastern Colorado—pass immense herds of cattle as our first-class locomotive rushes us along—two or three times crossing the Arkansas, which we follow many miles, and of which river I get fine views, sometimes for quite a distance, its stony, upright, not very high, palisade banks, and then its muddy flats. We pass Fort Lyon—lots of adobe houses—limitless pasturage, appropriately flecked with those herds of cattle—in due time the declining sun in the west—a sky of limpid pearl over all—and so evening on the Great Plains. A calm, pensive, boundless landscape—the perpendicular rocks of north Arkansas, hued in twilight—a thin line of violet on the southwestern horizon—the palpable coolness and slight aroma—a belated cowboy with some unruly member of his herd—an emigrant wagon toiling yet a little further, the horses slow and tired—two men, apparently father and son, jogging along on foot—and around all the indescribable *chiaroscuro* and sentiment (profounder than anything at sea) athwart these endless wilds.

AMERICA'S CHARACTERISTIC LAND-SCAPE ℘ Speaking generally as to the capacity and sure future destiny of that plain and prairie area (larger than any European kingdom) it is the inexhaustible land of wheat, maize, wool, flax, coal, iron, beef and pork, butter and cheese, apples and grapes—land of ten million virgin farms—to the eye at present wild and unproductive—yet experts say that upon it when irrigated may easily be grown enough wheat to feed the world. Then as to scenery (giving my own thought and feeling), while I know the standard claim is that Yosemite, Niagara Falls, the upper Yellowstone and the like, afford the greatest natural shows, I am not so sure but the prairies and plains, while less stunning at first sight, last longer, fill the esthetic sense fuller, precede all the rest, and make North America's characteristic landscape. ℘ Indeed through the whole of this journey, with all its shows and varieties, what most impressed me, and will longest remain with me, are these same prairies. Day after day, and night after night, to my eyes, to all my senses—the esthetic one most of all—they silently and broadly unfolded. Even their simplest statistics are sublime.

EARTH'S MOST IMPORTANT STREAM ℘ The valley of the Mississippi river and its tributaries (this stream and its adjuncts involve a big part of the question) comprehends more than twelve hundred thousand square miles, the greater part prairies. It is by far the most important stream on the globe, and would seem to have been marked out by design, slow-flowing from north to south, through a dozen climates, all fitted for man's healthy occupancy, its outlet unfrozen all the year, and its line forming a safe, cheap continental avenue for commerce and passage from the north temperate to the torrid zone. Not even the mighty Amazon (though larger in volume) on its line of east and west—not the Nile in Africa, nor the Danube in Europe, nor the three great rivers of China, compare with it. Only the Mediterranean Sea has played some such part in history, and all through the past, as the Mississippi is destined to play in the future. By its demesnes, watered and welded by its branches, the Missouri, the Ohio, the Arkansas, the Red, the Yazoo, the St. Francis, and others, it already compacts twenty-five millions of people, not merely the most peaceful and money-making, but the most restless and warlike on earth. Its valley, or reach, is rapidly concentrating the political power of the American Union. One almost thinks it *is* the Union—or soon will be. Take it out, with its radiations, and what would be left? From the car windows through Indiana, Illinois, Missouri, or stopping some days along the Topeka and Sante Fe road, in southern Kansas, and indeed wherever I went, hundreds and thousands of miles through this region, my eyes feasted on primitive and rich meadows, some of them partially inhabited, but far, immensely far more untouched, unbroken—and much of it more lovely and fertile in its unplowed innocence than the fair and valuable fields of New York's, Pennsylvania's, Maryland's, or Virginia's richest farms.

PRAIRIE ANALOGIES—THE TREE QUES-
TION ᕧ The word *prairie* is French, and means literally meadow. The cosmical analogies of our North
American plains are the Steppes of Asia, the Pampas
and Llanos of South America, and perhaps the Saharas
of Africa. Some think the plains have been originally
lake beds; others attribute the absence of forests to the
fires that almost annually sweep over them (the cause, in
vulgar estimation, of Indian summer). The tree question
will soon become a grave one. Although the Atlantic
slope, the Rocky Mountain region, and the southern
portion of the Mississippi valley are well wooded, there
are here stretches of hundreds and thousands of miles
where either not a tree grows, or often useless destruction has prevailed; and the matter of the cultivation and
spread of forests may well be pressed upon thinkers who
look to the coming generations of the prairie States.

MISSISSIPPI VALLEY LITERATURE ᕧ
Lying by one rainy day in Missouri to rest after quite a
long exploration—first trying a big volume I found
there of *Milton, Young, Gray, Beattie, and Collins,* but
giving it up for a bad job—enjoying however for awhile,
as often before, the reading of Walter Scott's poems,
Lay of the Last Minstrel, Marmion, and so on—I stopped
and laid down the book, and pondered the thought of a
poetry that should in due time express and supply the
teeming region I was in the midst of and have briefly
touched upon. One's mind needs but a moment's deliberation anywhere in the United States to see clearly
enough that all the prevalent book and library poets,
either as imported from Great Britain, or followed and
doppelganged here, are foreign to our States, copiously
as they are read by us all. But to fully understand not
only how absolutely in opposition to our times and
lands, and how little and cramped, and what anachro-
nisms and absurdities many of their pages are, for American purposes, one must dwell or travel awhile in Missouri, Kansas, and Colorado, and get rapport with their
people and country. ᕧ Will the day ever come—no
matter how long deferred—when those models and lay
figures from the British islands—and even the precious
traditions of the classics will—be reminiscences, studies
only? The pure breath, primitiveness, boundless prodigality and amplitude, strange mixture of delicacy and
power, of continence, of real and ideal, and of all original and first-class elements, of these prairies, the Rocky
Mountains, and of the Mississippi and Missouri Rivers—
will they ever appear in, and in some sort form a standard for our poetry and art? (I sometimes think that even
the ambition of my friend Joaquin Miller to put them in,
and illustrate them, places him ahead of the whole
crowd.) ᕧ Not long ago I was down New York Bay,

on a steamer, watching the sunset over the dark-green
heights of Navesink, and viewing all that inimitable
spread of shore, shipping, and sea, around Sandy Hook.
But an intervening week or two, and my eyes catch the
shadowy outlines of the Spanish Peaks. In the more than
two thousand miles between, though of infinite and
paradoxical variety, a curious and absolute fusion is
doubtless steadily annealing, compacting, identifying
all. But subtler and wider and more solid (to produce
such compaction) than the laws of the states, or the
common ground of Congress or the Supreme Court, or
the grim welding of our national wars, or the steel ties of
railroads, or all the kneading and fusing processes of our
material and business history, past or present, would in
my opinion be a great throbbing, vital, imaginative
work, or series of works, or literature, in constructing
which the plains, the prairies, and the Mississippi River,
with the demesnes of its varied and ample valley, should
be the concrete background, and America's humanity,
passions, struggles, hopes, there and now—an *éclaircissement* as it is and is to be, on the stage of the New World,
of all Time's hitherto drama of war, romance, and evolution—should furnish the lambent fire, the ideal.

AN INTERVIEWER'S ITEM ᕧ OCT. 17, '79
ᕧ Today one of the newspapers of St. Louis prints the
following informal remarks of mine on American, especially Western literature: "We called on Mr. Whitman
yesterday and after a somewhat desultory conversation
abruptly asked him: 'Do you think we are to have a
distinctively American literature?' 'It seems to me,' said
he, 'that our work at present is to lay the foundations of
a great nation in products, in agriculture, in commerce,
in networks of intercommunication, and in all that relates to the comforts of vast masses of men and families,
with freedom of speech, ecclesiasticism, etc. These we
have founded and are carrying out on a grander scale
than ever hitherto, and Ohio, Illinois, Indiana, Missouri,
Kansas, and Colorado seem to me to be the seat and field
of these very facts and ideas. Materialistic prosperity in
all its varied forms, with those other points that I mentioned, intercommunication and freedom, are first to be
attended to. When those have their results and get settled, then a literature worthy of us will begin to be defined. Our American superiority and vitality are in the
bulk of our people, not in a gentry like the old world.
The greatness of our army during the Secession War was
in the rank and file, and so with the nation. Other lands
have their vitality in a few, a class, but we have it in the
bulk of the people. Our leading men are not of much
account and never have been, but the average of the
people is immense, beyond all history. Sometimes I
think in all departments, literature and art included, that

will be the way our superiority will exhibit itself. We will not have great individuals or great leaders, but a great average bulk, unprecedentedly great.' "

THE WOMEN OF THE WEST ℘ KANSAS CITY ℘ I am not so well satisfied with what I see of the women of the prairie cities. I am writing this where I sit leisurely in a store in Main Street, Kansas City, a streaming crowd on the sidewalks flowing by. The ladies (and the same in Denver) are all fashionably dressed, and have the look of "gentility" in face, manner, and action; but they do *not* have, either in physique or the mentality appropriate to them, any high native originality of spirit or body (as the men certainly have, appropriate to them). They are "intellectual" and fashionable, but dyspeptic-looking and generally doll-like; their ambition evidently is to copy their eastern sisters. Something far different and in advance must appear, to tally and complete the superb masculinity of the West, and maintain and continue it.

THE SILENT GENERAL ℘ SEPT. 28, '79 ℘ So General Grant, after circumambiating the world, has arrived home again—landed in San Francisco yesterday, from the ship *City of Tokio* from Japan. What a man he is! what a history! what an illustration—his life—of the capacities of that American individuality common to us all. Cynical critics are wondering "what the people can see in Grant" to make such a hubbub about. They aver (and it is no doubt true) that he has hardly the average of our day's literary and scholastic culture, and absolutely no pronounced genius or conventional eminence of any sort. Correct: but he proves how an average western farmer, mechanic, boatman, carried by tides of circumstances, perhaps caprices, into a position of incredible military or civic responsibilities (history has presented none more trying, no born monarch's, no mark more shining for attack or envy), may steer his way fitly and steadily through them all, carrying the country and himself with credit year after year—command over a million armed men—fight more than fifty pitched battles—rule for eight years a land larger than all the kingdoms of Europe combined—and then, retiring, quietly (with a cigar in his mouth) make the promenade of the whole world, through its courts and coteries, and kings and czars and mikados, and splendidest glitters and etiquettes, as phlegmatically as he ever walked the portico of a Missouri hotel after dinner. I say all this is what people like—and I am sure I like it. Seems to me it transcends Plutarch. How those old Greeks, indeed, would have seized on him! A mere plain man—no art, no poetry—only practical sense, ability to do, or try his best to do, what devolved upon him. A common trader, moneymaker, tanner, farmer of Illinois—general for the republic, in its terrific struggle with itself, in the war of attempted secession—President following (a task of peace, more difficult than the war itself)—nothing heroic, as the authorities put it—and yet the greatest hero. The gods, the destinies, seem to have concentrated upon him.

PRESIDENT HAYES'S SPEECHES ℘ SEPT. 30 ℘ I see President Hayes has come out West, passing quite informally from point to point, with his wife and a small cortege of big officers, receiving ovations, and making daily and sometimes double-daily addresses to the people. To these addresses—all impromptu, and some would call them ephemeral—I feel to devote a memorandum. They are shrewd, good-natured, face-to-face speeches, on easy topics not too deep; but they give me some revised ideas of oratory—of a new, opportune theory and practice of that art, quite changed from the classic rules, and adapted to our days, our occasions, to American democracy, and to the swarming populations of the West. I hear them criticised as wanting in dignity, but to me they are just what they should be, considering all the circumstances, who they come from, and whom they are addressed to. Underneath, his objects are to compact and fraternize the States, encourage their materialistic and industrial development, soothe and expand their self-poise, and tie all and each with resistless double ties not only of intertrade barter, but human comradeship. ℘ From Kansas City I went on to St. Louis, where I remained nearly three months, with my brother, T. J. W., and my dear nieces.

ST. LOUIS MEMORANDA ℘ OCT., NOV., AND DEC., '79 ℘ The points of St. Louis are its position, its absolute wealth (the long accumulations of time and trade, solid riches, probably a higher average thereof than any city), the unrivaled amplitude of its well-laid-out environage of broad plateaus, for future expansion —and the great state of which it is the head. It fuses northern and southern qualities, perhaps native and foreign ones, to perfection, rendezvous the whole stretch of the Mississippi and Missouri Rivers, and its American electricity goes well with its German phlegm. Fourth, Fifth, and Third Streets are store streets, showy, modern, metropolitan, with hurrying crowds, vehicles, horsecars, hubbub, plenty of people, rich goods, plate-glass windows, iron fronts often five or six stories high. You can purchase anything in St. Louis (in most of the big western cities for the matter of that) just as readily and cheaply as in the Atlantic marts. Often in going about the town you see reminders of old, even decayed civilization. The water of the west, in some places, is not good, but they make it up here by plenty of very fair wine and inexhaustible quantities of the best beer in the world. There are immense establishments for slaughtering beef and pork—and I saw flocks of sheep, 5,000 in a flock. (In Kansas City I had visited a packing establishment that kills and packs an average of 2,500 hogs a day the whole year round, for export. Another in Atchison, Kansas, same extent; others nearly equal elsewhere. And just as big ones here.)

NIGHTS ON THE MISSISSIPPI ൠ OCT. 29TH, 30TH, AND 31ST ൠ Wonderfully fine, with the full harvest moon, dazzling and silvery. I have haunted the river every night lately, where I could get a look at the bridge by moonlight. It is indeed a structure of perfection and beauty unsurpassable, and I never tire of it. The river at present is very low; I noticed today it had much more of a blue-clear look than usual. I hear the slight ripples, the air is fresh and cool, and the view, up or down, wonderfully clear, in the moonlight. I am out pretty late: it is so fascinating, dreamy. The cool night air, all the influences, the silence, with those far-off eternal stars, do me good. I have been quite ill of late. And so, well-near the center of our national demesne, these night views of the Mississippi.

UPON OUR OWN LAND ൠ "Always, after supper, take a walk half a mile long," says an old proverb, dryly adding, "and if convenient let it be upon your own land." I wonder does any other nation but ours afford opportunity for such a jaunt as this? Indeed has any previous period afforded it? No one, I discover, begins to know the real geographic, democratic, indissoluble American Union in the present, or suspect it in the future, until he explores these Central States, and dwells awhile observantly on their prairies, or amid their busy towns, and the mighty father of waters. A ride of two or three thousand miles, "on one's own land," with hardly a disconnection, could certainly be had in no other place than the United States, and at no period before this. If you want to see what the railroad is, and how civilization and progress date from it—how it is the conqueror of crude nature, which it turns to man's use, both on small scales and on the largest—come hither to inland America. ൠ I returned home, east, Jan. 5, 1880, having traversed, to and fro and across, 10,000 miles and more. I soon resumed my seclusions down in the woods, or by the creek, or gaddings about cities, and an occasional disquisition, as will be seen following.

EDGAR POE'S SIGNIFICANCE ൠ JAN. 1, '80 ൠ In diagnosing this disease called humanity—to assume for the nonce what seems a chief mood of the personality and writings of my subject—I have thought that poets, somewhere or other on the list, present the most marked indications. Comprehending artists in a mass, musicians, painters, actors, and so on, and considering each and all of them as radiations or flanges of that furious whirling wheel, poetry, the centre and axis of the whole, where else indeed may we so well investigate the causes, growths, tally marks of the time—the age's matter and malady? ൠ By common consent there is nothing better for man or woman than a perfect and noble life, morally without flaw, happily balanced in activity, physically sound and pure, giving its due proportion, and no more, to the sympathetic, the human emotional element—a life, in all these, unhasting, unresting, untiring to the end. And yet there is another shape of personality dearer far to the artist sense (which likes the play of strongest lights and shades), where the perfect character, the good, the heroic, although never attained, is never lost sight of, but through failures, sorrows, temporary downfalls, is returned to again and again, and while often violated, is passionately adhered to as long as mind, muscles, voice, obey the power we call volition. This sort of personality we see more or less in Burns, Byron, Schiller, and George Sand. But we do not see it in Edgar Poe. (All this is the result of reading at intervals the last three days a new volume of his poems— I took it in my rambles down by the pond, and by degrees read it all through there.) While to the character first outlined the service Poe renders is certainly that entire contrast and contradiction which is next best to fully exemplifying it. ൠ Almost without the first sign of moral principle, or of the concrete or its heroisms, or the simpler affections of the heart, Poe's verses illustrate an intense faculty for technical and abstract beauty, with the rhyming art to excess, an incorrigible propensity toward nocturnal themes, a demoniac undertone behind every page—and, by final judgment, probably belong among the electric lights of imaginative literature, brilliant and dazzling, but with no heat. There is an indescribable magnetism about the poet's life and reminiscences, as well as the poems. To one who could work out their subtle retracing and retrospect, the latter would make a close tally no doubt between the author's birth and antecedents, his childhood and youth, his physique, his so-called education, his studies and associates, the literary and social Baltimore, Richmond, Philadelphia, and New York, of those times—not only the places and circumstances in themselves, but often, very often, in a strange spurning of, and reaction from, them all. ൠ The following from a report in the Washington *Star* of November 16, 1875, may afford those who care for it something further of my point of view toward this interesting figure and influence of our era.

There occurred about that date in Baltimore a public reburial of Poe's remains, and dedication of a monument over the grave: *Being in Washington on a visit at the time, "the old gray" went over to Baltimore, and though ill from paralysis, consented to hobble up and silently take a seat on the platform, but refused to make any speech, saying, "I have felt a strong impulse to come over and be here today myself in memory of Poe, which I have obeyed, but not the slightest impulse to make a speech, which, my dear friends, must also be obeyed." In an informal circle, however, in conversation after the ceremonies, Whitman said: "For a long while, and until lately, I had a distaste for Poe's writings. I wanted, and still want for poetry, the clear sun shining, and fresh air blowing—the strength and power of health, not of delirium, even amid the stormiest passions—with always the background of the eternal moralities. Noncomplying with these requirements, Poe's genius has yet conquered a special recognition for itself, and I too have come to fully admit it, and appreciate it and him.* ❧ *In a dream I once had, I saw a vessel on the sea, at midnight, in a storm. It was no great full-rigged ship, nor majestic steamer, steering firmly through the gale, but seemed one of those superb little schooner yachts I had often seen lying anchored, rocking so jauntily, in the waters around New York, or up Long Island Sound—now flying uncontrolled with torn sails and broken spars through the wild sleet and winds and waves of the night. On the deck was a slender, slight, beautiful figure, a dim man, apparently enjoying all the terror, the murk, and the dislocation of which he was the center and the victim. That figure of my lurid dream might stand for Edgar Poe, his spirit, his fortunes, and his poems—themselves all lurid dreams."* ❧ Much more may be said, but I most desired to exploit the idea put at the beginning. By its popular poets the calibres of an age, the weak spots of its embankments, its sub-currents (often more significant than the biggest surface ones) are unerringly indicated. The lush and the weird that have taken such extraordinary possession of nineteenth-century verse-lovers—what mean they? The inevitable tendency of poetic culture to morbidity, abnormal beauty—the sickliness of all technical thought or refinement in itself—the abnegation of the perennial and democratic concretes at first hand, the body, the earth and sea, sex and the like—and the substitution of something for them at second or third hand—what bearings have they on current pathological study?

BEETHOVEN'S SEPTET ❧ FEB. 11, '80 ❧ At a good concert tonight in the foyer of the Opera House, Philadelphia—the band a small but first-rate one. Never did music more sink into and soothe and fill me—never so prove its soul-rousing power, its impossibility of statement. Especially in the rendering of one of Beethoven's master septets by the well-chosen and perfectly combined instruments (violins, viola, clarionet, horn, 'cello, and contrabass) was I carried away, seeing, absorbing many wonders. Dainty abandon, sometimes as if Nature laughing on a hillside in the sunshine; serious and firm monotonies, as of winds; a horn sounding through the tangle of the forest, and the dying echoes; soothing floating of waves, but presently rising in surges, angrily lashing, muttering, heavy; piercing peals of laughter, for interstices; now and then weird, as Nature herself is in certain moods—but mainly spontaneous, easy, careless—often the sentiment of the postures of naked children playing or sleeping. It did me good even to watch the violinists drawing their bows so masterly—every motion a study. I allowed myself, as I sometimes do, to wander out of myself. The conceit came to me of a copious grove of singing birds, and in their midst a simple harmonic duo, two human souls, steadily asserting their own pensiveness, joyousness.

A HINT OF WILD NATURE ❧ FEB. 13 ❧ As I was crossing the Delaware today, saw a large flock of wild geese, right overhead, not very high up, ranged in V-shape in relief against the noon clouds of light smoke-color. Had a capital though momentary view of them, and then of their course on and on southeast, till gradually fading (my eyesight yet first rate for the open air and its distances, but I use glasses for reading). Queer thoughts melted into me the two or three minutes, or less, seeing these creatures cleaving the sky—the spacious, airy realm—even the prevailing smoke-gray color everywhere (no sun shining)—the water below—the rapid flight of the birds, appearing just for a minute—flashing to me such a hint of the whole spread of Nature, with her eternal unsophisticated freshness, her never-visited recesses of sea, sky, shore—and then disappearing in the distance.

LOAFING IN THE WOODS ❧ MARCH 8 ❧ I write this down in the country again, but in a new spot, seated on a log in the woods, warm, sunny, midday. Have been loafing here deep among the trees, shafts of tall pines, oak, hickory, with a thick undergrowth of laurels and grapevines—the ground covered everywhere by debris, dead leaves, breakage, moss—everything solitary, ancient, grim. Paths (such as they are) leading hither and yon (how made I know not, for nobody seems to come here, nor man nor cattle-kind). Temperature today about 60, the wind through the pine-tops; I sit and listen to its hoarse sighing above (and to the *stillness*) long and long, varied by aimless rambles in the old roads and paths, and by exercise pulls at the young saplings, to keep my joints from getting stiff. Bluebirds, robins, meadowlarks begin to appear. ❧

NEXT DAY, 9TH ᵅ A snowstorm in the morning, and continuing most of the day. But I took a walk over two hours, the same woods and paths, amid the falling flakes. No wind, yet the musical low murmur through the pines, quite pronounced, curious, like waterfalls, now stilled, now pouring again. All the senses—sight, sound, smell—delicately gratified. Every snowflake lay where it fell on the evergreens, holly trees, laurels, etc., the multitudinous leaves and branches piled, bulging white, defined by edge lines of emerald—the tall straight columns of the plentiful bronze-topped pines—a slight resinous odor blending with that of the snow. (For there is a scent to everything, even the snow, if you can only detect it—no two places, hardly any two hours, anywhere, exactly alike. How different the odor of noon from midnight, or winter from summer, or a windy spell from a still one.)

A CONTRALTO VOICE ᵅ MAY 9, SUNDAY ᵅ Visit this evening to my friends the J.'s—good supper, to which I did justice—lively chat with Mrs. J. and I. and J. As I sat out front on the walk afterward, in the evening air, the church choir and organ on the corner opposite gave Luther's hymn, *Ein feste Berg*, very finely. The air was borne by a rich contralto. For nearly half an hour there in the dark (there was a good string of English stanzas) came the music, firm and unhurried, with long pauses. The full silver starbeams of Lyra rose silently over the church's dim roof ridge. Varicolored lights from the stained-glass windows broke through the tree shadows. And under all—under the Northern Crown up there, and in the fresh breeze below, and the *chiaroscuro* of the night, that liquid-full contralto.

SEEING NIAGARA TO ADVANTAGE ᵅ JUNE 4, '80 ᵅ For really seizing a great picture or book, or piece of music, or architecture, or grand scenery—or perhaps for the first time even the common sunshine, or landscape or maybe even the mystery of identity, most curious mystery of all—there comes some lucky five minutes of a man's life, set amid a fortuitous concurrence of circumstances, and bringing in a brief flash the culmination of years of reading and travel and thought. The present case, about two o'clock this afternoon, gave me Niagara, its superb severity of action and color and majestic grouping, in one short, indescribable show. We were very slowly crossing the Suspension Bridge—not a full stop anywhere, but next to it—the day clear, sunny, still—and I out on the platform. The falls were in plain view about a mile off, but very distinct, and no roar—hardly a murmur. The river tumbling green and white, far below me; the dark high banks, the plentiful umbrage, many bronze cedars, in

shadow and tempering and arching all the immense materiality, a clear sky overhead with a few white clouds, limpid, spiritual, silent. Brief, and as quiet as brief, that picture—a remembrance always afterward. Such are the things, indeed, I lay away with my life's rare and blessed bits of hours, reminiscent, past—the wild sea storm I once saw one winter day, off Fire Island—the elder Booth in *Richard*, that famous night forty years ago in the old Bowery—or Alboni in the children's scene in *Norma*—or night views, I remember, on the field, after battles in Virginia—or the peculiar sentiment of moonlight and stars over the Great Plains, western Kansas—or scooting up New York Bay, with a stiff breeze and a good yacht off Navesink. With these, I say, I henceforth place that view, that afternoon, that combination complete, that five minutes' perfect absorption of Niagara—not the great majestic gem alone by itself, but set complete in all its varied, full indispensable surroundings.

JAUNTING TO CANADA ᵅ To go back a little, I left Philadelphia, 9th and Green Streets, at 8 o'clock P.M., June 3, on a first-class sleeper, by the Lehigh Valley (North Pennsylvania) route, through Bethlehem, Wilkes Barre, Waverly, and so (by Erie) on through Corning to Hornellsville, where we arrived at 8, morning, and had a bounteous breakfast. I must say I never put in such a good night on any railroad track—smooth, firm, the minimum of jolting, and all the swiftness compatible with safety. So without change to Buffalo, and thence to Clifton, where we arrived early afternoon; then on to London, Ontario, Canada, in four more—less than twenty-two hours altogether. I am domiciled at the hospitable house of my friends Dr. and Mrs. Bucke, in the ample and charming garden and lawns of the asylum.

SUNDAY WITH THE INSANE ᵅ JUNE 6 ᵅ Went over to the religious services (Episcopal), main Insane Asylum, held in a lofty, good-sized hall, third story. Plain boards, whitewash, plenty of cheap chairs, no ornament or color, yet all scrupulously clean and sweet. Some three hundred persons present, mostly patients. Everything—the prayers, a short sermon, the firm orotund voice of the minister, and most of all, beyond any portraying or suggesting, *that audience*—deeply impressed me. I was furnished with an armchair near the pulpit, and sat facing the motley, yet perfectly well-behaved and orderly congregation. The quaint dresses and bonnets of some of the women, several very old and gray, here and there like the heads in old pictures. O the looks that came from those faces! There were two or three I shall probably never forget. Nothing at all markedly repulsive or hideous—strangely enough I did not see one such. Our common humanity, mine and yours, everywhere:

The same old blood—the same red running blood

yet behind most, an inferred arrière of such storms, such wrecks, such mysteries, fires, love, wrong, greed for wealth, religious problems, crosses—mirrored from those crazed faces (yet now temporarily so calm, like still waters), all the woes and sad happenings of life and death—now from every one the devotional element radiating—was it not, indeed, *the peace of God that passeth all understanding*, strange as it may sound? I can only say that I took long and searching eye-sweeps as I sat there, and it seemed so, rousing unprecedented thoughts, problems unanswerable. A very fair choir, and melodeon accompaniment. They sang "Lead, kindly light," after the sermon. Many joined in the beautiful hymn, to which the minister read the introductory text, "*In the daytime also He led them with a cloud, and all the night with a light of fire.*" Then the words:

> *Lead, kindly light, amid th' encircling gloom,*
> *Lead thou me on.*
> *The night is dark, and I am far from home;*
> *Lead thou me on.*
> *Keep thou my feet; I do not ask to see*
> *The distant scene; one step enough for me.*
>
> *I was not ever thus, nor prayed that thou*
> *Shouldst lead me on;*
> *I loved to choose and see my path; but now,*
> *Lead thou me on.*
> *I loved the garish day, and spite of fears,*
> *Pride ruled my will; remember not past years.*

᳇ A couple of days after, I went to the "Refractory Building," under special charge of Dr. Beemer, and through the wards pretty thoroughly, both the men's and women's. I have since made many other visits of the kind through the asylum, and around among the detached cottages. As far as I could see, this is among the most advanced, perfected, and kindly and rationally carried on, of all its kind in America. It is a town in itself, with many buildings and a thousand inhabitants. ᳇ I learn that Canada, and especially this ample and populous province, Ontario, has the very best and plentiest benevolent institutions in all departments.

REMINISCENCE OF ELIAS HICKS ᳇ JUNE 8 ᳇ Today a letter from Mrs. E. S. L., Detroit, accompanied in a little Post Office roll by a rare old engraved head of Elias Hicks (from a portrait in oil by Henry Inman, painted for J. V. S., must have been 60 years or more ago, in New York)—among the rest the following excerpt about E. H. in the letter: *I have listened to his preaching so often when a child, and sat with my mother at social gatherings where he was the center, and everyone so pleased and stirred by his conversation. I hear that you contemplate writing or speaking about him, and I wondered whether you had a picture of him. As I am the owner of two, I send you one.*

GRAND NATIVE GROWTH ᳇ In a few days I go to Lake Huron and may have something to say of that region and people. From what I already see, I should say the young native population of Canada was growing up, forming a hardy, democratic, intelligent, radically sound, and just as American, good-natured, and *individualistic* race as the average range of best specimens among us. As among us, too, I please myself by considering that this element, though it may not be the majority, promises to be the leaven which must eventually leaven the whole lump.

A ZOLLVEREIN BETWEEN THE U. S. AND CANADA ᳇ Some of the more liberal of the presses here are discussing the question of a *zollverein* between the United States and Canada. It is proposed to form a union for commercial purposes—to altogether abolish the frontier tariff line, with its double sets of customhouse officials now existing between the two countries, and to agree upon one tariff for both, the proceeds of this tariff to be divided between the two governments on the basis of population. It is said that a large proportion of the merchants of Canada are in favor of this step, as they believe it would materially add to the business of the country, by removing the restrictions that now exist on trade between Canada and the States. Those persons who are opposed to the measure believe that it would increase the material welfare of the country, but it would loosen the bonds between Canada and England; and this sentiment overrides the desire for commercial prosperity. Whether the sentiment can continue to bear the strain put upon it is a question. It is thought by many that commercial considerations must in the end prevail. It seems also to be generally agreed that such a *zollverein*, or common customs union, would bring practically more benefits to the Canadian provinces than to the United States. (It seems to me a certainty of time, sooner or later, that Canada shall form two or three grand states, equal and independent, with the rest of the American Union. The St. Lawrence and lakes are not for a frontier line, but a grand interior or mid-channel.)

THE ST. LAWRENCE LINE ❧ AUGUST 20 ❧ Premising that my three or four months in Canada were intended, among the rest, as an exploration of the line of the St. Lawrence, from Lake Superior to the sea (the engineers here insist upon considering it as one stream, over 2,000 miles long, including lakes and Niagara and all)—that I have only partially carried out my program; but for the seven or eight hundred miles so far fulfilled, I find that the *Canada question* is absolutely controlled by this vast water line, with its first-class features and points of trade, humanity, and many more—here I am writing this nearly a thousand miles north of my Philadelphia starting point (by way of Montreal and Quebec) in the midst of regions that go to a further extreme of grimness, wildness of beauty, and a sort of still and pagan *scaredness*, while yet Christian, inhabitable, and partially fertile, than perhaps any other on earth. The weather remains perfect; some might call it a little cool, but I wear my old gray overcoat and find it just right. The days are full of sunbeams and oxygen. Most of the forenoons and afternoons I am on the forward deck of the steamer.

THE SAVAGE SAGUENAY ❧ Up these black waters, over a hundred miles—always strong, deep (hundreds of feet, sometimes thousands), ever with high, rocky hills for banks, green and gray—at times a little like some parts of the Hudson, but much more pronounced and defiant. The hills rise higher—keep their ranks more unbroken. The river is straighter and of more resolute flow, and its hue, though dark as ink, exquisitely polished and sheeny under the August sun. Different, indeed, this Saguenay from all other rivers—different effects—a bolder, more vehement play of lights and shades. Of a rare charm of singleness and simplicity. (Like the organ chant at midnight from the old Spanish convent, in *Favorita*—one strain only, simple and monotonous and unornamented—but indescribably penetrating and grand and masterful.) Great place for echoes; while our steamer was tied at the wharf at Tadoussac (taj-oo-sac) waiting, the escape pipe letting off steam, I was sure I heard a band at the hotel up in the rocks—could even make out some of the tunes. Only when our pipe stopped, I knew what caused it. Then at Cape Eternity and Trinity Rock, the pilot with his whistle producing similar marvelous results, echoes indescribably weird, as we lay off in the still bay under their shadows.

CAPES ETERNITY AND TRINITY ❧ But the great, haughty, silent capes themselves: I doubt if any crack points, or hills, or historic places of note, or anything of the kind elsewhere in the world, outvies

these objects (I write while I am before them face to face). They are very simple, they do not startle—at least they did not me—but they linger in one's memory forever. They are placed very near each other, side by side, each a mountain rising flush out of the Saguenay. A good thrower could throw a stone on each in passing—at least it seems so. Then they are as distinct in form as a perfect physical man or a perfect physical woman. Cape Eternity is bare, rising, as just said, sheer out of water, rugged and grim (yet with an indescribable beauty) nearly two thousand feet high. Trinity Rock, even a little higher, also rising flush, top rounded like a great head with close-cut verdure of hair. I consider myself well repaid for coming my thousand miles to get the sight and memory of the unrivalled duo. They have stirred me more profoundly than anything of the kind I have yet seen. If Europe or Asia had them, we should certainly hear of them in all sorts of sent-back poems, rhapsodies, etc., a dozen times a year through our papers and magazines.

CHICOUTIMI AND HA-HA BAY ❧ No, indeed—life and travel and memory have offered and will preserve to me no deeper-cut incidents, panorama, or sights to cheer my soul than these at Chicoutimi and Ha-Ha Bay, and my days and nights up and down this fascinating savage river—the rounded mountains, some bare and gray, some dull red, some draped close all over with matted green verdure or vines—the ample, calm, eternal rocks everywhere—the long streaks of motley foam, a milk-white curd on the glistening breast of the stream—the little two-masted schooner, dingy yellow, with patched sails, set wing-and-wing, nearing us, coming saucily up the water with a couple of swarthy, black-haired men aboard—the strong shades falling on the light gray or yellow outlines of the hills all through the forenoon, as we steam within gunshot of them—while ever the pure and delicate sky spreads over all. And the splendid sunsets, and the sights of evening—the same old stars (relatively a little different, I see, so far north), Arcturus and Lyra, and the Eagle, and great Jupiter like a silver globe, and the constellation of the Scorpion. Then Northern Lights nearly every night.

THE INHABITANTS—GOOD LIVING ❧ Grim and rocky and black-watered as the demesne hereabout is, however, you must not think genial humanity, and comfort, and good living are not to be met. Before I began this memorandum I made a first-rate breakfast of sea trout, finishing off with wild raspberries. I find smiles and courtesy everywhere—physiognomies in general curiously like those in the United States (I was astonished to find the same resemblance all through the province of Quebec). In general the inhabitants of this rugged country (Charlevois, Chicoutimi and Tadoussac Counties, and Lake St. John region) a simple, hardy population, lumbering, trapping furs, boating, fishing, berry-picking and a little farming. I was watching a group of young boatmen eating their early dinner—nothing but an immense loaf of bread, had apparently been the size of a bushel measure, from which they cut chunks with a jackknife. Must be a tremendous winter country this, when the solid frost and ice fully set in.

CEDAR-PLUMS LIKE—NAMES ɞ BACK AGAIN IN CAMDEN AND DOWN IN JERSEY ɞ One time I thought of naming this collection "Cedar-Plums Like" (which I still fancy wouldn't have been a bad name, nor inappropriate). A mélange of loafing, looking, hobbling, sitting, traveling—a little thinking thrown in for salt, but very little—not only summer but all seasons—not only days but nights—some literary meditations—books, authors examined, Carlyle, Poe, Emerson tried (always under my cedar tree, in the open air, and never in the library)—mostly the scenes everybody sees, but some of my own caprices, meditations, egotism—truly an open-air and mainly summer formation—singly, or in clusters—wild and free and somewhat acrid—indeed more like cedar-plums than you might guess at first glance. ɞ But do you know what they are? (To city man, or some sweet parlor lady, I now talk.) As you go along roads, or barrens, or across country, anywhere through these states, middle, eastern, western, or southern, you will see, certain seasons of the year, the thick woolly tufts of the cedar mottled with bunches of china-blue berries, about as big as fox grapes. But first a special word for the tree itself: everybody knows that the cedar is a healthy, cheap, democratic wood, streaked red and white—an evergreen—that it is not a *cultivated* tree—that it keeps away moths—that it grows inland or seaboard, all climates, hot or cold, any soil—in fact rather prefers sand and bleak side spots—content if the plow, the fertilizer, and the trimming ax will but keep away and let it alone. After a long rain, when everything looks bright, often have I stopped in my wood saunters, south or north, or far west, to take in its dusky green, washed clean and sweet, and specked copiously with its fruit of clear, hardy blue. The wood of the cedar is of use—but what profit on earth are those sprigs of acrid plums? A question impossible to answer satisfactorily. True, some of the herb doctors give them for stomachic affections, but the remedy is as bad as the disease. Then in my rambles down in Camden County I once found an old crazy woman gathering the clusters with zeal and joy. She showed, as I was told afterward, a sort of infatuation for them, and every year placed and kept profuse bunches

high and low about her room. They had a strange charm on her uneasy head, and effected docility and peace. (She was harmless, and lived near by with her well-off married daughter.) Whether there is any connection between those bunches, and being out of one's wits, I cannot say, but I myself entertain a weakness for them. Indeed, I love the cedar, anyhow—its naked ruggedness, its just palpable odor (so different from the perfumer's best), its silence, its equable acceptance of winter's cold and summer's heat, of rain or drought—its shelter to me from those, at times—its associations (well, I never could explain *why* I love anybody, or anything). The service I now specially owe to the cedar is, while I cast around for a name for my proposed collection, hesitating, puzzled—after rejecting a long, long string, I lift my eyes, and lo! the very term I want. At any rate, I go no further—I tire in the search. I take what some invisible kind spirit has put before me. Besides, who shall say there is not affinity enough between (at least the bundle of sticks that produced) many of these pieces, or granulations, and those blue berries? their uselessness growing wild—a certain aroma of Nature I would so like to have in my pages—the thin soil whence they come—their content in being let alone—their stolid and deaf repugnance to answering questions (this latter the nearest, dearest trait affinity of all). ɞ Then, reader dear, in conclusion, as to the point of the name for the present collection, let us be satisfied to *have* a name—something to identify and bind it together, to concrete all its vegetable, mineral, personal memoranda, abrupt raids of criticism, crude gossip of philosophy, varied sands and clumps—without bothering ourselves because certain pages do not present themselves to you or me as coming under their own name with entire fitness or amiability. (It is profound, vexatious, never-explicable matter—this of names. I have been exercised deeply about it my whole life.*) ɞ After all of which the name "Cedar-Plums Like" got its nose put out of joint; but I cannot afford to throw away what I penciled down the lane there, under the shelter of my old friend, one warm October noon. Besides, it wouldn't be civil to the cedar tree.

* In the pocket of my receptacle book I find a list of suggested and rejected names for this volume, or parts of it—such as following:

As the wild bee hums in May,
& August mulleins grow,
& Winter snowflakes fall,
& stars in the sky roll round.

Away from Books—away from Art,
Now for the Day and Night—the lesson done,
Now for the Sun and Stars.

DEATH OF THOMAS CARLYLE ❧ FEB. 10, '81 ❧ And so the flame of the lamp, after long wasting and flickering, has gone out entirely. ❧ As a representative author, a literary figure, no man else will bequeath to the future more significant hints of our stormy era, its fierce paradoxes, its din, and its struggling parturition periods, than Carlyle. He belongs to our own branch of the stock too; neither Latin nor Greek, but altogether Gothic. Rugged, mountainous, volcanic, he was himself more a French Revolution than any of his volumes. In some respects, so far in the nineteenth century, the best-equipped, keenest mind, even from the college point of view, of all Britain; only he had an ailing body. Dyspepsia is to be traced in every page, and now and then fills the page. One may include among the lessons of his life—even though that life stretched to amazing length—how behind the tally of genius and morals stands the stomach, and gives a sort of casting vote. ❧ Two conflicting agonistic elements seem to have contended in the man, sometimes pulling him different ways like wild horses. He was a cautious, conservative Scotchman, fully aware what a fetid gasbag much of modern radicalism is; but then his great heart demanded reform, demanded change—often terribly at odds with his scornful brain. No author ever put so much wailing and despair into his books, sometimes palpable, oftener latent. He reminds me of that passage in Young's poems where as death presses closer and closer for his prey, the soul rushes hither and thither, appealing, shrieking, berating, to escape the general doom. ❧ Of shortcomings, even positive blur-spots, from an American point of view, he had serious share. ❧ Not for his merely literary merit (though that was great)—not as "maker of books," but as launching into the self-complacent atmosphere of our days a rasping, questioning, dislocating agitation and shock, is Carlyle's final value. It is time the English-speaking peoples had some true idea about the verteber of genius, namely power. As if they must always have it

cut and biased to the fashion, like a lady's cloak! What a needed service he performs! How he shakes our comfortable reading circles with a touch of the old Hebraic anger and prophecy—and indeed it is just the same. Not Isaiah himself more scornful, more threatening: "The crown of pride, the drunkards of Ephraim, shall be trodden under feet: And the glorious beauty which is on the head of the fat valley shall be a fading flower." (The word prophecy is much misused; it seems narrowed to prediction merely. That is not the main sense of the Hebrew word translated "prophet"; it means one whose mind bubbles up and pours forth as a fountain, from inner, divine spontaneities revealing God. Prediction is a very minor part of prophecy. The great matter is to reveal and outpour the Godlike suggestions pressing for birth in the soul. This is briefly the doctrine of the Friends or Quakers.) ❧ Then the simplicity and amid ostensible frailty the towering strength of this man—a hardy oak knot, you could never wear out—an old farmer dressed in brown clothes, and not handsome—his very foibles fascinating. Who cares that he wrote about Dr. Francia, and "Shooting Niagara"—and "the Nigger Question"—and didn't at all admire our United States? (I doubt if he ever thought or said half as bad words about us as we deserve.) How he splashes like leviathan in the seas of modern literature and politics! Doubtless, respecting the latter, one needs first to realize, from actual observation, the squalor, vice, and doggedness ingrained in the bulk population of the British Islands, with the red tape, the fatuity, the flunkeyism everywhere, to understand the last meaning in his pages. Accordingly, though he was no chartist or radical, I consider Carlyle's by far the most indignant comment or protest anent the fruits of feudalism today in Great Britain—the increasing poverty and degradation of the homeless, landless twenty millions, while a few thousands, or rather a few hundreds, possess the entire soil, the money, and the fat berths. Trade and shipping, and clubs and culture, and prestige, and guns, and a fine select class of gentry and aristocracy, with every modern improvement, cannot begin to salve or defend such stupendous hoggishness. ❧ The way to test how much he has left his country were to consider, or try to consider, for a moment, the array of British thought, the resultant ensemble of the last fifty years, as existing to-day, *but with Carlyle left out.* It would be like an army with no artillery. The show were still a gay and rich one —Byron, Scott, Tennyson, and many more—horsemen and rapid infantry, and banners flying—but the last heavy roar so dear to the ear of the trained soldier, and that settles fate and victory, would be lacking. ❧ For the last three years we in America have had transmitted glimpses of a thin-bodied, lonesome, wifeless, childless,

---

(*Footnote continued:*)

Notes of a Half-Paralytic	As Voices in the Dusk, from
Week in and Week out	Speakers far or hid
Embers of Ending Days	Autochthons . . . . . Embryons
Ducks and Drakes	Wing-and-Wing
Flood Tide and Ebb	Notes and Recallés
Gossip at Early Candlelight	Only Mulleins and Bumblebees
Echoes and Escapades	Pond Babble . . . . . Tête-a-Têtês
Such as I . . . . Evening Dews	Echoes of a Life in the 19th
Notes after Writing a Book	Century in the New World
Far and Near at 63	Flanges of Fifty Years
Drifts and Cumulus	Abandons . . . . . Hurry Notes
Maize-Tassels . . . . . Kindlings	A Life Mosaic . . . . . Native
Fore and Aft . . . . . Vestibules	Moments
Scintilla at 60 and after	Types and Semitones
Sands on the Shores of 64	Oddments . . . . . Sand Drifts
	Again and Again

very old man, lying on a sofa, kept out of bed by indomitable will, but of late, never well enough to take the open air. I have noted this news from time to time in brief descriptions in the papers. A week ago I read such an item just before I started out for my customary evening stroll between eight and nine. In the fine cold night, unusually clear (Feb. 5, '81), as I walked some open grounds adjacent, the condition of Carlyle, and his approaching—perhaps even then actual—death, filled me with thoughts eluding statement, and curiously blending with the scene. The planet Venus, an hour high in the west, with all her volume and luster recovered (she has been shorn and languid for nearly a year), including an additional sentiment I never noticed before—not merely voluptuous, Paphian, steeping, fascinating—now with calm commanding seriousness and hauteur—the Milo Venus now. Upward to the zenith, Jupiter, Saturn, and the moon past her quarter, trailing in procession, with the Pleiades following, and the constellation Taurus, and red Aldebaran. Not a cloud in heaven. Orion strode through the southeast, with his glittering belt—and a trifle below hung the sun of the night, Sirius. Every star dilated, more vitreous, nearer than usual. Not as in some clear nights when the larger stars entirely outshine the rest. Every little star or cluster just as distinctly visible, and just as nigh. Berenice's Hair showing every gem, and new ones. To the northeast and north the Sickle, the Goat and the Kids, Cassiopeia, Castor and Pollux, and the two Dippers. While through the whole of this silent indescribable show, inclosing and bathing my whole receptivity, ran the thought of Carlyle dying. (To soothe and spiritualize, and, as far as may be, solve the mysteries of death and genius, consider them under the stars at midnight.) ꝫ And now that he has gone hence, can it be that Thomas Carlyle, soon to chemically dissolve in ashes and by winds, remains an identity still? In ways perhaps eluding all the statements, lore, and speculations of ten thousand years—eluding all possible statements to mortal sense—does he yet exist, a definite, vital being, a spirit, an individual—perhaps now wafted in space among those stellar systems, which, suggestive and limitless as they are, merely edge more limitless, far more suggestive systems? I have no doubt of it. In silence, of a fine night, such questions are answered to the soul, the best answers that can be given. With me, too, when depressed by some specially sad event or tearing problem, I wait till I go out under the stars for the last voiceless satisfaction.

CARLYLE FROM AMERICAN POINTS OF VIEW ꝫ LATER THOUGHTS AND JOTTINGS ꝫ There is surely at present an inexplicable *rapport* (all the more piquant from its contradictoriness) between that deceased author and our United States of America —no matter whether it lasts or not.* As we Westerners assume definite shape, and result in formations and fruitage unknown before, it is curious with what a new sense our eyes turn to representative outgrowths of crises and personages in the Old World. Beyond question, since Carlyle's death, and the publication of Froude's memoirs, not only the interest in his books, but every personal bit regarding the famous Scotchman—his dyspepsia, his buffetings, his parentage, his paragon of a wife, his career in Edinburgh, in the lonesome nest on Craigenputtock moor, and then so many years in London—is probably wider and livelier today in this country than in his own land. Whether I succeed or no, I, too, reaching across the Atlantic and taking the man's dark fortune-telling of humanity and politics, would offset it all (such is the fancy that comes to me), by a far more profound horoscope-casting of those themes—G. F. Hegel's.† ꝫ First, about a chance, a never-fulfilled vacuity of this pale cast of thought—this British Hamlet from Cheyne Row, more puzzling than the Danish one, with his contrivances for settling the broken and spavined joints of the world's government, especially its democratic dislocation. Carlyle's grim fate was cast to live and dwell in, and largely embody, the parturition agony and qualms of the old order, amid crowded accumulations of ghastly morbidity, giving birth to the new. But conceive of him (or his parents before him) coming to America, recuperated by the cheering realities and activity of our people and country—growing up and delving face-to-face

---

* It will be difficult for the future—judging by his books, personal dissympathies, etc.—to account for the deep hold this author has taken on the present age, and the way he has colored its method and thought. I am certainly at a loss to account for it all as affecting myself. But there could be no view, or even partial picture, of the middle and latter part of our nineteenth century that did not markedly include Thomas Carlyle. In his case (as so many others, literary productions, works of art, personal identities, events) there has been an impalpable something more effective than the palpable. Then I find no better text (it is always important to have a definite, special, even oppositional, living man to start from) for sending out certain speculations and comparisons for home use. Let us see what they amount to—those reactionary doctrines, fears, scornful analyses of democracy—even from the most erudite and sincere mind of Europe.

† Not the least mentionable part of the case (a streak, it may be, of that humor with which history and fate love to contrast their gravity) is that although neither of my great authorities during their lives considered the United States worthy of serious mention, all the principal works of both might not inappropriately be this day collected and bound up under the conspicuous title: "*Speculations for the Use of North America, and Democracy There, with the Relations of the Same to Metaphysics, including Lessons and Warnings (Encouragements too, and of the Vastest) from the Old World to the New.*"

resolutely among us here, especially at the West—inhaling and exhaling our limitless air and eligibilities—devoting his mind to the theories and developments of this Republic amid its practical facts as exemplified in Kansas, Missouri, Illinois, Tennessee, or Louisiana. I say *facts*, and face-to-face confrontings—so different from books, and all those quiddities and mere reports in the libraries, upon which the man (it was wittily said of him at the age of thirty, that there was no one in Scotland who had gleaned so much and seen so little) almost wholly fed, and which even his sturdy and vital mind but reflected at best. ஒ Something of the sort narrowly escaped happening. In 1835, after more than a dozen years of trial and non-success, the author of *Sartor Resartus* removing to London, very poor, a confirmed hypochondriac, *Sartor* universally scoffed at, no literary prospects ahead, deliberately settled on one last casting-throw of the literary dice—resolved to compose and launch forth a book on the subject of *The French Revolution*—and if that won no higher guerdon or prize than hitherto, to sternly abandon the trade of author forever and emigrate for good to America. But the venture turned out a lucky one, and there was no emigration. ஒ Carlyle's work in the sphere of literature, as he commenced and carried it out, is the same in one or two leading respects that Immanuel Kant's was in speculative philosophy. But the Scotchman had none of the stomachic phlegm and never-perturbed placidity of the Königsberg sage, and did not, like the latter, understand his own limits and stop when he got to the end of them. He clears away jungle and poison vines and underbrush —at any rate hacks valiantly at them, smiting hip and thigh. Kant did the like in his sphere, and it was all he professed to do; his labors have left the ground fully prepared ever since—and greater service was probably never performed by mortal man. But the pang and hiatus of Carlyle seem to me to consist in the evidence everywhere that amid a whirl of fog and fury and cross-purposes, he firmly believed he had a clue to the medication of the world's ills, and that his bounden mission was to exploit it.* ஒ There were two anchors, or sheet-anchors, for steadying, as a last resort, the Carlylean ship. One will be specified presently. The other, perhaps the main, was only to be found in some marked form of personal force, an extreme degree of competent urge

and will, a man or men "born to command." Probably there ran through every vein and current of the Scotchman's blood something that warmed up to this kind of trait and character above aught else in the world, and which makes him in my opinion the chief celebrater and promulgator of it in literature—more than Plutarch, more than Shakespeare. The great masses of humanity stand for nothing—at least nothing but nebulous raw material; only the big planets and shining suns for him. To ideas almost invariably languid or cold, a number-one forceful personality was sure to rouse his eulogistic passion and savage joy. In such case, even the standard of duty hereinafter raised, was to be instantly lowered and veiled. All that is comprehended under the terms republicanism and democracy were distasteful to him from the first, and as he grew older they became hateful and contemptible. For an undoubtedly candid and penetrating faculty such as his, the bearings he persistently ignored were marvelous. For instance, the promise, nay certainty of the democratic principle, to each and every state of the current world, not so much of helping it to perfect legislators and executives, but as the only effectual method for surely, however slowly, training people on a large scale toward voluntarily ruling and managing themselves (the ultimate aim of political and all other development)—to gradually reduce the fact of *governing* to its minimum, and to subject all its staffs and their doings to the telescopes and microscopes of committees and parties—and greatest of all, to afford—not stagnation and obedient content, which went well enough with the feudalism and ecclesiasticism of the antique and medieval world, but—a vast and sane and recurrent ebb and tide action for those floods of the great deep that have henceforth palpably burst forever their old bounds —seem never to have entered Carlyle's thought. It was splendid how he refused any compromise to the last. He was curiously antique. In that harsh, picturesque, most potent voice and figure, one seems to be carried back from the present to the British Islands more than two thousand years, to the range between Jerusalem and Tarsus. His fullest best biographer justly says of him: *He was a teacher and a prophet, in the Jewish sense of the word. The prophecies of Isaiah and Jeremiah have become a part of the permanent spiritual inheritance of mankind, because events proved that they had interpreted correctly the signs of their own times, and their prophecies were fulfilled. Carlyle, like them, believed that he had a special message to deliver to the present age. Whether he was correct in that belief, and whether his message was a true message, remains to be seen. He has told us that our most cherished ideas of political liberty, with their kindred corollaries, are mere illusions, and that the progress which has seemed to go along with them is a progress towards anarchy and social dissolution. If he was wrong, he has misused*

---

* I hope I shall not myself fall into the error I charge upon him, of prescribing a specific for indispensable evils. My utmost pretension is probably but to offset that old claim of the exclusively curative power of first-class individual men, as leaders and rulers, by the claims, and general movement and result, of ideas. Something of the latter kind seems to me the distinctive theory of America, of democracy, and of the modern—or rather, I should say, it *is* democracy, and *is* the modern.

his powers. The principles of his teachings are false. He has offered himself as a guide upon a road of which he had no knowledge; and his own desire for himself would be the speediest oblivion both of his person and his works. If, on the other hand, he has been right; if, like his great predecessors, he has read truly the tendencies of this modern age of ours, and his teaching is authenticated by facts, then Carlyle, too, will take his place among the inspired seers. ℘ To which I add an amendment that under no circumstances, and no matter how completely time and events disprove his lurid vaticinations, should the English-speaking world forget this man, nor fail to hold in honor his unsurpassed conscience, his unique method, and his honest fame. Never were convictions more earnest and genuine. Never was there less of a flunkey or temporizer. Never had political progressivism a foe it could more heartily respect. ℘ The second main point of Carlyle's utterance was the idea of *duty being done*. (It is simply a new codicil—if it be particularly new, which is by no means certain—on the time-honored bequest of dynasticism, the mold-eaten rules of legitimacy and kings.) He seems to have been impatient sometimes to madness when reminded by persons who thought at least as deeply as himself, that this formula, though precious, is rather a vague one, and that there are many other considerations to a philosophical estimate of each and every department either in general history or individual affairs. ℘ Altogether, I don't know anything more amazing than these persistent strides and throbbings so far through our nineteenth century of perhaps its biggest, sharpest, and most erudite brain, in defiance and discontent with everything; contemptuously ignoring (either from constitutional inaptitude, ignorance itself, or more likely because he demanded a definite cure-all here and now) the only solace and solvent to be had. ℘ There is, apart from mere intellect, in the make-up of every superior human identity (in its moral completeness, considered as ensemble, not for that moral alone, but for the whole being, including physique), a wondrous something that realizes without argument, frequently without what is called education (though I think it the goal and apex of all education deserving the name)—an intuition of the absolute balance, in time and space, of the whole of this multifarious, mad chaos of fraud, frivolity, hoggishness —this revel of fools, and incredible make-believe and general unsettledness, we call *the world*; a soul-sight of that divine clue and unseen thread which holds the whole congeries of things, all history and time, and all events, however trivial, however momentous, like a leashed dog in the hand of the hunter. Such soul-sight and root-center for the mind—mere optimism explains only the surface or fringe of it—Carlyle was mostly, perhaps entirely without. He seems instead to have been

haunted in the play of his mental action by a specter, never entirely laid from first to last (Greek scholars, I believe, find the same mocking and fantastic apparition attending Aristophanes' comedies)—the specter of world destruction. ℘ How largest triumph or failure in human life, in war or peace, may depend on some little hidden centrality, hardly more than a drop of blood, a pulsebeat, or a breath of air! It is certain that all these weighty matters, democracy in America, Carlylism, and the temperament for deepest political or literary exploration, turn on a simple point in speculative philosophy. ℘ The most profound theme that can occupy the mind of man—the problem on whose solution science, art, the bases and pursuits of nations, and everything else, including intelligent human happiness (here today, 1882, New York, Texas, California, the same as all times, all lands), subtly and finally resting, depends for competent outset and argument, is doubtless involved in the query: What is the fusing explanation and tie—what the relation between the (radical, democratic) Me, the human identity of understanding, emotions, spirit, etc., on the one side, of and with the (conservative) Not Me, the whole of the material objective universe and laws, with what is behind them in time and space, on the other side? Immanuel Kant, though he explained, or partially explained, as may be said, the laws of the human understanding, left this question an open one. Schelling's answer, or suggestion of answer, is (and very valuable and important, as far as it goes) that the same general and particular intelligence, passion, even the standards of right and wrong, which exist in a conscious and formulated state in man, exist in an unconscious state, or in perceptible analogies, throughout the entire universe of external Nature, in all its objects large or small, and all its movements and processes—thus making the impalpable human mind, and concrete Nature, notwithstanding their duality and separation, convertible, and in centrality and essence one. But G. F. Hegel's fuller statement of the matter probably remains the last best word that has been said upon it, up to date. Substantially adopting the scheme just epitomized, he so carries it out and fortifies it and merges everything in it, with certain serious gaps now for the first time filled, that it becomes a coherent metaphysical system, and substantial answer (as far as there can be any answer) to the foregoing question—a system which, while I distinctly admit that the brain of the future may add to, revise, and even entirely reconstruct, at any rate beams forth today in its entirety, illuminating the thought of the universe, and satisfying the mystery thereof to the human mind, with a more consoling scientific assurance than any yet. ℘ According to Hegel the whole earth (an old nucleus thought, as in the Vedas, and no doubt before, but never hitherto brought so absolutely to the front, fully surcharged with modern scientism and facts, and made the sole entrance to each and all), with its infinite variety, the past, the surroundings of today, or what may happen in the future, the contrarities of material with spiritual, and of natural with artificial, are all, to the eye of the *ensemblist*, but necessary sides and unfoldings, different steps or links, in the endless process of creative thought, which, amid numberless apparent failures and contradictions, is held together by central and never-broken unity—not contradictions or failures at all, but radiations of one consistent and eternal purpose; the whole mass of everything steadily, unerringly tending and flowing toward the permanent *utile* and *morale*, as rivers to oceans. As life is the whole law and incessant effort of the visible universe, and death only the other or invisible side of the same, so the *utile*, so truth, so health, are the continuous-immutable laws of the moral universe, and vice and disease, with all their perturbations, are but transient, even if ever-so-prevalent expressions. ᕗ To politics throughout, Hegel applies the like catholic standard and faith. Not any one party, or any one form of government, is absolutely and exclusively true. Truth consists in the just relations of objects to each other. A majority or democracy may rule as outrageously and do as great harm as an oligarchy or despotism—though far less likely to do so. But the great evil is either a violation of the relations just referred to, or of the moral law. The specious, the unjust, the cruel, and what is called the unnatural, though not only permitted but in a certain sense (like shade to light) inevitable in the divine scheme, are by the whole constitution of that scheme, partial, inconsistent, temporary, and though having ever-so-great an ostensible majority, are certainly destined to failure, after causing great suffering. ᕗ Theology, Hegel translates into science.* All apparent contradictions in the statement of the deific nature by different ages, nations, churches, points of view, are but fractional and imperfect expressions of one essential unity, from which they all proceed—crude endeavors or distorted parts, to be regarded both as distinct and united. In short (to put it in our own form, or summing up), that thinker or analyzer or overlooker who by an inscrutable combination of trained wisdom and natural intuition most fully accepts in perfect faith the moral unity and sanity of the creative scheme, in history, science, and all life and time, present and future, is both the truest cosmical devotee or religioso, and the profoundest philosopher. While he who, by the spell of himself and his circumstances, sees darkness and despair in the sum of the workings of God's providence, and

who, in that, denies or prevaricates, is, no matter how much piety plays on his lips, the most radical sinner and infidel. ᕗ I am the more assured in recounting Hegel a little freely here,* not only for offsetting the Carlylean letter and spirit—cutting it out all and several from the very roots, and below the roots—but to counterpoise, since the late death and deserved apotheosis of Darwin, the tenets of the evolutionists. Unspeakably precious as those are to biology, and henceforth indispensable to a right aim and estimate in study, they neither comprise or explain everything—and the last word or whisper still remains to be breathed, after the utmost of those claims, floating high and forever above them all, and above technical metaphysics. While the contributions which German Kant and Fichte and Schelling and Hegel have bequeathed to humanity—and which English Darwin has also in his field—are indispensable to the erudition of America's future, I should say that in all of them, and the best of them, when compared with the lightening flashes and flights of the old prophets and *exaltés*, the spiritual poets and poetry of all lands (as in the Hebrew Bible), there seems to be, nay certainly is, something lacking—something cold, a failure to satisfy the deepest emotions of the soul—a want of living glow, fondness, warmth, which the old *exaltés* and poets supply, and which the keenest modern philosophers so far do not. ᕗ Upon the whole, and for our purposes, this man's name certainly belongs on the list with the just-specified, first-class moral physicians of our current era—and with Emerson and two or three others—though his prescription is drastic, and perhaps destructive, while theirs is assimilating, normal, and tonic. Feudal at the core, and mental offspring and radiation of feudalism as are his books, they afford ever-valuable lessons and affinities to democratic America. Nations or individuals, we surely learn deepest from unlikeness, from a sincere opponent, from the light thrown even scornfully on dangerous spots and liabilities. (Michelangelo invoked heaven's special protection against his friends and affectionate flatterers; palpable foes he could manage for himself.) In many particulars Carlyle was indeed, as Froude terms him, one of those far-off Hebraic utterers, a new Micah or Habbakuk. His words at times bubble forth with abysmic

---

* I have deliberately repeated it all, not only in offset to Carlyle's ever-lurking pessimism and world decadence, but as presenting the most thoroughly *American points of view* I know. In my opinion the above formulas of Hegel are an essential and crowning justification of New World democracy in the creative realms of time and space. There is that about them which only the vastness, the multiplicity, and the vitality of America would seem able to comprehend, to give scope and illustration to, or to be fit for, or even originate. It is strange to me that they were born in Germany, or in the old world at all. While a Carlyle, I should say, is quite the legitimate European product to be expected.

---

* I am much indebted to J. Gostick's abstract.

inspiration. Always precious, such men; as precious now as any time. His rude, rasping, taunting, contradictory tones—what ones are more wanted amid the supple, polished, money-worshiping, Jesus-and-Judas-equalizing, suffrage-sovereignty echoes or current America? He has lit up our nineteenth century with the light of a powerful, penetrating, and perfectly honest intellect of the first class, turned on British and European politics, social life, literature, and representative personages— thoroughly dissatisfied with all, and mercilessly exposing the illness of all. But while he announces the malady, and scolds and raves about it, he himself, born and bred in the same atmosphere, is a marked illustration of it.

A COUPLE OF OLD FRIENDS—A COLERIDGE BIT ᕫ LATTER APRIL ᕫ Have run down in my country haunt for a couple of days, and am spending them by the pond. I had already discovered my kingfisher here (but only one—the mate not here yet). This fine bright morning, down by the creek, he has come out for a spree, circling, flirting, chirping, at a round rate. While I am writing these lines he is disporting himself in scoots and rings over the wider parts of the pond, into whose surface he dashes, once or twice making a loud *souse*—the spray flying in the sun—beautiful! I see his white and dark-gray plumage and peculiar shape plainly, as he has deigned to come very near me. The noble, graceful bird! Now he is sitting on the limb of an old tree, high up, bending over the water—seems to be looking at me while I memorandize. I almost fancy he knows me. *Three days later*—My second kingfisher is here with his (or her) mate. I saw the two together flying and whirling around. I had heard, in the distance, what I thought was the clear rasping staccato of the birds several times already—but I couldn't be sure the notes came from both until I saw them together. Today at noon they appeared, but apparently either on business or for a little limited exercise only. No wild frolic now, full of free fun and motion, up and down for an hour. Doubtless, now they have cares, duties, incubation responsibilities. The frolics are deferred till summer-close. ᕫ I don't know as I can finish today's memorandum better than with Coleridge's lines, curiously appropriate in more ways than one:

All Nature seems at work—slugs leave their lair,
The bees are stirring—birds are on the wing,
And winter, slumbering in the open air,
Wears on his smiling face a dream of spring;
And I, the while, the sole unbusy thing,
Nor honey make, nor pair, nor build, nor sing.

A WEEK'S VISIT TO BOSTON ᕫ MAY 1, '81 ᕫ Seems as if all the ways and means of American travel

today had been settled, not only with reference to speed and directness, but for the comfort of women, children, invalids, and old fellows like me. I went on by a through train that runs daily from Washington to the Yankee metropolis without change. You get in a sleeping car soon after dark in Philadelphia, and after ruminating an hour or two, have your bed made up if you like, draw the curtains, and go to sleep in it—fly on through Jersey to New York—hear in your half-slumbers a dull jolting and bumping sound or two—are unconsciously toted from Jersey City by a midnight steamer around the Battery and under the big bridge to the track of the New Haven road—resume your flight eastward, and early the next morning you wake up in Boston. All of which was my experience. I wanted to go to the Revere House. A tall unknown gentleman (a fellow passenger on his way to Newport, he told me; I had just chatted a few moments before with him) assisted me out through the depot crowd, procured a hack, put me in it with my traveling bag, saying smilingly and quietly, "Now I want you to let this be *my* ride," paid the driver, and before I could remonstrate, bowed himself off. ᕫ The occasion of my jaunt, I suppose I had better say here, was for a public reading of "The death of Abraham Lincoln" essay, on the sixteenth anniversary of that tragedy, which reading duly came off, night of April 15. Then I lingered a week in Boston—felt pretty well (the mood propitious, my paralysis lulled)—went around everywhere, and saw all that was to be seen, especially human beings. Boston's immense material growth— commerce, finance, commission stores, the plethora of goods, the crowded streets, and sidewalks—made of course the first surprising show. In my trip out West, last year, I thought the wand of future prosperity, future empire, must soon surely be wielded by St. Louis, Chicago, beautiful Denver, perhaps San Francisco; but I see the said wand stretched out just as decidedly in Boston, with just as much certainty of staying; evidences of copious capital—indeed no center of the New World ahead of it (half the big railroads in the West are built with Yankees' money, and they take the dividends). Old Boston with its zigzag streets and multitudinous angles (crush up a sheet of letter paper in your hand, throw it down, stamp it flat, and that is a map of old Boston)— new Boston with its miles upon miles of large and costly houses—Beacon Street, Commonwealth Avenue, and a hundred others. But the best new departures and expansions of Boston, and of all the cities of New England, are in another direction.

THE BOSTON OF TODAY ᕫ In the letters we get from Dr. Schliemann (interesting but fishy) about his excavations there in the far-off Homeric area, I notice cities, ruins, etc., as he digs them out of their graves, are certain to be in layers—that is to say, upon the foundation of an old concern, very far down indeed, is always another city or set of ruins, and upon that another super-added—and sometimes upon that still another—each representing either a long or rapid stage of growth and development, different from its predecessor, but unerringly growing out of and resting on it. In the moral, emotional, heroic, and human growths (the main of a race in my opinion), something of this kind has certainly taken place in Boston. The New England metropolis of today may be described as sunny (there is something else that makes warmth, mastering even winds and meteorologies, though those are not to be sneezed at), joyous, receptive, full of ardor, sparkle, a certain element of yearning, magnificently tolerant, yet not to be fooled; fond of good eating and drinking—costly in costume as its purse can buy; and all through its best average of houses, streets, people, that subtle something (generally thought to be climate, but it is not—it is something indefinable in the *the race*, the turn of its development) which effuses behind the whirl of animation, study, business, a happy and joyous public spirit, as distinguished from a sluggish and saturnine one. Makes me think of the glints we get (as in Symonds's books) of the jolly old Greek cities. Indeed there is a good deal of the Hellenic in B., and the people are getting handsomer too—padded out, with freer motions, and with color in their faces. I never saw (although this is not Greek) so many *fine-looking gray-haired women*. At my lecture I caught myself pausing more than once to look at them, plentiful everywhere through the audience—healthy and wifely and motherly, and wonderfully charming and beautiful—I think such as no time or land but ours could show.

MY TRIBUTE TO FOUR POETS ⮞ APRIL 16 ⮞ A short but pleasant visit to Longfellow. I am not one of the calling kind, but as the author of *Evangeline* kindly took the trouble to come and see me three years ago in Camden, where I was ill, I felt not only the impulse of my own pleasure on that occasion, but a duty. He was the only particular eminence I called on in Boston, and I shall not soon forget his lit-up face and glowing warmth and courtesy, in the modes of what is called the old school. ⮞ And now just here I feel the impulse to interpolate something about the mighty four who stamp this first American century with its birthmarks of poetic literature. In a late magazine one of my reviewers, who ought to know better, speaks of my "attitude of contempt and scorn and intolerance" toward the leading poets—of my "deriding" them, and preaching their "uselessness." If anybody cares to know what I think—

and have long thought and avowed—about them, I am entirely willing to propound. I can't imagine any better luck befalling these States for a poetical beginning and initiation than has come from Emerson, Longfellow, Bryant, and Whittier. Emerson, to me, stands unmistakably at the head, but for the others I am at a loss where to give any precedence. Each illustrious, each rounded, each distinctive. Emerson for his sweet, vital-tasting melody, rhymed philosophy, and poems as amber-clear as the honey of the wild bee he loves to sing. Longfellow for rich color, graceful forms and incidents—all that makes life beautiful and love refined—competing with the singers of Europe on their own ground, and, with one exception, better and finer work than that of any of them. Bryant pulsing the first interior verse-throbs of a mighty world—bard of the river and the wood, ever conveying a taste of open air, with scents as from hayfields, grapes, birch borders—always lurkingly fond of threnodies—beginning and ending his long career with chants of death, with here and there through all, poems, or passages of poems, touching the highest universal truths, enthusiasms, duties—morals as grim and eternal, if not as stormy and fateful, as anything in Aeschylus. While in Whittier, with his special themes (his outcropping love of heroism and war, for all his Quakerdom, his verses at times like the measured step of Cromwell's old veterans)—in Whittier lives the zeal, the moral energy that founded New England—the splendid rectitude and ardor of Luther, Milton, George Fox—I must not, dare not, say the willfulness and narrowness—though doubtless the world needs now, and always will need, almost above all, just such narrowness and willfulness.

MILLET'S PICTURES—LAST ITEMS ⮞ APRIL 18 ⮞ Went out three or four miles to the house of Quincy Shaw, to see a collection of J. F. Millet's pictures. Two rapt hours. Never before have I been so penetrated by this kind of expression. I stood long and long before "The Sower." I believe what the picture-men designate "The First Sower," as the artist executed a second copy, and a third, and, some think, improved in each. But I doubt it. There is something in this that could hardly be caught again—a sublime murkiness and original pent fury. Besides this masterpiece, there were many others (I shall never forget the simple evening scene, "Watering the Cow"), all inimitable, all perfect as pictures, works of mere art; and then it seemed to me, with that last impalpable ethic purpose from the artist (most likely unconscious to himself) which I am always looking for. To me all of them told the full story of what went before and necessitated the great French Revolution—the long precedent crushing of the masses of a heroic people into the earth, in abject poverty, hunger— every right denied, humanity attempted to be put back for generations—yet Nature's force, titanic here, the stronger and hardier for that repression—waiting terribly to break forth, revengeful—the pressure on the dikes, and the bursting at last—the storming of the Bastille—the execution of the king and queen—the tempest of massacres and blood. Yet who can wonder?

Could we wish humanity different?
Could we wish the people made of wood or stone?
Or that there be no justice in destiny or time?

OPPOSITE: *The Sower*   ABOVE: *Field People Reposing*   BELOW: *Watering the Cow*

The true France, base of all the rest, is certainly in these pictures. I comprehend "Field People Reposing," "The Diggers," and "The Angelus" in this opinion. Some folks always think of the French as a small race, five or five-and-a-half feet high, and ever frivolous and smirking. Nothing of the sort. The bulk of the personnel of France, before the revolution, were large-sized, serious, industrious as now, and simple. The revolution and Napoleon's wars dwarfed the standard of human size, but it will come up again. If for nothing else, I should dwell on my brief Boston visit for opening to me the new world of Millet's pictures. Will America ever have such an artist out of her own gestation, body, soul? SUNDAY, APRIL 17 An hour and a half, late this afternoon, in silence and half light, in the great nave of Memorial Hall, Cambridge, the walls thickly covered with mural tablets, bearing the names of students and graduates of the university who fell in the Secession War. APRIL 23 It was well I got away in fair order, for if I had stayed another week I should have been killed with kindness, and with eating and drinking.

BIRDS—AND A CAUTION MAY 14
Home again; down temporarily in the Jersey woods. Between 8 and 9 A.M. a full concert of birds, from different quarters, in keeping with the fresh scent, the peace, the naturalness all around me. I am lately noticing the russet-back, size of the robin or a trifle less, light breast and shoulders, with irregular dark stripes—tail long—sits hunched up by the hour these days, top of a tall bush, or some tree, singing blithely. I often get near and listen as he seems tame; I like to watch the working of his bill and throat, the quaint sidle of his body, and flex of his long tail. I hear the woodpecker, and night and early morning the shuttle of the whippoorwill—noons, the gurgle of thrush delicious, and *meo-o-ow* of the catbird. Many I cannot name; but I do not very particularly seek information. (You must not know too much, or be too precise or scientific about birds and trees and flowers and water craft; a certain free margin, and even vagueness—perhaps ignorance, credulity—helps your enjoyment of these things, and of the sentiment of feathered, wooded, river, or marine Nature generally. I repeat it—don't want to know too exactly, or the reasons why. My own notes have been written off hand in the latitude of middle New Jersey. Though they describe what I saw—what appeared to me—I dare say the expert ornithologist, botanist, or entomologist will detect more than one slip in them.)

SAMPLES OF MY COMMONPLACE BOOK
I ought not to offer a record of these days, interests, recuperations, without including a certain old, well-thumbed commonplace book*, filled with favorite excerpts, I carried in my pocket for three summers, and absorbed over and over again, when the mood invited. I find so much in having a poem or fine suggestion sink into me (a little then goes a great ways) prepared by these vacant-sane and natural influences.

---

* SAMPLES OF MY COMMONPLACE BOOK
DOWN AT THE CREEK

I have—says old Pindar—many swift arrows in my quiver which speak to the wise, though they need an interpreter to the thoughtless.

Such a man as it takes ages to make, and ages to understand.   H. D. THOREAU

If you hate a man, don't kill him, but let him live.   BUDDHISTIC

Famous swords are made of refuse scraps, thought worthless.

Poetry is the only verity—the expression of a sound mind speaking after the ideal—and not after the apparent.   EMERSON

The form of oath among the Shoshone Indians is, "The earth hears me. The sun hears me. Shall I lie?"

The true test of civilization is not the census, nor the size of cities, nor the crops—no, but the kind of a man the country turns out.
                                   EMERSON

The whole wide ether is the eagle's sway:
The whole earth is a brave man's fatherland.
                                   EURIPIDES

Spices crushed, their pungence yield,
Trodden scents their sweets respire;
Would you have its strength revealed?
Cast the incense in the fire.

Matthew Arnold speaks of "the huge Mississippi of falsehood called History."

The wind blows north, the wind blows south,
The wind blows east and west;
No matter how the free wind blows,
Some ship will find it best.

Preach not to others what they should eat, but eat as becomes you, and be silent.
                                   EPICTETUS

Victor Hugo makes a donkey meditate and apostrophize thus:
My brother, man, if you would know the truth,
We both are by the same dull walls shut in;

MY NATIVE SAND AND SALT ONCE MORE ⁂ JULY 25, '81—FAR ROCKAWAY, L.I. ⁂ A good day here, on a jaunt, amid the sand and salt, a steady breeze setting in from the sea, the sun shining, the sedge odor, the noise of the surf, a mixture of hissing and booming, the milk-white crests curling over. I had a leisurely bath and naked ramble as of old, on the warm-gray shore sands, my companions off in a boat in deeper water (I shouting to them Jupiter's menaces against the gods, from Pope's Homer). ⁂ JULY 28—TO LONG BRANCH ⁂ 8:30 A.M., on the steamer *Plymouth Rock*, foot of 23d Street, New York, for Long Branch. Another fine day, fine sights, the shores, the shipping and bay—everything comforting to the body and spirit of me. (I find the human and objective atmosphere of New York City and Brooklyn more affiliative to me than any other.) *An hour later*—Still on the steamer, now sniffing the salt very plainly—the long pulsating *swash* as our boat steams seaward—the hills of Navesink and many passing vessels—the air the best part of all. At

---

The gate is massive and the dungeon strong.
But you look through the keyhole out beyond,
And call this knowledge; yet have not at hand
The key wherein to turn the fatal lock.

"William Cullen Bryant surprised me once," relates a writer in a New York paper, "by saying that prose was the natural language of composition, and he wondered how anybody came to write poetry."

Farewell! I did not know thy worth;
But thou art gone, and now 'tis prized:
So angels walked unknown on earth,
But when they flew were recognized.
                                          HOOD

John Burroughs, writing of Thoreau, says: "He improves with age—in fact requires age to take off a little of his asperity, and fully ripen him. The world likes a good hater and refuser almost as well as it likes a good lover and accepter—only it likes him farther off."

LOUISE MICHEL
AT THE BURIAL OF BLANQUI (1881):
Blanqui drilled his body to subjection to his grand conscience and his noble passions, and commencing as a young man, broke with all that is sybaritish in modern civilization. Without the power to sacrifice self, great ideas will never bear fruit.

Out of the leaping furnace flame
A mass of molten silver came;
Then, beaten into pieces three,
Went forth to meet its destiny.
The first a crucifix was made,
Within a soldier's knapsack laid;
The second was a locket fair,
Where a mother kept her dead child's hair;
The third—a bangle, bright and warm,
Around a faithless woman's arm.

A mighty pain to love it is,
And 'tis a pain that pain to miss;
But of all pain the greatest pain,
It is to love, but love in vain.

MAURICE F. EGAN
ON DE GUÉRIN:
A pagan heart, a Christian soul had he,
He followed Christ, yet for dead Pan he sighed,
Till earth and heaven met within his breast:
As if Theocritus in Sicily
Had come upon the Figure crucified,
And lost his gods in deep, Christ-given rest.

And if I pray, the only prayer
That moves my lips for me,
Is, leave the mind that now I bear,
And give me Liberty.
                              EMILY BRONTË

I travel on not knowing,
I would not if I might;
I would rather walk with God in the dark,
Than go alone in the light;
I would rather walk with Him by faith
Than pick my way by sight.

PROF. HUXLEY IN A LATE LECTURE:
I myself agree with the sentiment of Thomas Hobbes, of Malmesbury, that "the scope of all speculation is the performance of some action or thing to be done." I have not any very great respect for, or interest in, mere "knowing," as such.

PRINCE METTERNICH:
Napoleon was of all men in the world the one who most profoundly despised the race. He had a marvellous insight into the weaker sides of human nature (and all our passions are either foibles themselves, or the cause of foibles). He was a very small man of imposing character. He was ignorant, as a sublieutenant generally is: a remarkable instinct supplied the lack of knowledge. From his mean opinion of men, he never had any anxiety lest he should go wrong. He ventured everything, and gained thereby an immense step toward success. Throwing himself upon a prodigious arena, he amazed the world, and made himself master of it, while others cannot even get so far as being masters of their own hearth. Then he went on and on, until he broke his neck.

[113]

Long Branch the bulk of the day, stopped at a good hotel, took all very leisurely, had an excellent dinner, and then drove for over two hours about the place, especially Ocean Avenue, the finest drive one can imagine, seven or eight miles right along the beach. In all directions costly villas, palaces, millionaires (but few among them I opine like my friend George W. Childs, whose personal integrity, generosity, unaffected simplicity, go beyond all worldly wealth).

HOT WEATHER NEW YORK ᴑ AUGUST ᴑ In the big city awhile. Even the height of the dogdays, there is a good deal of fun about New York, if you only avoid fluster and take all the buoyant wholesomeness that offers. More comfort, too, than most folks think. A middle-aged man, with plenty of money in his pocket tells me that he has been off for a month to all the swell places, has disbursed a small fortune, has been hot and out of kilter everywhere, and has returned home and lived in New York City the last two weeks quite contented and happy. People forget when it is hot here, it is generally hotter still in other places. New York is so situated, with the great ozonic brine on both sides, it comprises the most favorable health chances in the world. (If only the suffocating crowding of some of its tenement houses could be broken up.) I find I never sufficiently realized how beautiful are the upper two-thirds of Manhattan Island. I am stopping at Mott Haven, and have been familiar now for ten days with the region above One-Hundredth Street, and along the Harlem River and Washington Heights. Am dwelling a few days with my friends, Mr. and Mrs. J. H. J., and a merry houseful of young ladies. Am putting the last touches on the printer's copy of my new volume of *Leaves of Grass*—the completed book at last. Work at it two or three hours, and then go down and loaf along the Harlem River; have just had a good spell of this recreation. The sun sufficiently veiled, a soft south breeze, the river full of small or large shells (light taper boats) darting up and down, some singly, now and then long ones with six or eight young fellows practicing—very inspiriting sights. Two fine yachts lie anchored off the shore. I linger long, enjoying the sundown, the glow, the streaked sky, the heights, distances, shadows. ᴑ AUG. 10 ᴑ As I haltingly ramble an hour or two this forenoon by the more secluded parts of the shore, or sit under an old cedar halfway up the hill, the city near in view, many young parties gather to bathe or swim, squads of boys, generally twos or threes, some larger ones, along the sand bottom, or off an old pier close by. A peculiar and pretty carnival—at its height a hundred lads or young men, very democratic, but all decent-behaving. The laughter, voices, calls, responses—the springing and diving of the bathers from the great stringpiece of the decayed pier, where climb or stand long ranks of them, naked, rose-colored, with movements, postures ahead of any sculpture. To all this, the sun, so bright, the dark green shadow of the hills the other side, the amber rolling waves, changing as the tide comes in to a transparent tea color—the frequent splash of the playful boys, sousing—the glittering drops sparkling, and the good western breeze blowing.

"CUSTER'S LAST RALLY" ᴑ Went today to see this just-finished painting by John Mulvany, who has been out in far Dakota, on the spot, at the forts, and among the frontiersmen, soldiers, and Indians for the last two years, on purpose to sketch it in from reality, or the best that could be got of it. Sat for over an hour before the picture, completely absorbed in the first view. A vast canvas, I should say twenty or twenty-two feet by twelve, all crowded, and yet not crowded, conveying such a vivid play of color, it takes a little time to get used to it. There are no tricks; there is no throwing of shades in masses; it is all at first painfully real, overwhelming, needs good nerves to look at it. Forty or fifty figures, perhaps more, in full finish, and detail in the midground with three times that number, or more, through the rest—swarms upon swarms of savage Sioux, in their war bonnets, frantic, mostly on ponies, driving through the background, through the smoke, like a hurricane of demons. A dozen of the figures are wonderful. Altogether a Western, autochthonic phase of America, the frontiers, culminating, typical, deadly, heroic to the uttermost—nothing in the books like it, nothing in Homer, nothing in Shakespeare; more grim and sublime than either, all native, all our own, and all a fact. A great lot of muscular, tan-faced men, brought to bay under terrible circumstances—death ahold of them, yet every man undaunted, not one losing his head, wringing out every cent of the pay before they sell their lives. Custer (his hair cut short) stands in the middle, with dilated eye and extended arm, aiming a huge cavalry pistol. Captain Cook is there, partially wounded, blood on the white handkerchief around his head, aiming his carbine cooly, half-kneeling (his body was afterwards found close by Custer's). The slaughtered or half-slaughtered horses, for breastworks, make a peculiar feature. Two dead Indians, herculean, lie in the foreground, clutching their Winchester rifles, very characteristic. The many soldiers, their faces and attitudes, the carbines, the broad-brimmed western hats, the powder smoke in puffs, the dying horses with their rolling eyes almost human in their agony, the clouds of war-bonneted Sioux in the background, the figures of Custer and Cook—with indeed the whole scene, dreadful, yet with an attraction and beauty that will remain in my memory. With all its color and fierce action, a certain Greek continence pervades it. A sunny sky and clear light envelop all. There is an almost entire absence of the stock traits of European war pictures. The physiognomy of the work is realistic and Western. I only saw it for an hour or so; but it needs to be seen many times—needs to be studied over and over again. I could look on such a work at brief intervals all my life without tiring; it is very tonic to me; then it has an ethic purpose below all, as all great art must have. The artist said the sending of the picture abroad, probably to London, had been talked of. I advised him if it went abroad to take it to Paris. I think they might appreciate it there—nay, they certainly would. Then I would like to show Messieur Crapeau that some things can be done in America as well as others.

SOME OLD ACQUAINTANCES—MEMORIES ᐤ AUG. 16 ᐤ "Chalk a big mark for today," was one of the sayings of an old sportsman friend of mine, when he had had unusually good luck—come home thoroughly tired, but with satisfactory results of fish or birds. Well, today might warrant such a mark for me. Everything propitious from the start. An hour's fresh stimulation, coming down ten miles of Manhattan Island by railroad and 8 o'clock stage. Then an excellent breakfast at Pfaff's restaurant, 24th Street. Our host himself, an old friend of mine, quickly appeared on the scene to welcome me and bring up the news, and, first opening a big fat bottle of the best wine in the cellar, talk about antebellum times, '59 and '60, and the jovial suppers at his then Broadway place, near Bleecker Street. Ah, the friends and names and frequenters, those times, that place. Most are dead—Ada Clare, Wilkins, Daisy Sheppard, O'Brien, Henry Clapp, Stanley, Mullin, Wood, Brougham, Arnold—all gone. And there Pfaff and I, sitting opposite each other at the little table, gave a remembrance to them in a style they would have themselves full confirmed, namely, big, brimming, filled-up champagne glasses, drained in abstracted silence, very leisurely, to the last drop. (Pfaff is a generous German *restaurateur*, silent, stout, jolly, and I should say the best selector of champagne in America.)

A DISCOVERY OF OLD AGE ᐤ Perhaps the best is always cumulative. One's eating and drinking one wants fresh, and for the nonce, right off, and have done with it—but I would not give a straw for that person or poem, or friend, or city, or work of art, that was not more grateful the second time than the first—and more still the third. Nay, I do not believe any grandest eligibility ever comes forth at first. In my own experience (persons, poems, places, characters) I dis-

cover the best hardly ever at first (no absolute rule about it, however), sometimes suddenly bursting forth, or stealthily opening to me, perhaps after years of unwitting familiarity, unappreciation, usage.

A VISIT, AT THE LAST, TO R. W. EMERSON ᐤ CONCORD, MASS. ᐤ One here on a visit—elastic, mellow, Indian-summery weather. Came to-day from Boston (a pleasant ride of 40 minutes by steam, through Somerville, Belmont, Waltham, Stony Brook, and other lively towns), convoyed by my friend F. B. Sanborn, and to his ample house, and the kindness and hospitality of Mrs. S. and their fine family. Am writing this under the shade of some old hickories and elms, just after 4 P.M., on the porch, within a stone's throw of the Concord River. Off against me, across stream, on a meadow and side-hill, haymakers are gathering and wagoning-in probably their second or third crop. The spread of emerald green and brown, the knolls, the score or two of little haycocks dotting the meadow, the loaded-up wagons, the patient horses, the slow-strong action of the men and pitchforks—all in the just-waning afternoon, with patches of yellow sunsheen, mottled by long shadows—a cricket shrilly chirping, herald of the dusk—a boat with two figures noiselessly gliding along the little river, passing under the stone bridge-arch—the slight settling haze of aerial moisture, the sky and the peacefulness expanding in all directions and overhead—fill and soothe me. ᐤ SAME EVENING ᐤ Never had I a better piece of luck befall me: a long and blessed evening with Emerson, in a way I couldn't have wished better or different. For nearly two hours he has been placidly sitting where I could see his face in the best light, near me. Mrs. S.'s back-parlor well filled with people, neighbors, many fresh and charming faces, women, mostly young, but some old. My friend A. B. Alcott and his daughter Louisa were there early. A good deal of talk, the subject Henry Thoreau—some new glints of his life and fortunes, with letters to and from him—one of the best by Margaret Fuller, others by Horace Greeley, Channing, etc.—one from Thoreau himself, most quaint and interesting. (No doubt I seemed very stupid to the roomful of company, taking hardly any part in the conversation; but I had "my own pail to milk in," as the Swiss proverb puts it.) My seat and the relative arrangement were such that, without being rude, or anything of the kind, I could just look squarely at E., which I did a good part of the two hours. On entering, he had spoken very briefly and politely to several of the company, then settled himself in his chair, a trifle pushed back, and, though a listener and apparently an alert one, remained silent through the whole talk and discussion. A lady friend quietly took a seat next him, to give special attention. A good color in his face, eyes clear, with the well-known expression of sweetness, and the old clear-peering aspect quite the same. ❧ NEXT DAY ❧ Several hours at E's house, and dinner there. An old familiar house (he has been in it thirty-five years), with surroundings, furnishment, roominess, and plain elegance and fullness, signifying democratic ease, sufficient opulence, and an admirable old-fashioned simplicity—modern luxury, with its mere sumptuousness and affectation, either touched lightly upon or ignored altogether. Dinner the same. Of course the best of the occasion (Sunday, September 18, '81) was the sight of E. himself. As just said, a healthy color in the cheeks, and good light in the eyes, cheery expression, and just the amount of talking that best suited, namely, a word or short phrase only where needed, and almost always with a smile. Besides Emerson himself, Mrs. E., with their daughter Ellen, the son Edward and his wife, with my friend F. S. and Mrs. S., and others, relatives and intimates. Mrs. Emerson, resuming the subject of the evening before (I sat next to her), gave me further and fuller information about Thoreau, who, years ago, during Mr. E.'s absence in Europe, had lived for some time in the family, by invitation.

OTHER CONCORD NOTATIONS ❧ Though the evening at Mr. and Mrs. Sanborn's, and the memorable family dinner at Mr. and Mrs. Emerson's, have most pleasantly and permanently filled my memory, I must not slight other notations of Concord. I went to the old Manse, walked through the ancient garden, entered the rooms, noted the quaintness, the unkempt grass and bushes, the little panes in the windows, the low ceiling, the spicy smell, the creepers embowering the light. Went to the Concord battleground, which is close by, scanned French's statue, "The Minuteman," read Emerson's poetic inscription on the base, lingered a long while on the bridge, and stopped by the grave of the unnamed British soldiers, buried there the day after the fight in April '75. Then riding on (thanks to my friend Miss M. and her spirited white ponies, she driving them), a half-hour at Hawthorne's and Thoreau's graves. I got out and went up of course on foot, and stood a long while and pondered. They lie close together in a pleasant wooded spot well up the cemetery hill, "Sleepy Hollow." The flat surface of the first was densely covered by myrtle, with a border of arbor vitae, and the other had a brown headstone, moderately elaborate, with inscriptions. By Henry's side lies his brother John, of whom much was expected but he died young. Then to Walden Pond, that beautifully embowered sheet of water, and spent over an hour there. On the spot in the woods where Thoreau had his solitary house is now quite a

cairn of stones, to mark the place; I too carried one and deposited on the heap. As we drove back, saw the "School of Philosophy," but it was shut up, and I would not have it opened for me. Near by stopped at the house of W. T. Harris, the Hegelian, who came out, and we had a pleasant chat while I sat in the wagon. I shall not soon forget those Concord drives, and especially that charming Sunday forenoon one with my friend Miss M., and the white ponies.

BOSTON COMMON—MORE OF EMERSON ❧ OCT. 10–13 ❧ I spend a good deal of time on the Common these delicious days and nights—every midday from 11:30 to about 1—and almost every sunset another hour. I know all the big trees, especially the old elms along Tremont and Beacon Streets, and have come to a sociable-silent understanding with most of them, in the sunlit air (yet crispy cool enough), as I saunter along the wide unpaved walks. Up and down this breadth by Beacon Street, between these same old elms, I walked for two hours, of a bright sharp February midday twenty-one years ago, with Emerson, then in his prime, keen, physically and morally magnetic, armed at every point, and when he chose, wielding the emotional just as well as the intellectual. During those two hours he was the talker and I the listener. It was an argument-statement, reconnoitering, review, attack, and pressing home (like an army corps in order, artillery, cavalry, infantry) of all that could be said against that part (and a main part) in the construction of my poems, *Children of Adam.* More precious than gold to me, that dissertation—it afforded me, ever after, this strange and paradoxical lesson; each point of E.'s statement was unanswerable, no judge's charge ever more complete or convincing, I could never hear the points better put—and then I felt down in my soul the clear and unmistakable conviction to disobey all, and pursue my own way. "What have you to say then to such things?" said E., pausing in conclusion. "Only that while I can't answer them at all, I feel more settled than ever to adhere to my own theory, and exemplify it," was my candid response. Whereupon we went and had a good dinner at the American House. And thenceforward I never wavered or was touched with qualms (as I confess I had been two or three times before).

AN OSSIANIC NIGHT—DEAREST FRIENDS ❧ NOV., '81 ❧ Again back in Camden. As I cross the Delaware in long trips tonight, between 9 and 11, the scene overhead is a peculiar one—swift sheets of flitting vapor gauze, followed by dense clouds throwing an inky pall on everything. Then a spell of that transparent steel-gray black sky I have noticed under similar circumstances, on which the moon would beam for a few moments with calm luster, throwing down a broad dazzle of highway on the waters; then the mists careering again. All silently, yet driven as if by the furies they sweep along, sometimes quite thin, sometimes thicker —a real Ossianic night—amid the whirl, absent or dead friends, the old, the past, somehow tenderly suggested —while the Gael strains chant themselves from the mists ("Be thy soul blest, O Carril! in the midst of thy eddying winds. O that thou wouldst come to my hall when I am alone by night! And thou dost come, my friend. I hear often thy light hand on my harp, when it hangs on the distant wall, and the feeble sound touches my ear. Why dost thou not speak to me in my grief, and tell me when I shall behold my friends? But thou passest away in thy murmuring blast; the wind whistles through the gray hairs of Ossian"). ❧ But most of all, those changes of moon and sheets of hurrying vapor and black clouds, with the sense of rapid action in weird silence, recall the far-back Erse belief that such above were the preparations for receiving the wraiths of just-slain warriors ("We sat that night in Selma, round the strength of the shell. The wind was abroad in the oaks. The spirit of the mountain roared. The blast came rustling through the hall, and gently touched my harp. The sound was mournful and low, like the song of the tomb. Fingal heard it the first. The crowded sighs of his bosom rose. Some of my heroes are low, said the gray-haired king of Morven. I hear the sound of death on the harp. Ossian, touch the trembling string. Bid the sorrow rise, that their spirits may fly with joy to Morven's woody hills. I touched the harp before the king; the sound was mournful and low. Bend forward from your clouds, I said, ghosts of my fathers! Bend. Lay by the red terror of your course. Receive the falling chief; whether he comes from a distant land, or rises from the rolling sea. Let his robe of mist be near; his spear that is formed of a cloud. Place a half-extinguished meteor by his side, in the form of a hero's sword. And oh! let his countenance be lovely, that his friends may delight in his presence. Bend from your clouds, I said, ghosts of my fathers, bend. Such was my song in Selma, to the lightly trembling harp"). ❧ How or why I know not, just at the moment, but I too muse and think of my best friends in their distant homes —of William O'Connor, of Maurice Bucke, of John Burroughs, and of Mrs. Gilchrist—friends of my soul— stanchest friends of my other soul, my poems.

ONLY A NEW FERRYBOAT ❧ JAN. 12, '82
❧ Such a show as the Delaware presented an hour before sundown yesterday evening, all along between Philadelphia and Camden, is worth weaving into an item. It was full tide, a fair breeze from the southwest, the water of a pale tawny color, and just enough motion to make things frolicsome and lively. Add to these an approaching sunset of unusual splendor, a broad tumble of clouds, with much golden haze and profusion of beaming shaft and dazzle. In the midst of all, in the clear drab of the afternoon light, there steam'd up the river the large, new boat, the *Wenonah*, as pretty an object as you could wish to see, lightly and swiftly skimming along, all trim and white, covered with flags, transparent red and blue, streaming out in the breeze. Only a new ferryboat, and yet in its fitness comparable with the prettiest product of Nature's cunning, and rivaling it. High up in the transparent ether gracefully balanced and circled four or five great sea hawks, while here below, amid the pomp and picturesqueness of sky and river, swam this creation of artificial beauty and motion and power, in its way no less perfect.

DEATH OF LONGFELLOW ❧ CAMDEN, APRIL 3, '82 ❧ I have just returned from an old forest haunt, where I love to go occasionally away from parlors, pavements, and the newspapers and magazines— and where, of a clear forenoon, deep in the shade of pines and cedars and a tangle of old laurel trees and vines, the news of Longfellow's death first reached me. For want of anything better, let me lightly twine a sprig of the sweet ground ivy trailing so plentifully through the dead leaves at my feet, with reflections of that half-hour alone, there in the silence, and lay it as my contribution on the dead bard's grave. ❧ Longfellow in his voluminous works seems to me not only to be eminent in the style and forms of poetical expression that mark the present age (an idiosyncrasy, almost a sickness, of verbal melody), but to bring what is always dearest as poetry to the general human heart and taste, and probably must be so in the nature of things. He is certainly the sort of bard and counteractant most needed for our materialistic, self-assertive, money-worshiping, Anglo-Saxon races, and especially for the present age in America—an age tyrannically regulated with reference to the manufacturer, the merchant, the financier, the politician, and the day workman—for whom and among whom he comes as the poet of melody, courtesy, deference—poet of the mellow twilight of the past in Italy, Germany, Spain, and in Northern Europe—poet of all sympathetic gentleness—and universal poet of women and young people. I should have to think long if I were asked to name the man who has done more, and in more valuable directions, for America. ❧ I doubt if there ever was before such a fine intuitive judge and selecter of poems. His translations of many German and Scandinavian pieces are said to be better than the vernaculars. He does not urge or lash. His influence is like good drink or air.

He is not tepid either, but always vital, with flavor, motion, grace. He strikes a splendid average, and does not sing exceptional passions, or humanity's jagged escapades. He is not revolutionary, brings nothing offensive or new, does not deal hard blows. On the contrary, his songs soothe and heal, or if they excite, it is a healthy and agreeable excitement. His very anger is gentle, is at second hand (as in the "Quadroon Girl" and the "Witnesses"). ᴥ There is no undue element of pensiveness in Longfellow'ss trains. Even in the early translation, the Manrique, the movement is as of strong and steady wind or tide, holding up and buoying. Death is not avoided through his many themes, but there is something almost winning in his original verses and renderings on that dread subject—as, closing the "Happiest Land" dispute,

> And then the landlord's daughter
> Up to heaven raised her hand,
> And said, "Ye may no more contend,
> There lies the happiest land."

ᴥ To the ungracious complaint-charge of his want of racy nativity and special originality, I shall only say that America and the world may well be reverently thankful —can never be thankful enough—for any such singing bird vouchsafed out of the centuries, without asking that the notes be different from those of other songsters; adding what I have heard Longfellow himself say, that ere the New World can be worthily original, and announce herself and her own heroes, she must be well saturated with the originality of others, and respectfully consider the heroes that lived before Agamemnon.

STARTING NEWSPAPERS ᴥ Reminiscences (from the *Camden Courier*)—As I sat taking my evening sail across the Delaware in the staunch ferryboat *Beverly*, a night or two ago, I was joined by two young reporter friends. "I have a message for you," said one of them; "the C. folks told me to say they would like a piece signed by your name, to go in their first number. Can you do it for them?" "I guess so," said I; "what might it be about?" "Well, anything on newspapers, or perhaps what you've done yourself, starting them." And off the boys went, for we had reached the Philadelphia side. The hour was fine and mild, the bright half-moon shining; Venus, with excess of splendor, just setting in the west, and the great Scorpion rearing its length more than half up in the southeast. As I crossed leisurely for an hour in the pleasant night scene, my young friend's words brought up quite a string of reminiscences. ᴥ I commenced when I was but a boy of eleven or twelve writing sentimental bits for the old *Long Island Patriot*, in Brooklyn; this was about 1832. Soon after, I had a piece or two in George P. Morris's then celebrated and fashionable *Mirror*, of New York City. I remember with what half-suppressed excitement I used to watch for the big, fat, red-faced, slow-moving, very old English carrier who distributed the *Mirror* in Brooklyn; and when I got one, opening and cutting the leaves with trembling fingers. How it made my heart double-beat to see *my piece* on the pretty white paper, in nice type. ᴥ My first real venture was the *Long Islander*, in my own beautiful town of Huntington, in 1839. I was about twenty years old. I had been teaching country school for two or three years in various parts of Suffolk and Queens Counties, but liked printing; had been at it while a lad, learned the trade of compositor, and was encouraged to start a paper in the region where I was born. I went to New York, bought a press and types, hired some little help, but did most of the work myself, including the presswork. Everything seemed turning out well (only my own restlessness prevented me gradually establishing a permanent property there). I bought a good horse, and every week went all around the country serving my papers, devoting one day and night to it. I never had happier jaunts—going over to south side, to Babylon, down the south road, across to Smithtown and Comac, and back home. The experiences of those jaunts, the dear old-fashioned farmers and their wives, the stops by the hay-fields, the hospitality, nice dinners, occasional evenings, the girls, the rides through the brush, come up in my memory to this day. ᴥ I next went to the *Aurora* daily in New York City—a sort of free lance. Also wrote regularly for the *Tattler*, an evening paper. With these and a little outside work was occupied off and on, until I went to edit the *Brooklyn Eagle*, where for two years I had one of the pleasantest sits of my life—a good owner, good pay, and easy work and hours. The troubles in the Democratic party broke forth about those times (1848–'49) and I split off with the radicals, which led to rows with the boss and "the party," and I lost my place. ᴥ Being now out of a job, I was offered impromptu (it happened between the acts one night in the lobby of the old Broadway theater near Pearl Street, New York City) a good chance to go down to New Orleans on the staff of the *Crescent*, a daily to be started there with plenty of capital behind it. One of the owners, who was north buying material, met me walking in the lobby, and though it was our first acquaintance, after fifteen minutes' talk (and a drink) we made a formal bargain, and he paid me two hundred dollars down to bind the contract and bear my expenses to New Orleans. I started two days afterward; had a good leisurely time, as the paper wasn't to be out in three weeks. I enjoyed my journey and Louisiana life much. Returning to Brooklyn a year or two afterward I started the *Freeman*, first as a weekly, then daily. Pretty soon the Secession War broke out, and I, too, got drawn in the current southward, and spent the following three years there (as memorandized preceding). ᵃᵉ Besides starting them as aforementioned, I have had to do, one time or another, during my life, with a long list of papers, at divers places, sometimes under queer circumstances. During the war, the hospitals at Washington, among other means of amusement, printed a little sheet among themselves, surrounded by wounds and death, the *Armory Square Gazette*, to which I contributed. The same long afterward, casually, to a paper—I think it was called the *Jimplecute*—out in Colorado where I stopped at the time. When I was in Quebec province, in Canada, in 1880, I went into the queerest little old French printing office near Tadoussac. It was far more primitive and ancient than my Camden friend William Kurtz's place up on Federal Street. I remember, as a youngster, several characteristic old printers of a kind hard to be seen these days.

THE GREAT UNREST OF WHICH WE ARE PART ᵃᵉ

My thoughts went floating on vast and mystic currents as I sat today in solitude and half-shade by the creek—returning mainly to two principal centers. One of my cherished themes for a never-achieved poem has been the two impetuses of man and the universe—in the latter, creation's incessant unrest,* exfoliation (Darwin's evolution, I suppose). Indeed, what is Nature but change, in all its visible, and still more its invisible processes? Or what is humanity in its faith, love, heroism, poetry, even morals, but *emotion?*

BY EMERSON'S GRAVE ᵃᵉ MAY 6, '82 ᵃᵉ

We stand by Emerson's new-made grave without sadness—indeed a solemn joy and faith, almost hauteur—our soul-benison no more

> *Warrior, rest, thy task is done,*

for one beyond the warriors of the world lies surely symbolized here. A just man, poised on himself, all-loving, all-inclosing, and sane and clear as the sun. Nor

---

* "Fifty thousand years ago the constellation of the Great Bear or Dipper was a starry cross; a hundred thousand years hence the imaginary dipper will be upside down, and the stars which form the bowl and handle will have changed places. The misty nebulae are moving, and besides are whirling around in great spirals, some one way, some another. Every molecule of matter in the whole universe is swinging to and fro; every particle of ether which fills space is in jellylike vibration. Light is one kind of motion, heat another, electricity another, magnetism another, sound another. Every human sense is the result of motion; every perception, every thought is but motion of the molecules of the brain translated by that incomprehensible thing we call mind. The processes of growth, of existence, of decay, whether in worlds, or in the minutest organisms, are but motion."

does it seem so much Emerson himself we are here to honor—it is conscience, simplicity, culture, humanity's attributes at their best, yet applicable if need be to average affairs, and eligible to all. So used are we to suppose a heroic death can only come from out of battle or storm, or mighty personal contest, or amid dramatic incidents or danger (have we not been taught so for ages by all the plays and poems?) that few even of those who most sympathizingly mourn Emerson's late departure will fully appreciate the ripened grandeur of that event, with its play of calm and fitness, like evening light on the sea. ᵃᵉ How I shall henceforth dwell on the blessed hours when, not long since, I saw that benignant face, the clear eyes, the silently smiling mouth, the form yet upright in its great age—to the very last, with so much spring and cheeriness, and such an absence of decrepitude, that even the term *venerable* hardly seemed fitting. ᵃᵉ Perhaps the life now rounded and completed in its mortal development, and which nothing can change or harm more, has its most illustrious halo, not in its splendid intellectual or esthetic products, but as forming in its entirety one of the few (alas! how few!) perfect and flawless excuses for being, of the entire literary class. ᵃᵉ We can say, as Abraham Lincoln at Gettysburg, It is not we who come to consecrate the dead—we reverently come to receive, if so it may be, some consecration to ourselves and daily work from him.

AT PRESENT WRITING—PERSONAL ᵃᵉ

A LETTER TO A GERMAN FRIEND—EXTRACT ᵃᵉ MAY 31, '82 ᵃᵉ "From today I enter upon my 64th year. The paralysis that first affected me nearly ten years ago has since remained, with varying course—seems to have settled quietly down, and will probably continue. I easily tire, am very clumsy, cannot walk far; but my spirits are first-rate. I go around in public almost every day—now and then take long trips, by railroad or boat, hundreds of miles—live largely in the open air—am sunburned and stout (weigh 190)—keep up my activity and interest in life, people, progress, and the questions of the day. About two-thirds of the time I am quite comfortable. What mentality I ever had remains entirely unaffected; though physically I am a half-paralytic, and likely to be so, long as I live. But the principal object of my life seems to have been accomplished—I have the most devoted and ardent of friends, and affectionate relatives—and of enemies I really make no account."

AFTER TRYING A CERTAIN BOOK ᵃᵉ

I tried to read a beautifully printed and scholarly volume on *The Theory of Poetry*, received by mail this morning from England—but gave it up at last for a bad job. Here are some capricious pencilings that followed, as I find them in my notes: ℘ In youth and maturity Poems are charged with sunshine and varied pomp of day; but as the soul more and more takes precedence (the sensuous still included), the Dusk becomes the poet's atmosphere. I too have sought, and ever seek, the brilliant sun, and make my songs according. But as I grow old, the half-lights of evening are far more to me. ℘ The play of Imagination, with the sensuous objects of Nature for symbols and Faith—with Love and Pride as the unseen impetus and moving power of all, make up the curious chessgame of a poem. ℘ Common teachers or critics are always asking "What does it mean?" Symphony of fine musician, or sunset, or sea waves rolling up the beach—what do they mean? Undoubtedly in the most subtle-elusive sense they mean something—as love does, and religion does, and the best poem; but who shall fathom and define those meanings? (I do not intend this as a warrant for wildness and frantic escapades—but to justify the soul's frequent joy in what cannot be defined to the intellectual part, or to calculation.) ℘ At its best, poetic lore is like what may be heard of conversation in the dusk, from speakers far or hid, of which we get only a few broken murmurs. What is not gathered is far more—perhaps the main thing. ℘ Grandest poetic passages are only to be taken at free removes, as we sometimes look for stars at night, not by gazing directly toward them, but off one side. ℘ TO A POETIC STUDENT AND FRIEND ℘ I only seek to put you in rapport. Your own brain, heart, evolution, must not only understand the matter, but largely supply it.

FINAL CONFESSIONS—LITERARY TESTS

℘ So draw near their end these garrulous notes. There have doubtless occurred some repetitions, technical errors in the consecutiveness of dates, in the minutiæ of botanical, astronomical, etc., exactness, and perhaps elsewhere; for in gathering up, writing, peremptorily dispatching copy, this hot weather (last of July and through August, '82), and delaying not the printers, I have had to hurry along, no time to spare. But in the deepest veracity of all—in reflections of objects, scenes, Nature's outpourings, to my senses and receptivity, as they seemed to me—in the work of giving those who care for it, some authentic glints, specimen days of my life—and in the *bona fide* spirit and relations, from author to reader, on all the subjects designed, and as far as they go, I feel to make unmitigated claims. ℘ The synopsis of my early life, Long Island, New York City, and so forth, and the diary jottings in the Secession War, tell their own story. My plan in starting what constitutes most of the middle of the book, was originally for hints and data of a Nature poem that should carry one's experiences a few hours, commencing at noon-flush, and

so through the afterpart of the day—I suppose led to such idea by my own life-afternoon now arrived. But I soon found I could move at more ease by giving the narrative at first hand. (Then there is a humiliating lesson one learns, in serene hours, of a fine day or night. Nature seems to look on all fixed-up poetry and art as something almost impertinent.) ℘ Thus I went on, years following, various seasons and areas, spinning forth my thought beneath the night and stars (or as I was confined to my room by half-sickness), or at midday looking out upon the sea, or far north steaming over the Saguenay's black breast, jotting all down in the loosest sort of chronological order, and here printing from my impromptu notes, hardly even the seasons grouped together, or anything corrected—so afraid of dropping what smack of outdoors or sun or starlight might cling to the lines, I dared not try to meddle with or smooth them. Every now and then (not often, but for a foil) I carried a book in my pocket—or perhaps tore out from some broken or cheap edition a bunch of loose leaves; most always had something of the sort ready, but only took it out when the mood demanded. In that way, utterly out of reach of literary conventions, I reread many authors. ℘ I cannot divest my appetite of literature, yet I find myself eventually trying it all by Nature—*first premises* many call it, but really the crowning results of all, laws, tallies, and proofs. (Has it never occurred to anyone how the last deciding tests applicable to a book are entirely outside of technical and grammatical ones, and that any truly first-class production has little or nothing to do with the rules and calibres of ordinary critics? or the bloodless chalk of Allibone's Dictionary? I have fancied the ocean and the daylight, the mountain and the forest, putting their spirit in a judgment on our books. I have fancied some disembodied human soul giving its verdict.)

NATURE AND DEMOCRACY—MORALITY

℘ Democracy most of all affiliates with the open air, is sunny and hardy and sane only with Nature—just as much as Art is. Something is required to temper both —to check them, restrain them from excess, morbidity. I have wanted, before departure, to bear special testimony to a very old lesson and requisite. American democracy, in its myriad personalities, in factories, workshops, stores, offices—through the dense streets and houses of cities, and all their manifold sophisticated life —must either be fibered, vitalized, by regular contact with outdoor light and air and growths, farm scenes, animals, fields, birds, sun-warmth and free skies, or it will certainly dwindle and pale. We cannot have grand races of mechanics, work people, and commonalty (the only specific purpose of America) on any less terms. I conceive of no flourishing and heroic elements of democracy in the United States or of democracy maintaining itself at all, without the Nature element forming a main part—to be its health element and beauty element—to really underlie the whole politics, sanity, religion, and art of the New World. ◈ Finally, the morality: "Virtue," said Marcus Aurelius, "what is it? Only a living and enthusiastic sympathy with Nature." Perhaps indeed the efforts of the true poets, founders, religions, literatures, all ages, have been, and ever will be, our time and times to come, essentially the same—to bring people back from their persistent strayings and sickly abstractions, to the costless average, divine, original concrete.

NOTE ◈ LONDON EDITION, 1887 ◈ As I write these lines I still continue living in Camden, New Jersey, America. Coming this way from Washington City, on my road to the sea-shore (and a temporary rest, as I supposed) in the early summer of 1873, I broke down disabled, and have dwelt here, as my central residence, all the time since—almost 14 years. In the preceding pages I have described how, during those years, I partially recuperated (in 1876) from my worst paralysis by going down to Timber Creek, living close to Nature, and domiciling with my dear friends, George and Susan Stafford. From 1877 or '8 to '83 or '4 I was well enough to travel around, considerably—journeyed westward to Kansas, leisurely exploring the Prairies, and on to Denver and the Rocky Mountains; another time north to Canada, where I spent most of the summer with my friend Dr. Bucke, and jaunted along the great lakes, and the St. Lawrence and Saguenay rivers; another time to Boston, to properly print the final edition of my poems (I was there over two months, and had a "good time.")

I have so brought out the completed *Leaves of Grass* during this period; also *Specimen Days*, of which the foregoing is a transcript; collected and re-edited the *Democratic Vistas* cluster—commemorated Abraham Lincoln's death, on the successive anniversaries of its occurrence, by delivering my lecture on it ten or twelve times; and "put in," through many a month and season, the aimless and resultless ways of most human lives. ◈ Thus the last 14 years have passed. At present (end-days of March, 1887—I am nigh entering my 69th year) I find myself continuing on here, quite dilapidated and even wrecked bodily from the paralysis, etc.—but in *good heart* (to use a Long Island country phrase,) and with about the same mentality as ever. The worst of it is, I have been growing feebler quite rapidly for a year, and now can't walk around—hardly from one room to the next. I am forced to stay indoors and in my big chair nearly all the time. We have had a sharp, dreary winter too, and it has pinched me. I am alone most of the time; every week, indeed almost every day, write some—reminiscences, essays, sketches, for the magazines; and read, or rather I should say dawdle over books and papers a good deal—spend half the day at that. ◈ Nor can I finish this note without putting on record—wafting over sea from hence—my deepest thanks to certain friends and helpers (I would specify them all and each by name, but imperative reasons, outside of my own wishes, forbid,) in the British Islands, as well as in America. Dear, even in the abstract, is such flattering unction always no doubt to the soul! Nigher still, if possible, I myself have been, and am to-day indebted to such help for my very sustenance, clothing, shelter, and continuity. And I would not go to the grave without briefly, but plainly, as I here do, acknowledging—may I not say even glorifying in it?

✗ (print 200 copies ~~each one~~) size of this
~~this sized card~~ white paper

card not very _thick_ — you are to
adhere to this sized card
through _all_ the prints (as you
~~will~~ have several)

Use yr own judgment ab't
color & other technicalities
— make a _good_ job of course
☞

print the 3/4 standing figure
same — (same sized card)

(They are all (will be 6 or 7
on 8 of them) to be collected together
& put in a very handsome
strong proper sized mail envelope
labeled in gilt & sold as _Pictures_
from life of _W W_ —
(perhaps made in a small album)

see notes
aug 4 '89

122. Courtesy of the Library of Congress, Charles E. Feinberg Collection.

PICTURES FROM LIFE OF WALT WHITMAN

Opposite, Whitman's directions for an edition of photographs called *Pictures from Life of WW*:

Print 200 copies each card – this sized card – size of this white paper – card not very thick – you are to adhere to this sized card through all the prints (as you will have several) – Use y'r own judgment ab't color & other technicalities – make a good job of course – Print the 3/4 standing figure same (same sized card) – They are all (will be 6 or 7 or 8 of them) to be collected together & put in a very handsome strong proper sized mail envelope label'd in gilt & sold as PICTURES FROM LIFE OF WW – *(perhaps made in a small album) Aug 4 '89*

From *A Backward Glance O'er Travel'd Roads*:

LEAVES OF GRASS *indeed (I cannot too often reiterate) has mainly been the outcropping of my own emotional and other personal nature – an attempt, from first to last, to put a Person, a human being (myself, in the latter half of the Nineteenth Century, in America,) freely, fully and truly on record. I could not find any similar personal record in current literature that satisfied me.*

From *Song of Myself*:

I celebrate myself, and sing myself,
And what I assume you shall assume,
For every atom belonging to me as good belongs to you.

The following descriptions of Whitman were written by his close friend, Dr. Richard Maurice Bucke (see pp. 99–100), and were published in *Cosmic Consciousness: A Study in the Evolution of the Human Mind*, pp. 179–186:

He did not generally wait for a formal introduction; upon meeting any person for the first time he very likely stepped forward, held out his hand (either left or right, whichever happened to be disengaged), and the person and he were acquainted at once.

Walt Whitman's dress was always extremely plain. He usually wore in pleasant weather a light-gray suit of good woolen cloth. The only thing peculiar about his dress was that he had no necktie at any time, and always wore shirts with very large turn-down collars, the button at the neck some five or six inches lower than usual, so that the throat and upper part of the breast were exposed. . . . His clothes might (and often did) show signs of wear, or they might be torn or have holes in them, but they never looked soiled. Indeed, an exquisite aroma of cleanliness has always belonged to his clothes, his breath, his whole body, his eating and drinking, his conversation, and no one could know him for an hour without seeing that it penetrated his mind and life, and was in fact the expression of a purity which was physical as much as moral and moral as much as physical.

As there were those who instinctively loved him, so there were others, here and there, who instinctively disliked him. As his poetic utterances were so ridiculous to many, even his personal appearance, in not a few cases, aroused equally sarcastic remark. His large figure, his red face, his copious beard, his loose and free attire, his rolling and unusually ample shirt-collar, without necktie and always wide open at the throat, all met at times with jeers and explosive laughter.

He never spoke deprecatingly of any nationality or class of men, or time in the world's history, or feudalism, or against any trades or occupations – not even against any animals, insects, plants or inanimate things, nor any of the laws of nature, or any of the results of those laws, such as illness, deformity or death. He never complained or grumbled either at the weather, pain, illness or at anything else. He never in conversation, in any company, or under any circumstances, used language that could be thought indelicate (of course he has used language that could be thought indelicate, but none that is so). . . . He never swore; he could not very well, since as far as I know he never spoke in anger, and apparently never was angry. He never exhibited fear, and I do not believe he ever felt it. His conversation, mainly toned low, was always agreeable and usually instructive. He never made compliments, very seldom apologised, used the common forms of civility, such as "if you please" and "thank you," quite sparingly, usually made a smile or a nod answer for them. . . . He never gossiped. He seldom talked about private people, even to say something good of them, except to answer a question or remark, and then he always gave what he said a turn favorable to the person spoken of.

His conversation, speaking generally, was of current affairs, work of the day, political and historical news, European as well as American, a little of books, much of the aspects of nature – as scenery, the stars, birds, flowers and trees. He read the newspapers regularly, liked good descriptions and reminiscences. He did not, on the whole, talk much anyhow. His manner was invariably calm and simple, belonged to itself alone, and could not be fully described or conveyed.

124. 1846, age 27. Compositor for the New World, 1841. Edited and wrote for New York newspapers and magazines, 1842 to 1848. Courtesy of The Walt Whitman House, Camden, New Jersey. Saunders 1.1.

Walt Whitman in 1850 or '49

125. Age 30. Worked for *New Orleans Crescent*, 1848. Published a Free-Soil newspaper, *The Brooklyn Freeman*, 1849. Also supervised a printshop and bookstore, and worked as a carpenter. Courtesy of the Library of Congress, Charles E. Feinberg Collection. Saunders 2.

126. About 1854, age 35, just before the first publication of *Leaves of Grass* in Brooklyn. Courtesy of the Duke University Library, Trent Collection. Saunders 5.

127. 1854, age 35. This engraving by Samuel Hollyer, copied from a lost photograph, appeared instead of Whitman's name at the beginning of the first edition of *Leaves of Grass*. Courtesy of the Yale University Library.
Saunders 4. Enlarged here about three times.

128. About 1860, age 41. The second edition of *Leaves of Grass* had been published in 1856 by Fowler & Wells of New York. The third edition was published in 1860 by Thayer & Eldridge of Boston. Photograph might be by Matthew Brady. Courtesy of the Library of Congress, Charles E. Feinberg Collection. Not in Saunders.

129. 1862, age 43. In December he began his work in the war hospitals. Photograph by Matthew Brady. Courtesy of the National Archives. Saunders 16.

130. 1862. Photograph by Matthew Brady. Courtesy of the New York Public Library. Saunders 35.1.

131. 1862(?). Courtesy of the Library of Congress, Charles E. Feinberg Collection. Not in Saunders.

132. 1862(?). Courtesy of the Yale University Library. Saunders 19.

Walt Whitman in 1864

133. 1864, age 45. Courtesy of the Yale University Library. Saunders 23.

134. 1864, age 45. Photograph by Alexander Gardner, Washington, D.C. Courtesy of the Library of Congress, Charles E. Feinberg Collection. Saunders 22.

135. 1864(?). Photograph by Alexander Gardner, Washington, D.C. Courtesy of the Library of Congress, Charles E. Feinberg Collection. Saunders 21.

Washington D.C. 1865 — Walt Whitman & his rebel soldier friend Pete Doyle

136. "Washington, D.C. 1865—Walt Whitman & his rebel soldier friend Pete Doyle." Age 46. *Drum Taps* was published in New York. From January to June Whitman worked as a clerk in the Indian Bureau of the Department of the Interior. Discharged by James Harlan who reputedly considered *Leaves of Grass* immoral. Another clerkship was obtained in the Attorney General's office. Courtesy of the Library of Congress, Charles E. Feinberg Collection. Saunders 29.

137. 1867, age 48. The fourth edition of *Leaves of Grass* was published in New York by W. E. Chapin. Photograph by Matthew Brady. Courtesy of the National Archives. Saunders 24.

138. 1867–68(?). Courtesy of the Yale University Library. Saunders 45.

139. 1867(?). Photograph by Matthew Brady. Courtesy of the Library of Congress, Charles E. Feinberg Collection. Saunders 26.

140. 1869, age 50(?). Courtesy of the Yale University Library. Saunders 43.

141. 1869, age 50. Photograph by Frank Pearsall. Courtesy of the New York Public Library. Saunders 31.

142. 1869–71(?). *Democratic Vistas* was published in book form in 1871. Courtesy of the Yale University Library. Saunders 41.

143. 1871, age 52(?). The fifth edition of *Leaves of Grass* was published in New York by J. S. Redfield. Courtesy of the Library of Congress, Charles E. Feinberg Collection. Saunders 27.

144. 1871(?). Courtesy of the Library of Congress, Charles E. Feinberg Collection. Saunders 47.

145. 1871(?). Courtesy of the Library of Congress, Charles E. Feinberg Collection. Not in Saunders.

146. 1871. Photograph by Henry Ulke and Brothers, Washington, D.C. Courtesy of the Library of Congress, Charles E. Feinberg Collection. Saunders 34.

147. 1872, age 53. Delivered "As strong as a bird on pinions free" at the Dartmouth College commencement. Photograph by Frank Pearsall. Courtesy of the New York Public Library. Saunders 32.

148. 1872. Photograph by Frank Pearsall. Courtesy of the New York Public Library. Saunders 36.

149. 1872(?). Courtesy of the Yale University Library. Not in Saunders.

150. 1875(?). In February, 1873, age 53, he was stricken by paralysis. In May his mother died. A substitute did his work at the Attorney General's office, and in 1874 he was formally discharged from his clerkship. In 1874 he wrote "Prayer of Columbus", which is reprinted on page 195. Courtesy of the Library of Congress, Charles E. Feinberg Collection. Not in Saunders.

151. 1875(?). He spent the summer at the Stafford's farm on Timber Creek in Camden County, New Jersey. Courtesy of the Yale University Library. Not in Saunders.

152. 1879, age 60. With the children of Mr. & Mrs. J. H. Johnston of New York. Whitman gave a lecture on Abraham Lincoln in New York on April 14. The sixth edition of *Leaves of Grass* had been published in Camden in 1876. Courtesy of the Yale University Library. Saunders 68.

W. KURTZ.　　　MADISON SQUARE

153. 1879. On September 10 he began his journey by train across the United States. Courtesy of the Library of Congress, Charles E. Feinberg Collection. Saunders 67.

154. 1879. Courtesy of the New York Public Library. Saunders 71.

155. 1879. Courtesy of the New York Public Library. Saunders 89.

156. 1879. Courtesy of the New York Public Library. Saunders 57.

157. 1879. Courtesy of the Library of Congress, Charles E. Feinberg Collection. Saunders 37.1.

158. 1879. Courtesy of the New York Public Library. Saunders 64.

159. 1880, age 61. Returned from the West in January. Courtesy of the Yale University Library. Saunders 74.

160. 1880. Courtesy of the Library of Congress, Charles E. Feinberg Collection. Saunders 80.

Walt Whitman
London Canada Sept 22 1880

161. 1880. Visited Dr. Richard M. Bucke, good friend, biographer, and director of the insane asylum in London, Ontario. Courtesy of the Duke University Library, Saunders 75.

162. 1880. Photograph by Edy Brothers, London, Ontario. Courtesy of the Library of Congress, Charles E. Feinberg Collection. Saunders 111.

163. 1880. Photograph by Edy Brothers, London, Ontario. Courtesy of the Library of Congress, Charles E. Feinberg Collection. Saunders 76.

164. 1881, age 62. The seventh edition of *Leaves of Grass* was published by J. R. Osgood of Boston. Photograph by Bartlett F. Kenny, Boston. Courtesy of the Library of Congress, Charles R. Feinberg Collection. Not in Saunders.

165. 1881. Photograph by W. Shaw Warren, Boston. Courtesy of the New York Public Library. Saunders 82.

Walt
Whitman
May 25ᵗ 1882

166. 1882, age 63. *Specimen Days and Collect* were published by Rees Welsh of Philadelphia. Courtesy of the Yale University Library. Saunders 101.

167. 1882. In February the seventh edition of *Leaves of Grass* was judged immoral by the Society for the Suppression of Vice, and the publishers, J. R. Osgood of Boston, gave the printing plates to Whitman. Rees Welch and Co., and then David McKay of Philadelphia became Whitman's publishers. Courtesy of the New York Public Library. Saunders 84.1.

Walt Whitman

168. 1883, age 64. Dr. R. M. Bucke's biography of Whitman was published. Photographed at Ocean Grove by Phillips & Taylor of Philadelphia. Courtesy of the Library of Congress, Charles E. Feinberg Collection. Saunders 48.

169. 1884, age 65. Income from book sales enabled Whitman to buy a house on Mickle Street in Camden, New Jersey. He lived there from March 26, 1884 until his death on March 26, 1892. Courtesy of the Library of Congress, Charles E. Feinberg Collection. Saunders 58.

170. 1885, age 66. His paralysis worsened after a sunstroke in July. Many friends contributed to buy this horse and phaeton for Whitman who could walk only with great effort. Bill Duckett is sitting next to him. Courtesy of the Yale University Library. Saunders 90.

171. 1886(?). Again with Bill Duckett. Tintype courtesy of the New York Public Library. Saunders 79.1.

172. 1887, age 68. Photograph attributed to Thomas Eakins who painted Whitman's portrait this year. The painting is in the Pennsylvania Academy of Fine Arts, Philadelphia. An oil sketch of Whitman by Eakins is in the Museum of Fine Arts, Boston. Courtesy of the Yale University Library. Saunders 103.

Walt Whitman

173. 1887. This and the next four photographs were taken by George C. Cox in New York while Whitman was visiting to speak in honor of Abraham Lincoln at the Madison Square Theater. Courtesy of the Yale University Library. Saunders 92.

Walt Whitman 1887

174. 1887. Photograph by George C. Cox, New York. Courtesy of the New York Public Library. Saunders 95.

175. 1887. Photograph by George C. Cox, New York. Courtesy of the Library of Congress, Charles E. Feinberg Collection. Saunders 94.

176. 1887. With Nigel and Catherine Jeanette Chomeley-Jones. Photograph by George C. Cox, New York. Courtesy of the Smithsonian Institution. Saunders 97.3.

177. 1887. Courtesy of the Smithsonian Institution. Not in Saunders.

178. 1887. Courtesy of the Duke University Library. Saunders 96.

Walt Whitman
Sept: '87

179. 1887. Courtesy of the Yale University Library. Saunders 98.

180. 1888. age 69, *November Boughs* was published by David McKay in Philadelphia. Whitman suffered another paralytic stroke in June. The eighth edition of *Leaves of Grass* was published, including "Sands at Seventy", "A Backward Glance O'er Travel'd Roads", and *Portraits from Life*. Courtesy of the Yale University Library. Saunders 102.

My 71st year arrives; the fifteen past months nearly all illness or half illness — until a tolerable day (Aug: 6 1889) & convoy'd by Mr. B and Ed: W. I have been carriaged across to Philadelphia (how sunny & fresh & good look'd the river, the people, the vehicles, & Market & Arch streets!) & have sat for this photo: wh: satisfies me.

Walt Whitman

181. 1889, age 70. Photograph by Gutekunst, Philadelphia. Courtesy of the Library of Congress, Charles E. Feinberg Collection. Saunders 112.

182. 1890, age 71. On the wharf, probably near his Mickle Street house in Camden. Photograph by Dr. John Johnston, author of *Diary Notes of a Visit to Walt Whitman and Some of His Friends, in 1890*, published by the Labour Press, Manchester, England, in 1898. Courtesy of the Duke University Library. Saunders 110.

183. 1890. With his nurse, Warren Fritzenger. Also photographed by Dr. John Johnston. Courtesy of the Library of Congress, Charles E. Feinberg Collection. Saunders 108.

184. 1890. Courtesy of the New York Public Library. Saunders 115.

185. 1891, May, age 72. *Good-bye, My Fancy* was published this year. The ninth edition of *Leaves of Grass* was published in 1892, and is known as the Deathbed Edition. The tenth edition was published posthumously by his literary executors, Dr. R. M. Bucke, Thomas Harned, and Horace Traubel, and included "Old Age Echoes." The last edition was prefaced with Whitman's wish: . . . *I place upon you the injunction that whatever may be added to the* Leaves *shall be supplementary, avowed as such, leaving the book complete as I left it, consecutive to the point I left off, marking always an unmistakable, deep down, unobliterable division line. In the long run the world will do as it pleases with the book. I am determined to have the world know what I was pleased to do.* These last four photographs were taken by Thomas Eakins. This one courtesy of the Yale University Library.

186. 1891. Photograph by Thomas Eakins. Courtesy of the Yale University Library. Saunders 123.

187. 1891. Photograph by Thomas Eakins. Courtesy of the Philadelphia Museum of Art. Saunders 122.

188. Photograph by Thomas Eakins. Courtesy of the Library of Congress, Charles E. Feinberg Collection. Saunders 118.

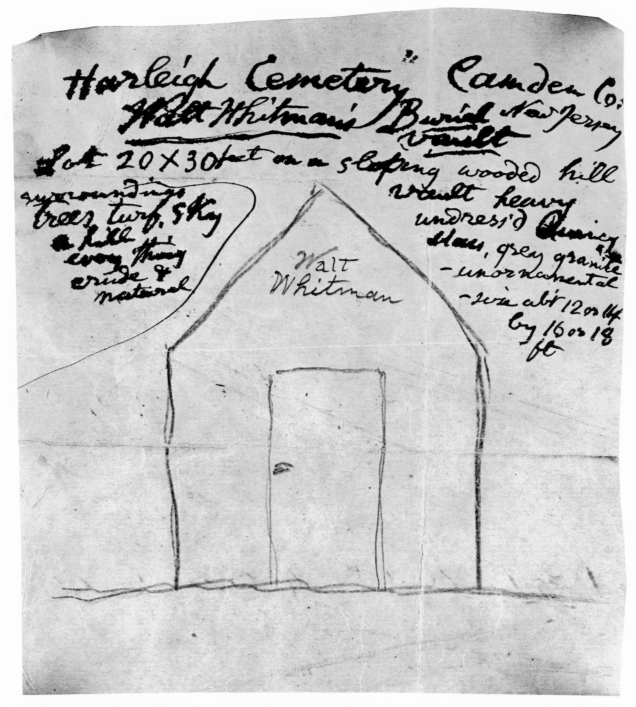

189. Whitman's design for his tomb: *Harleigh Cemetery, Camden Co., New Jersey. Walt Whitman's Burial Vault. Lot 20×30 feet on a sloping wooded hill, surroundings trees, turf, sky, a hill, everything crude & natural. Vault heavy undress'd (?) grey granite—unornamental—size ab't 12 or 14 by 16 or 18 ft.* Courtesy of the Library of Congress, Charles E. Feinberg Collection.

Photo by Laurens Maynard

Feby. 16. 1895

190. Inscribed on reverse: *Photographed Feby. 16, 1895. Traubel next to tomb—I am standing in shadow—Laurens Maynard. For Dr. R M. Bucke*. Courtesy of the New York Public Library.

LEAVES OF GRASS

SELECTIONS FROM THE 1882 EDITION

FACES

1

Sauntering the pavement or riding the country by-road, lo,
    such faces!
Faces of friendship, precision, caution, suavity, ideality,
The spiritual-prescient face, the always welcome common
    benevolent face,
The face of the singing of music, the grand faces of natural
    lawyers and judges broad at the back-top,
The faces of hunters and fishers bulged at the brows, the
    shaved blanch'd faces of orthodox citizens,
The pure, extravagant, yearning, questioning artist's face,
The ugly face of some beautiful soul, the handsome
    detested or despised face,
The sacred faces of infants, the illuminated face of the
    mother of many children,
The face of an amour, the face of veneration,
The face as of a dream, the face of an immobile rock,
The face withdrawn of its good and bad, a castrated face,
A wild hawk, his wings clipp'd by the clipper,
A stallion that yielded at last to the thongs and knife of the
    gelder.

Sauntering the pavement thus, or crossing the ceaseless
    ferry, faces and faces and faces,
I see them and complain not, and am content with all.

2

Do you suppose I could be content with all if I thought
    them their own finalè?

This now is too lamentable a face for a man,
Some abject louse asking leave to be, cringing for it,
Some milk-nosed maggot blessing what lets it wrig to its
    hole.

This face is a dog's snout sniffing for garbage,
Snakes nest in that mouth, I hear the sibilant threat.

This face is a haze more chill than the arctic sea,
Its sleepy and wabbling icebergs crunch as they go.

This is a face of bitter herbs, this an emetic, they need no
    label,
And more of the drug-shelf, laudanum, caoutchouc, or
    hog's-lard.

This face is an epilepsy, its wordless tongue gives out the
    unearthly cry,
Its veins down the neck distend, its eyes roll till they
    show nothing but their whites,
Its teeth grit, the palms of the hands are cut by the turn'd-in
    nails,
The man falls struggling and foaming to the ground, while
    he speculates well.

This face is bitten by vermin and worms,
And this is some murderer's knife with a half-pull'd
    scabbard.

This face owes to the sexton his dismalest fee,
An unceasing death-bell tolls there.

3

Features of my equals would you trick me with your creas'd
    and cadaverous march?
Well, you cannot trick me.

I see your rounded never-erased flow,
I see 'neath the rims of your haggard and mean disguises.

Splay and twist as you like, poke with the tangling fores
    of fishes or rats,
You'll be unmuzzled, you certainly will.

I saw the face of the most smear'd and slobbering idiot
    they had at the asylum,
And I knew for my consolation what they knew not,
I knew of the agents that emptied and broke my brother,
The same wait to clear the rubbish from the fallen
    tenement,
And I shall look again in a score or two of ages,
And I shall meet the real landlord perfect and unharm'd,
    every inch as good as myself.

4

The Lord advances, and yet advances,
Always the shadow in front, always the reach'd hand
    bringing up the laggards.

Out of this face emerge banners and horses—O superb! I
    see what is coming,
I see the high pioneer-caps, see staves of runners clearing
    the way,
I hear victorious drums.

This face is a life-boat,
This is the face commanding and bearded, it asks no odds
    of the rest,
This face is flavor'd fruit ready for eating,

This face of a healthy honest boy is the programme of all
    good.

These faces bear testimony slumbering or awake,
They show their descent from the Master himself.

Off the word I have spoken I except not one—red, white,
    black, are all deific,
In each house is the ovum, it comes forth after a thousand
    years.

Spots or cracks at the windows do not disturb me,
Tall and sufficient stand behind and make signs to me,
I read the promise and patiently wait.

This is a full-grown lily's face,
She speaks to the limber-hipp'd man near the garden
    pickets,
Come here she blushingly cries, Come nigh to me
    limber-hipp'd man,
Stand at my side till I lean as high as I can upon you,
Fill me with albescent honey, bend down to me,
Rub to me with your chafing beard, rub to my
    breast and shoulders.

5

The old face of the mother of many children,
Whist! I am fully content.

Lull'd and late is the smoke of the First-day morning,
It hangs low over the rows of trees by the fences,
It hangs thin by the sassafras and wild-cherry and cat-brier
    under them.

I saw the rich ladies in full dress at the soiree,
I heard what the singers were singing so long,
Heard who sprang in crimson youth from the white froth
    and the water-blue.

Behold a woman!
She looks out from her quaker cap, her face is clearer and
    more beautiful than the sky.

She sits in an armchair under the shaded porch of the
    farmhouse,
The sun just shines on her old white head.

Her ample gown is of cream-hued linen,
Her grandsons raised the flax, and her grand-daughters
    spun it with the distaff and the wheel.

The melodious character of the earth,

The finish beyond which philosophy cannot go and does
    not wish to go,
The justified mother of men.

YOU FELONS ON TRIAL IN COURTS

You felons on trial in courts,
You convicts in prison-cells, you sentenced assassins
    chain'd and handcuff'd with iron,
Who am I too that I am not on trial or in prison?
Me ruthless and devilish as any, that my wrists are not
    chain'd with iron, or my ankles with iron?

You prostitutes flaunting over the trottoirs or obscene in
    your rooms,
Who am I that I should call you more obscene than
    myself?
O culpable! I acknowledge—I exposé!
(O admirers, praise not me—compliment not me—you
    make me wince,
I see what you do not—I know what you do not.)

Inside these breast-bones I lie smutch'd and choked,
Beneath this face that appears so impassive hell's tides
    continually run,
Lusts and wickedness are acceptable to me,
I walk with delinquents with passionate love,
I feel I am of them—I belong to those convicts and
    prostitutes myself,
And henceforth I will not deny them—for how can I deny
    myself?

I SING THE BODY ELECTRIC

1

I sing the body electric,
The armies of those I love engirth me and I engirth them,
They will not let me off till I go with them, respond to
    them,
And discorrupt them, and charge them full with the
    charge of the soul.

Was it doubted that those who corrupt their own bodies
    conceal themselves?
And if those who defile the living are as bad as they who
    defile the dead?
And if the body does not do fully as much as the soul?
And if the body were not the soul, what is the soul?

2

The love of the body of man or woman balks account,
   the body itself balks account,
That of the male is perfect, and that of the female is
   perfect.

The expression of the face balks account,
But the expression of a well-made man appears not only
   in his face,
It is in his limbs and joints also, it is curiously in the
   joints of his hips and wrists,
It is in his walk, the carriage of his neck, the flex of his
   waist and knees, dress does not hide him,
The strong sweet quality he has strikes through the
   cotton and broadcloth,
To see him pass conveys as much as the best poem,
   perhaps more,
You linger to see his back, and the back of his neck and
   shoulder-side.

The sprawl and fulness of babes, the bosoms and heads of
   women, the folds of their dress, their style as we pass in
   the street, the contour of their shape downwards,
The swimmer naked in the swimming-bath, seen as he
   swims through the transparent green-shine, or lies with
   his face up and rolls silently to and fro in the heave of
   the water,
The bending forward and backward of rowers in row-
   boats, the horseman in his saddle,
Girls, mothers, house-keepers, in all their performances,
The group of laborers seated at noon-time with their
   open dinner-kettles, and their wives waiting,
The female soothing a child, the farmer's daughter in the
   garden or cow-yard,
The young fellow hoeing corn, the sleigh-driver driving
   his six horses through the crowd,
The wrestle of wrestlers, two apprentice-boys, quite
   grown, lusty, good-natured, native-born, out on the
   vacant lot at sundown after work,
The coats and caps thrown down, the embrace of love
   and resistance,
The upper-hold and under-hold, the hair rumpled over
   and blinding the eyes;
The march of firemen in their own costumes, the play of
   masculine muscle through clean-setting trowsers and
   waist-straps,
The slow return from the fire, the pause when the bell
   strikes suddenly again, and the listening on the alert,
The natural, perfect, varied attitudes, the bent head, the
   curv'd neck and the counting;
Such-like I love—I loosen myself, pass freely, am at the
   mother's breast with the little child,

Swim with the swimmers, wrestle with wrestlers,
   march in line with the firemen, and pause, listen, count.

3

I knew a man, a common farmer, the father of five sons,
And in them the fathers of sons, and in them the fathers
   of sons.
This man was of wonderful vigor, calmness, beauty of
   person,
The shape of his head, the pale yellow and white of his
   hair and beard, the immeasurable meaning of his black
   eyes, the richness and breadth of his manners,
There I used to go and visit him to see, he was wise also,
He was six feet tall, he was over eighty years old, his
   sons were massive, clean, bearded, tan-faced, handsome,
They and his daughters loved him, all who saw him
   loved him,
They did not love him by allowance, they loved him with
   personal love,
He drank water only, the blood show'd like scarlet
   through the clear-brown skin of his face,
He was a frequent gunner and fisher, he sail'd his boat
   himself, he had a fine one presented to him by a ship-
   joiner, he had fowling-pieces presented to him by men
   that loved him,
When he went with his five sons and many grand-sons to
   hunt or fish, you would pick him out as the most
   beautiful and vigorous of the gang,
You would wish long and long to be with him, you would
   wish to sit by him in the boat that you and he might
   touch each other.

4

I have perceiv'd that to be with those I like is enough,
To stop in company with the rest at evening is enough,
To be surrounded by beautiful, curious, breathing,
   laughing flesh is enough,
To pass among them or touch any one, or rest my arm ever
   so lightly round his or her neck for a moment, what is
   this then?
I do not ask any more delight, I swim in it as in a sea.

There is something in staying close to men and women
   and looking on them, and in the contact and odor of
   them, that pleases the soul well,
All things please the soul, but these please the soul well.

5

This is the female form,
A divine nimbus exhales from it from head to foot,

It attracts with fierce undeniable attraction,
I am drawn by its breath as if I were no more than a
   helpless vapor, all falls aside but myself and it,
Books, art, religion, time, the visible and solid earth, and
   what was expected of heaven or fear'd of hell, are now
   consumed,
Mad filaments, ungovernable shoots play out of it, the
   response likewise ungovernable,
Hair, bosom, hips, bend of legs, negligent falling hands all
   diffused, mine too diffused,
Ebb stung by the flow and flow stung by the ebb, love-
   flesh swelling and deliciously aching,
Limitless limpid jets of love hot and enormous, quivering
   jelly of love, white-blow and delirious juice,
Bridegroom night of love working surely and softly into
   the prostrate dawn,
Undulating into the willing and yielding day,
Lost in the cleave of the clasping and sweet-flesh'd day.

This the nucleus—after the child is born of woman,
   man is born of woman,
This the bath of birth, this the merge of small and large,
   and the outlet again.

Be not ashamed women, your privilege encloses the rest,
   and is the exit of the rest,
You are the gates of the body, and you are the gates of the
   soul.

The female contains all qualities and tempers them,
She is in her place and moves with perfect balance,
She is all things duly veil'd, she is both passive and active,
She is to conceive daughters as well as sons, and sons as
   well as daughters.

As I see my soul reflected in Nature,
As I see through a mist, One with inexpressible complete-
   ness, sanity, beauty,
See the bent head and arms folded over the breast, the
   Female I see.

6

The male is not less the soul nor more, he too is in his
   place,
He too is all qualities, he is action and power,
The flush of the known universe is in him,
Scorn becomes him well, and appetite and defiance
   become him well,
The wildest largest passions, bliss that is utmost, sorrow
   that is utmost become him well, pride is for him,
The full-spread pride of man is calming and excellent to
   the soul,

Knowledge becomes him, he likes it always, he brings
   every thing to the test of himself,
Whatever the survey, whatever the sea and the sail he
   strikes soundings at last only here,
(Where else does he strike soundings except here?)

The man's body is sacred and the woman's body is sacred,
No matter who it is, it is sacred—is it the meanest one in
   the laborers' gang?
Is it one of the dull-faced immigrants just landed on the
   wharf?
Each belongs here or anywhere just as much as the well-off,
   just as much as you,
Each has his or her place in the procession.

(All is a procession,
The universe is a procession with measured and perfect
   motion.)

Do you know so much yourself that you call the meanest
   ignorant?
Do you suppose you have a right to a good sight, and he
   or she has no right to a sight?
Do you think matter has cohered together from its diffuse
   float, and the soil is on the surface, and water runs and
   vegetation sprouts,
For you only, and not for him and her?

7

A man's body at auction,
(For before the war I often go to the slave-mart and watch
   the sale,)
I help the auctioneer, the sloven does not half know his
   business.

Gentlemen look on this wonder,
Whatever the bids of the bidders they cannot be high
   enough for it,
For it the globe lay preparing quintillions of years without
   one animal or plant,
For it the revolving cycles truly and steadily roll'd.

In this head the all-baffling brain,
In it and below it the makings of heroes.

Examine these limbs, red, black, or white, they are
   cunning in tendon and nerve,
They shall be stript that you may see them.

Exquisite senses, life-lit eyes, pluck, volition,
Flakes of breast-muscle, pliant backbone and neck, flesh not
   flabby, good-sized arms and legs,

And wonders within there yet.

Within there runs blood,
The same old blood! the same red-running blood!
There swells and jets a heart, there all passions, desires,
    reachings, aspirations,
(Do you think they are not there because they are not
    express'd in parlors and lecture-rooms?)

This is not only one man, this the father of those who
    shall be fathers in their turns,
In him the start of populous states and rich republics,
Of him countless immortal lives with countless embodi-
    ments and enjoyments.

How do you know who shall come from the offspring of his
    offspring through the centuries?
(Who might you find you have come from yourself, if you
    could trace back through the centuries?)

8

A woman's body at auction,
She too is not only herself, she is the teeming mother of
    mothers,
She is the bearer of them that shall grow and be mates to
    the mothers.

Have you ever loved the body of a woman?
Have you ever loved the body of a man?
Do you not see that these are exactly the same to all in all
    nations and times all over the earth?

If any thing is sacred the human body is sacred,
And the glory and sweet of a man is the token of manhood
    untainted,
And in man or woman a clean, strong, firm-fibred body,
    is more beautiful than the most beautiful face.

Have you seen the fool that corrupted his own live body?
    or the fool that corrupted her own live body?
For they do not conceal themselves, and cannot conceal
    themselves.

9

O my body! I dare not desert the likes of you in other
    men and women, nor the likes of the parts of you,
I believe the likes of you are to stand or fall with the likes
    of the soul, (and they that are the soul,)
I believe the likes of you shall stand or fall with my
    poems, and that they are my poems,
Man's, woman's, child's, youth's, wife's, husband's,
    mother's, father's, young man's, young woman's poems,

Head, neck, hair, ears, drop and tympan of the ears,
Eyes, eye-fringes, iris of the eye, eyebrows, and the
    waking or sleeping of the lids,
Mouth, tongue, lips, teeth, roof of the mouth, jaws, and
    the jaw-hinges,
Nose, nostrils of the nose, and the partition,
Cheeks, temples, forehead, chin, throat, back of the neck,
    neckslue,
Strong shoulders, manly beard, scapula, hind-shoulders,
    and the ample side-round of the chest,
Upper-arm, armpit, elbow-socket, lower-arm, arm-sinews,
    arm-bones,
Wrist and wrist-joints, hand, palm, knuckles, thumb,
    forefinger, finger-joints, finger-nails,
Broad breast-front, curling hair of the breast, breast-bone,
    breast-side,
Ribs, belly, backbone, joints of the backbone,
Hips, hip-sockets, hip-strength, inward and outward
    round, man-balls, man-root,
Strong set of thighs, well carrying the trunk above,
Leg-fibres, knee, knee-pan, upper-leg, under-leg,
Ankles, instep, foot-ball, toes, toe-joints, the heel;
All attitudes, all the shapeliness, all the belongings of my
    or your body or of any one's body, male or female,
The lung-sponges, the stomach-sac, the bowels sweet and
    clean,
The brain in its folds inside the skull-frame,
Sympathies, heart-valves, palate-valves, sexuality,
    maternity,
Womanhood, and all that is a woman, and the man that
    comes from woman,
The womb, the teats, nipples, breast-milk, tears, laughter,
    weeping, love-looks, love-perturbations and risings,
The voice, articulation, language, whispering, shouting
    aloud,
Food, drink, pulse, digestion, sweat, sleep, walking,
    swimming,
Poise on the hips, leaping, reclining, embracing, arm-
    curving and tightening,
The continual change of the flex of the mouth, and around
    the eyes,
The skin, the sunburnt shade, freckles, hair,
The curious sympathy one feels when feeling with the
    hand the naked meat of the body,
The circling rivers the breath, and breathing it in and out,
The beauty of the waist, and thence of the hips, and thence
    downward toward the knees,
The thin red jellies within you or within me, the bones
    and the marrow in the bones,
The exquisite realization of health;
O I say these are not the parts and poems of the body
    only, but of the soul,
O I say now these are the soul!

PRAYER OF COLUMBUS

A batter'd, wreck'd old man,
Thrown on this savage shore, far, far from home,
Pent by the sea and dark rebellious brows, twelve dreary
    months,
Sore, stiff with many toils, sicken'd and nigh to death,
I take my way along the island's edge,
Venting a heavy heart.

I am too full of woe!
Haply I may not live another day;
I cannot rest O God, I cannot eat or drink or sleep,
Till I put forth myself, my prayer, once more to Thee,
Breathe, bathe myself once more in Thee, commune with
    Thee,
Report myself once more to Thee.

Thou knowest my years entire, my life,
My long and crowded life of active work, not adoration
    merely;
Thou knowest the prayers and vigils of my youth,
Thou knowest my manhood's solemn and visionary
    meditations,
Thou knowest how before I commenced I devoted all to
    come to Thee,
Thou knowest I have in age ratified all those vows and
    strictly kept them,
Thou knowest I have not once lost nor faith nor ecstasy
    in Thee,
In shackles, prison'd, in disgrace, repining not,
Accepting all from Thee, as duly come from Thee.

All my emprises have been fill'd with Thee,
My speculations, plans, begun and carried on in thoughts
    of Thee,
Sailing the deep or journeying the land for Thee;
Intentions, purports, aspirations mine, leaving results to
    Thee.

O I am sure they really came from Thee,
The urge, the ardor, the unconquerable will,
The potent, felt, interior command, stronger than words,
A message from the Heavens whispering to me even in
    sleep,
These sped me on.

By me and these the work so far accomplish'd,
By me earth's elder cloy'd and stifled lands uncloy'd,
    unloos'd,
By me the hemispheres rounded and tied, the unknown to
    the known.

The end I know not, it is all in Thee,
Or small or great I know not—haply what broad fields,
    what lands,
Haply the brutish measureless human undergrowth I know,
Transplanted there may rise to stature, knowledge worthy
    Thee,
Haply the swords I know may there indeed be turn'd to
    reaping-tools,
Haply the lifeless cross I know, Europe's dead cross, may
    bud and blossom there.

One effort more, my altar this bleak sand;
That Thou O God my life hast lighted,
With ray of light, steady, ineffable, vouchsafed of Thee,
Light rare untellable, lighting the very light,
Beyond all signs, descriptions, languages;
For that O God, be it my latest word, here on my knees,
Old, poor, and paralyzed, I thank Thee.

My terminus near,
The clouds already closing in upon me,
The voyage balk'd, the course disputed, lost,
I yield my ships to Thee.

My hands, my limbs grow nerveless,
My brain feels rack'd, bewilder'd,
Let the old timbers part, I will not part,
I will cling fast to Thee, O God, though the waves
    buffet me,
Thee, Thee at least I know.

Is it the prophet's thought I speak, or am I raving?
What do I know of life? what of myself?
I know not even my own work past or present,
Dim ever-shifting guesses of it spread before me,
Of newer better worlds, their mighty parturition,
Mocking, perplexing me.

And these things I see suddenly, what mean they?
As if some miracle, some hand divine unseal'd my eyes,
Shadowy vast shapes smile through the air and sky,
And on the distant waves sail countless ships,
And anthems in new tongues I hear saluting me.

RECORDERS AGES HENCE

Recorders ages hence,
Come, I will take you down underneath this impassive
    exterior, I will tell you what to say of me,
Publish my name and hang up my picture as that of the
    tenderest lover,
The friend the lover's portrait, of whom his friend his
    lover was fondest,

Who was not proud of his songs, but of the measureless
ocean of love within him, and freely pour'd it forth,
Who often walk'd lonesome walks thinking of his dear
friends, his lovers,
Who pensive away from one he lov'd often lay sleepless
and dissatisfied at night,
Who knew too well the sick, sick dread lest the one he
lov'd might secretly be indifferent to him,
Whose happiest days were far away through fields, in
woods, on hills, he and another wandering hand in
hand, they twain apart from other men,
Who oft as he saunter'd the streets curv'd with his arm
the shoulder of his friend, while the arm of his friend
rested upon him also.

WHEN I HEARD
AT THE CLOSE OF THE DAY

When I heard at the close of the day how my name had
been receiv'd with plaudits in the capitol, still it was not
a happy night for me that follow'd,
And else when I carous'd, or when my plans were
accomplish'd, still I was not happy,

But the day when I rose at dawn from the bed of perfect
health, refresh'd, singing, inhaling the ripe breath of
autumn,
When I saw the full moon in the west grow pale and
disappear in the morning light,
When I wander'd alone over the beach, and undressing
bathed, laughing with the cool waters, and saw the sun
rise,
And when I thought how my dear friend my lover was on
his way coming, O then I was happy,
O then each breath tasted sweeter, and all that day my
food nourish'd me more, and the beautiful day pass'd well,
And the next came with equal joy, and with the next at
evening came my friend,
And that night while all was still I heard the waters roll
slowly continually up the shores,
I heard the hissing rustle of the liquid and sands as
directed to me whispering to congratulate me,
For the one I love most lay sleeping by me under the same
cover in the cool night,
In the stillness in the autumn moonbeams his face was
inclined toward me,
And his arm lay lightly around my breast—and that night
I was happy.